AUTHOR.M
B
TITLE.MORE
19
1ERS
D1629999

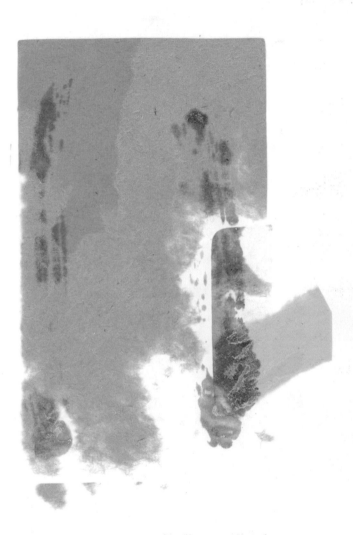

200 076 903 4E

MORE EQUAL THAN OTHERS

The Changing Fortunes of the
British and European Aristocracies

Also by Lord Montagu

MOTORING MONTAGUS

LOST CAUSES OF MOTORING

THE GORDON BENNETT RACES

JAGUAR — A BIOGRAPHY

ROLLS OF ROLLS-ROYCE

THE GILT AND THE GINGERBREAD

More Equal Than Others

The Changing Fortunes of the British and European Aristocracies

Lord Montagu of Beaulieu

Foreword by
SIR IAIN MONCREIFFE
OF THAT ILK Bt

LONDON
MICHAEL JOSEPH

WANDSWORTH PUBLIC LIBRARIES

First published in Great Britain by
MICHAEL JOSEPH LTD
52 Bedford Square
London, W.C.1
1970

© 1970 by Lord Montagu of Beaulieu

All Rights Reserved. No part of this publication may be reproduced, stored in a retrieval
system, or transmitted, in any form or by any
means, electronic, mechanical, photocopying,
recording or otherwise, without the prior permission of the Copyright owner

200076903

D312519

305. S223
MONT
323.31094 MON

7181 0690 3

Set and printed in Great Britain by
Tonbridge Printers Ltd, Peach Hall Works, Tonbridge, Kent
in Baskerville eleven on twelve point on paper supplied by
P. F. Bingham Ltd, and bound by James Burn
at Royal Mills, Esher, Surrey

Contents

Acknowledgements

First and foremost, I would like to acknowledge the assistance of Margaret Blunden, who carried out the major part of the historical research for this book. Her own excellent biography, *The Countess of Warwick*, published by Cassell, 1967, fitted her admirably to the task which she carried out efficiently and painstakingly.

Secondly, my special thanks to my old friend, Sir Iain Moncreiffe of that Ilk, whose introductory chapter sets the scene for the book with an expertise which few can command. I only hope that one day he will devote some time to expanding his ideas into a book of his own, and thus provide posterity with a permanent record of his knowledge and erudition. I also acknowledge my gratitude to Dr Johann George Hoyos and his son Philipp of Vienna, Austria for their help and criticism on the chapter concerning the history of the Austrian aristocracy.

Much of the material contained in the latter part of the book resulted from personal interviews which certain of my colleagues in the House of Lords kindly agreed to give, and I am most grateful to them for their co-operation. At the time of the interviews the Labour Government's proposals for the reform of the House of Lords were under consideration in the House of Commons. Although that Government changed its mind I am confident that in the longterm the peers will not change theirs. The large majority of us still want the House of Lords modernised and so constituted to enable it to play a useful part in the life of the country.

Whether or not it was, in the past, the desire of the aristocracies the world over to be 'more equal than others' recent events have clearly shown that the old myth of 'peers versus the people' is now dead. The future may well see the peers lined up with the people as a first line of defence against the over-authoritarian executive whose power grows daily.

The reasons why and how the British aristocracy finds itself in this unique and anachronistic position in the mid-twentieth century, I attempt to explain in this book.

Lord Montagu of Beaulieu

Foreword

by Sir Iain Moncreiffe of that Ilk Bt.

Lord Montagu of Beaulieu is one of the bastards to whom my colleague Don Pottinger and I referred in our book, *Blood Royal,* when we wrote the verse :

> 'The noble boys of Munster spring
> from William the Fourth, the Seaman King,[1]
> Richmond, Grafton, St Albans, Buccleuch,
> Southampton, Daventry, Montagu :
> These peers' families' fathers are reckoned
> Merrily back to King Charles the Second.'

But the fact that he descends from the Merry Monarch on the wrong side of the blanket through the Duke of Monmouth and Buccleuch, who was proved to be illegitimate in the trial by battle at Sedgemoor, is neither here nor there. Some Socialist M.P.s made great play (in their characteristically good-natured way) during the recent batty Lords Reform debates, on the royal bastards among our dukes. But dukedoms were originally introduced into Britain for the sons of kings, and were only given later to other noblemen to honour them with an equivalent status. And the Socialists themselves have been the leaders in saying that illegitimate sons should not be penalised for what is no fault of their own, but should have equal status with their lawful brothers. What is sauce for the dustmen is sauce for the dukes.

In his book, Lord Montagu compares the British peerage rather favourably with the nobility of certain other European countries. This is, of course, a matter of opinion, and not an opinion that I myself necessarily share (though perhaps I do), but he does give the facts on which he bases his opinion. Basically, his view is that the British aristocracy have always been

9

more closely linked to the land and to public affairs than their Continental counterparts, and have also tended on the whole to cultivate a sense of national responsibility as opposed to class advantage.

One of the difficulties of writing a book of this sort, is how to define the subject. We all know what we mean personally by 'noble' or 'aristocrat'; but do others think we are talking of the Scarlet Pimpernel, of the Duke of Devonshire, of Sir Winston Churchill, or of some kindly Trades Unionist Labour peer like the late Lord Mathers, one of the gentlest men that ever lived? For the purposes of this book, I think Lord Montagu means people like himself; hereditary peers with a long-term stake in the country. I don't think he's really thinking so much about the other peers, whether impoverished aristos or industrious middle-class Conservatives or show-biz Socialists, though they're extremely useful in providing our Legislature with a reasonably unbiased cross-section of the responsible age-groups in our community. Nor do I think he's thinking of the gentlemen, landed or otherwise: let alone of us Barts, who are neither as fishy nor as foul as Ruddigore would have us, but simply (in the nobiliary sense) good Red Herrings.

As a result, Lord Montagu has had to overcome considerable difficulty in writing about the Continental nobility. For in each country the definition differs. In Sweden, for example (one of the countries with which he doesn't deal) are we to suppose that the Bondes were 'ennobled' by being created counts in 1695 and (I rather think the senior branch) barons in 1802, when their ancestral uncle Karl Knutsson Bonde was already King of Sweden from 1448 to 1457? Again, Napoleon Buonaparte was born a Genoese noble, of a family who had been Patricians of Sarzana centuries before, but it's to be doubted that the average Englishman would regard him as a noble in the sense of the two field-marshals who managed to beat him on the battlefields of Leipzig and Waterloo: Prince Schwarzenberg and Lord Mornington's boy, the Duke of Wellington. For these reasons, and because Lord Montagu begins his book at the Reformation, it may be useful to give readers of this Foreword a brief but *panoptic* view of European aristocracy from the dawn of history. John Ball posed the interesting question :

10

'When Adam delved and Eve span
Who was then the gentleman?'

The answer is of course obvious: Adam. How could it have
been Eve? The viking Norse, from whom we have ultimately
derived so many of our institutions, would have had it otherwise; they held that in the Beginning there were created quite
separately jarl and carl and thrall, roughly corresponding with
what used to be called the upper, middle and lower classes. But
we devotees of Darwin know better; we all go back together to
the same aboriginal anthropoid gent. And think how interesting
a genealogical specimen any modern man would be who could
prove each generation of his pedigree and tell us of their lives
all the way back to the first *homo sapiens* to be evolved. However, the Norse were right that insofar as mankind had evolved
into separate (though interlocking) cousinhoods at the dawn of
history, it had already formed (almost everywhere civilised) three
roughly recognisable main groups, though individuals fluctuated
between them. This book, then, is about the jarl or 'upper'
branches of our common family tree.

Lord Montagu has been quoted as saying: 'After all, we
were all nouveaux riches once'. In a sense, this is obviously true;
in that all wealth has to have a beginning, if only in the first
hut that was ever built or the first pot ever moulded from
the prehistoric clay. In another sense it's also true, in that few
historic families could have continued to maintain the advanced
civilisation they have done so much to build up, without
repeated inter-marriages with the successful newly-rich. This is
what people mean by 'an injection of new blood'. In fact, there
is no such thing as 'new blood': all families are equally old.
Indeed, the dark horses are those who can't prove their lineage
before a certain date; we know that Lord Mountbatten
doesn't descend in the direct male line from Alfred the Great
(c. 848-900) because he can prove that his then forefather was
Count Reginar 'Long-Neck', the ruler of much of what is
now Belgium. But nobody has so far proved that Lord Attlee
does *not* descend in the direct male line (through the vicissitudes
of history) from Alfred the Great. What we call an 'old family'
is simply one, like the Kung family in China (the descendants of

11

Kung Fu-tze, better known as Confucius, or should I say the relations of Dr H. H. Kung, brother-in-law of both Madame Sun Yat-sen and Madame Chiang Kai-shek?) who have had the talent to hold distinguished positions over a long period, and have thus preserved their family records. But it's always nice to keep the family talents and freedom of manoeuvre up-to-date, and a *nouveau riche* heiress can hardly be wealthy unless her family had the brains to build up that wealth.

To take Lord Montagu himself as an example; he has inherited Beaulieu (of which he has made such a staggering success that its only rival in the stately homes business is the Tower of London) ultimately by descent from a coveted heiress of the line of Thomas Wriothesley, Earl of Southampton, K.G., P.C., Lord High Chancellor of England, who acquired Beaulieu Abbey in 1538. This all sounds very grand and (in the best Wodehouse manner) Wriothesley was pronounced 'Risley' just as Cholmondeley is pronounced 'Chumley'. But, unlike the Cholmondeleys, the noble Earl of Southampton – from the *riche* point of view at least – was as *nouveau* as *nouveau* could be. His real name was Writhe, and he was one of the cleverest of the clever boys who did well out the Reformation, a real tycoon under Henry VIII. Unlike a number of other Tudor politicians, he even managed to keep his head.

Nevertheless, Lord Montagu also represents the other side of the noble coin; and the one that I'm going to write about in this Foreword. In the direct male line, father to son all the way, and leaving nobody out, he descends through two lords (Montagu), five dukes and two earls (Buccleuch and Dalkeith), four kings (Charles II, Charles I, James I and the King Consort Henry, better known as Darnley), four more earls (Lennox), two Constables commanding the Scots against the English in France (Seigneurs d'Aubigny), four knightly barons (including one 'whose bravery Wallace praised above all men'), four hereditary Great Stewards of Scotland (among them a Crusader who was co-Regent of the realm), a Sheriff of Shropsire and a Seneschal of Dol, from a Breton noble called Alan, who was already hereditary Seneschal of Dol in Britanny a generation before the Norman Conquest. Now, there is reason to suppose – why, I have forgotten – that these hereditary Seneschals of Dol were related to the Counts of Dol and Dinan who were a branch of the reigning dynasty of Britanny. The Bretons in turn were Ancient Britons who had emigrated from Britain to the Armorican coast of Gaul under their dynastic leaders, and the Ancient Britons (as any Welshman could tell you) traced their leading families from the Celtic gods. Similarly, to take three very diverse aristocratic personalities, George Washington and Warwick the King-maker and Sir Alec Douglas-Home very possibly all sprang in the direct male line from Maldred (from whom we Moncreiffes believe that we too inherited our grass-grown hill-fort), brother of King Duncan who was slain by Macbeth; Maldred's father was an hereditary abbot of the Kindred of St Columba, himself a scion of the royal house of Niall of the Nine Hostages, Iron Age pagan King of the Gaels at Tara when the Romans were still fussing about in Britain; and King Niall, so far from being *nouveau* – though his raids on Britain made him exceedingly *riche* – was (as we all know) descended from a long line of kings, demi-gods and gods.

And here we get nearer the point. Nobility or aristocracy, using both words in their widest sense, ultimately derive from sacral royalty: 'the earliest religion of which we have any certain knowledge', in the words of the late Lord Raglan, President of the Royal Anthropological Institute. Among very intelligent and sophisticated peoples like the Jews or the Arabs, immemorial nobility is based on a sort of hereditary priestliness, for in their formative years it was inconceivable to their fore-fathers that the Godhead, or any part of the divine spirit, could be incarnate. So the Cohens, who alone can give the Priest's Blessing, are the seed of Aaron, the great High Priest who lived in the second millenium B.C., while King Hussein of Jordan and the King of Morocco both descend from the exquisite Fatima, daughter of the Prophet Mohammed who founded a different branch of what is fundamentally the same Faith. Similarly, in Japan (where the cult of the sacral emperor had nothing to do with supposing him infallible, contrary to the popular Anglo-American view) the greatest non-imperial family of the *kuge* or Court Nobility were the Princes Fujiwara, grandest branch of the priestly Nakatomi clan who (from the earliest recorded

Japanese history) 'recited twice a year the litany of the Great Purification'.

But most Europeans made do with an aristocracy whose forefathers had actually gone through the necessary rituals to incarnate a lucky divine spirit on behalf of their people; as indeed did the Pharaohs in Egypt, the Incas in Peru, the Kabakas in Buganda and the Rajputs in India. In Athens, for example, during one of the greatest periods of human scientific achievement, supermen like Plato and Solon were 'well-sired' *eupatrids* descended from Codrus, last Zeus-born sacral king of their world-shaking city. By the eleventh century A.D., however, the heirs of Greece and Rome were looking east from Byzantium; and the whole effective aristocracy of Europe, from Kiev to Dublin, and from Sweden to Sicily (with a very few Magyar and Slav and Celtic exceptions like Lord Montagu and me) were of what that crashing bore Hitler has inhibited us from referring to as *Nordic* origin – that is, out of primaeval forests sogging down from the Baltic. The Russian grand prince of Kiev, like his father-in-law King Harold of the Anglo-Saxons, was a scion of the mighty Skiöldung family that had once incarnated the storm-spirit Woden on the boundaries of Denmark. The king of Dublin and the duke of Normandy, equally, belonged to the ferocious Ynglingar dynasty who centuries before had been male incarnations of the goddess-spirit Freya, Mother Earth, and had been sacrificed at Uppsala in Sweden. The inter-relationship of this Nordic but international aristocracy, messing together from emperor to simple seigneur, is well demonstrated in Professor Forst de Battaglia's analysis of the sixty-four great-great-great-great-grandparents of St. Louis, King of France (1215-1270), where every country's nobility from Anne of Russia to the Cid is covered, and every rank from the King of England to the Seigneur de l'Isle Bouchard; but the only Celt is King Malcolm *Ceann-mor*. The rest are all Nordic dynasts, high or low, Goths or Franks or Saxons or Lombards or Normans.

The immemorial aristocracy of Europe (*uradel*, mistranslated *noblesse feodale* in the Neo-Gotha, since their earliest tenures were more probably allodial) stemmed from the cadet branches and other relations of these dynasts; for nobles are a bye-product of kings, and gentlemen (if that be a different term) are related to nobles. For instance, nobody was created a count in Normandy who wasn't related to the Frey-born ducal house; and an analysis of Scottish earldoms created as late as between 1390 and 1513 reveals a similar relationship to the Scottish royal house. Earls were truly 'cousins' of the sovereign, and are still officially so styled: that is why they wore crowns (what we now call coronets). So when King George VI made Lloyd George an earl in 1945, he was making him an honorary cousin of the Royal Family,[2] which would have been a pointless honour if Her present Majesty's own brother-in-law wasn't also made an earl. To give another example: long hair was originally a mark of royalty, for the royal hair was too sacred to be cut. So it became a symbol of nobility; the dynastic kindred. Tit. xxv of the Salic law laid down that only noble Franks could wear long hair, for a *puer crinitus* was thus distinguished from ordinary folk – and when the Carolingians deposed the last Merovingian king, they marked the occasion by cutting his hair. Note, a thousand years later, the popular distinction between the Cavaliers (hirsute horsey gents) and the Roundheads (short-haired squares). Even today middle-class and middle-aged majors, by some quirk of ancestral memory, are still driven hopping mad by the lengthy hair-does of the young (like my avant-garde cousin Weymouth), although such intrepid cavalry leaders as Prince Rupert and Lord Cardigan would have found crew-cuts much more repulsive in a gentleman.[3] Among aristos, only Dalrymples insist on short hair.

Incidentally, Professor Munch is probably right in deriving the very word king (Old Norse *konungr*) from *kon,* meaning kin, with the suffix *-ung* or *-ing* signifying descendant: i.e. "scion of *the* kindred", the sacral royal kindred. Among the Norse, all sons of the royal house who could raise a personal *hird* or noble bodyguard were styled kings. This system perhaps continued longest among the Scandinavian dynasts in Russia,[4] the Rurikids, all of whom bore the title of *kynaz* (probably derived from the same *kn* root as *konungr*). We translate *kynaz* as "prince", and later Russian rulers conferred the title in this form on other distinguished people. But this simply serves to illustrate the immemorial origins of European nobility: first

15

there were the sacral dynasts, then their kindred, then incomers accepted by giving them the same titular status in the community and marrying them to the daughters of their archetypes. In this context, it is interesting to observe that long before the Revolution, Russian princes were already following their well known modern avocations as restaurateurs and taxi-drivers, for in 1911 W. A. Phillips wrote of them : 'There may be three of four hundred princes bearing the same distinguished name; of these some may be great nobles, but others are not seldom found in quite humble capacities – waiters or droshky-drivers'.

Naturally disliking self-sacrifice, and accepting Our Lord's supreme sacrifice 'once only and for always' instead, most of the European dynasts converted themselves and their subjects during the first millenium A.D. The King of Sweden was a blood-sacrificing pagan as late as 1083, but by then most well-established royal dynasties had been churning out dozens of Christian saints, from St Edward the Confessor of England to St Wenzel of Bohemia, remembered in carols as Good King Wenceslas, although he was a mere duke : and including, I am happy to say, what I believe to be my own agnatic Columban relations Odhran[5] commemorated at Flisk as *St Muggins,* and his cousin *St Scandal* whose day is 5th May (in case you want to date your letters). Christianity brought to this collective and inter-related European aristocracy earnest clerks to give them a thick veneer of the bureaucratic and unromantic but essentially practical and utilitarian civilisation of the Mediterranean.

But underneath, thank goodness, there remained all the time (like touching wood or not walking under a ladder) much of the barbaric fun that eventually reached its zenith in tournaments and heraldry and Courtly Love. Mediaeval warfare was occasionally almost as unpleasant as modern warfare (I write as a Guards officer who was wounded in the back by the Royal Artillery at Monte Camino), though necessarily knightly combat was on a smaller scale than when the Hitlerite National *Socialists* of Germany took on the Stalinist Soviet *Socialists* of Russia. Nevertheless, though tongues can be held in cheeks, I rather think the *principles* of Chivalry were such that 'chivalrous' still has curiously enough a slightly different connotation from 'Nazi' or 'Bolshie'?

16

It is perhaps useful in this context to consider the original meaning of certain other words connected with the concept of aristocracy. The word 'noble' is from the Latin *nobilis* (known) and originally means a distinguished person; almost what our T.V. friends would call a celebrity.[6] Our word 'aristocracy' is from the Greek *aristos* (best) *kratia* (rule), and means government by the best people. The obvious danger is that, getting cocky in time unless modified and reinforced by rather *nouveau* best people, the older best people may degenerate and relax as 'the Best People'. Similarly, what is originally demanded from such a group specially equipped for good government is quality, but if it simply rests on its laurels such a group – unreinforced by new talent – can become merely 'the Quality'.

This does not, therefore, mean that we should offer a nobleman a political job simply because of his pedigree. But it shouldn't count against him either. With some 'intellectuals' it would, very very much, if his predecessors had distinguished themselves sufficiently (whether in war or in bed or even in juicy Commerce, the Life Blood of the Nation) for him to inherit a title. This is, on reflection, the negation both of *genuine* 'meritocracy' and of true democracy. For aristocrats are part of the People, and why shouldn't the People choose a meritorious aristocrat to lead them, if they like? Indeed, some students of Thucydides might think the Athenian democrats fared better when led by the aristocratic Pericles than when they elected Cleon the tanner (the Lloyd George of the Peloponnesian War that bled their civilisation white as he did ours). Yet a recent fashionable writer was 'certain . . . that not even the Tory party was likely to choose an aristocrat again to lead it'. They always say the middle class are the backbone of the country, but vertebrates need heads as well as backbones. However, our gritty, purposive, technological future is safe, boys; efficient plumbers obviously make better statesmen than Cecils or Russells—no more danger of Pitts the Younger, no more Winston Churchills, just an unending stimulating succession of all fourteen Mr Wilsons, alternating with their newly furbished 'image' Tory counterparts.

All the same, it may perhaps also be useful to compare the popular use of those words with their original meaning. For

17

from the days of natural expression by the ordinary people—then still in personal touch with the rural aristocracy and unaccustomed to the shrill propaganda catch-words of the Continent—it is interesting to examine the dictionary definitions of certain words, in the ways straightforward folk came to use them. A gentleman is among other things a 'man of chivalrous instincts, fine feelings, and good breeding' (Concise O.E.D.). To be noble is (also among other things) to be 'of lofty character or ideals . . . showing greatness of character, magnanimous, morally elevated . . . excellent, admirable'. *Noblesse oblige* means that 'privilege entails responsibility'. To teach this must surely be better than to pursue the chimera of equality, the natural enemy of quality.[7]

Alas, it is only fair to keep up with the times and point out that the dictionary word 'noble' also refers to an 'obsolete coin' usually 6/8d. However, in the days when the aristocracy was not allowed to be obsolete but instead ran this country, 6/8d. was the third of a real golden sovereign, and the noble too was made of gold in circumference larger than a modern half-crown (though thinner); even the quarter-noble was made of 30 grains of gold, which is after all perhaps a little more than our new masters would see fit to give us if they minted a $1/2\frac{1}{2}$d. piece in This Day and Age. The final accolade of the ordinary people is given in the phrase 'drunk as a lord'. But it is perhaps sobering to reflect that during the epic period when the aristocracy kept an eye on public affairs in England, from the mid sixteenth century until the Parliament Act of 1911, the £1 sterling was never devalued once, not even by so much as a farthing in your pockets. When we were governed by an Upper House of noblemen and a Lower House with a vast majority of gentlemen, they made us the greatest country the world has ever seen, painted the map red in anything but a Marxist sense and pioneeered liberty and democracy everywhere with sensible safeguards through what became known as the Mother of Parliaments. Sir Alec Douglas-Home's ancestor Lord Grey was the Prime Minister who forced through the Great Reform Bill with the help of Bertrand Russell's forefather Lord John Russell. Another of Sir Alec's ancestors, Lord Durham, was the 'Radical Jack' who devised Dominion status for the Colonies; and when the middle class in the Industrial Revolution neglected their factory workers, it was Lord Shaftesbury who led the Parliamentary pressure for reform. During this period too, our land wars were fought only by volunteers officered by gentlemen, yet we defeated the two successive greatest military powers on earth (both with vast conscript armies officered by experienced commanders) : Napoleonic France (on her own soil) and (also on her own soil) Czarist Russia. To hear anyone talk nowadays you would have thought we had lost the battles of the Alma and Inkerman and had failed to win the Crimean War. Nor should we forget thát that splendid and much-maligned victorious field-marshal Lord Raglan was a Plantagenet : of the same stock as Richard Coeur-de-Lion and the victors of Crécy and Poitiers and Agincourt – and one of the finest gentlemen there will ever have been.

But all this brings us to another point. What is a gentleman? Readers who are interested would be well advised to read, in the incomparable 11th edition of the Encyclopaedia Britannica, the counterweights to my present generalisations that appear under such headings as 'Nobility', 'Gentleman' and 'Prince'. Great confusion arises, in any study of aristocracy as between ourselves and the Continent – and even within ourselves – by lack of definition of the word 'noble'. In England, until the Wars of the Roses, there was no clear distinction between a noble and a gentleman. In the celebrated law-suit of Scrope v. Grosvenor, which lasted from 1385 to 1390 and at which people like Chaucer and Harry Hotspur gave evidence, it was repeatedly deponed (in the public schoolboy type of Norman-French then talked by the English knightly class) that the Scropes were socially O.K. and had a fundamental right to the famous bendor coat-of-arms *'qar ils sount de veille auncestrie & dez noblez & dez graundz gentils homes devenuz du temps de Conquest'* (because they are of old ancestry and of nobles and of grand gentlemen coming from the time of the Conquest). But by the Reformation, the English had come to make a conversational distinction between nobility and gentry : not always to the advantage of the former ('I can make you a lord, but only God can make you a gentleman,' observed King James I).

19

On the Continent, on the other hand, all gentlemen are nobles. In some countries – those formerly dominated by the German or eastern section of the Frankish Empire – whole families were normally given titles. In others – those that formerly looked to the French or Western section of the Frankish Empire – the tendency was for a title to pass only to the head of the family, chosen by primogeniture. But a title was not necessary to be a noble, and the vast majority of nobles abroad have always been untitled gentlemen. A noble is somebody who either belongs to the immemorial dynastic aristocracy who held their lands from the earliest records, or else somebody who has been created one by some sovereign (however trivial, nevertheless a fountain spouting honour) giving him a bit of paper elevating him and his descendants into the defined category. Although it is obviously fun to trace a family's fundamental nobility back to the dawn of history, it should perhaps be added as a counterbalance that, the more recent the parchment, the greater the immediate merit.

However, these patents of nobility do not necessarily create any *title,* and in status untitled foreign nobles correspond more or less to English gentlemen; so that in most Continental countries there are many thousands of untitled nobles.[8] All the same, titles add to the general fun and joy of life; what dull gossip columns we would have to endure without them.

In return for being ranked as nobles, however, families long suffered certain disabilities in many Continental countries. A noble in France, for instance, was expected to serve the Crown, i.e. the State, whether as soldier or churchman or diplomatist or judge, and not to seek to enrich himself in commerce for his own benefit. These conventions, springing from the dawn of the concept of nobility, were not always adhered to, but they had a certain original basic sense. The nobles were privileged in various ways, especially in taxation, but in return they had a duty to serve the nation rather than themselves. Most of their privileges were once duties: thus, in 1789 it was complained that the French peasantry (the most prosperous in Europe after the English farm-workers, and thus grown discontentedly independent-minded) still had to take their corn to the seigneur's mill to be ground, but it was overlooked that originally the seigneurs had been compelled by law to put up the cash to build the mills for their people in the first place, and that in return they had had a guarantee that the local folk wouldn't ever take their corn elsewhere once the mill was built. Again, it is the *metier* of the nobility to take an active part in public affairs, but literal aristocracy (the rule of the Best people) is incompatible with literal monarchy (rule by One, as in modern America and Wilson-Britain). So, during the era of Absolutism in Europe, the nobles were encouraged to hang about in the capital waiting for suitable state jobs (away from their estates where they might be popular and therefore dangerously independent-minded) and were discouraged from playing their proper part in public affairs (just as Sir Alec Douglas-Home has been now, from a different but equally jealous quarter); yet they were still disqualified by convention from engaging in business. Very grand nobles could shrug it off and get down to the doubloons, but very dicey nobles (the equivalent of our Impoverished Gentlewomen) could not afford to if they were to keep their honour. The English don't fuss too much about their pride and abstract honour, if a situation seems silly to them. So, although even in my youth there was a vague feeling that if you had enough money to jog along, a gentleman ought to serve his country rather than himself, either for a low salary or none at all, it never was thought wrong for an English gentleman to set out to make money; provided only in that case that he made a lot.

In conclusion, allow me to suggest that Scotland settles these matters best. We were so poor a country that we could not afford to distinguish between service to the state and service to the economy. As late as 1747 feudal barons (a different category with us from peers) had the duties of deciding between Life and Death in their Courts. But in 1736, to give an example, Baron Stobchon (John MacLaren of Wester Invernenty) was shot in the back by that ruffian Rob Roy's even nastier son *while the Baron was peacefully ploughing a field*. The MacLarens are, of course, immemorial noblesse, claiming kinship with the dynasts who were Earls of Strathearn 'by the Indulgence of God', and their remotest cadets were as proud as punch-drunk, however broke. To quote my own book on The Highland Clans: 'In 1498 Robin and Gilbert MacLaren joined the Scots Men-at-Arms

21

in the service of the King of France, and Colin and Simon MacLaren accompanied them as mounted Archers. They took part in the invasion of Italy in 1499, when Bernard Stuart, Marshal of France (cousin of the Earl of Lennox) captured Genoa and conquered all Lombardy. They were a touchy lot, their Highland pride mingling with that of their other Scottish comrades. "The men-at-arms were always of good lineage", as Chevalier Bayard affirmed to the Emperor Maximilian at the siege of Padua, which that sovereign and the French were then attacking. Bayard said the Scots men-at-arms were too well-born to assault the city alongside the mere German lansquenets, and that they must be allowed to "fight by the side of their equals".' In citing this, I do not mean these clansmen were right to be haughty about those poor krauts (how did they know the lansquenets did not all descend from natural sons of Charlemagne who were never recorded?), but that they were able to match the incredibly richer and infinitely grander French nobles like Bayard in pride of lineage though not in weight of pocket. Judicially, anybody recording his arms in Lyon Register is held to belong to the Scottish noblesse; although the term of art 'Estate of the Nobility' came to be used of the peers as opposed to the lairds. Scotland in general, and the Highlands in particular, have (in my opinion) thus arrived at the very best approach of all. For under the clan system every clansman came to feel (usually rightly) that he shared an immemorially noble and ultimately dynastic descent with his chief. So, instead of the horizontal divisions that separate the classes on the Continent – and to a much lesser extent in England – members of Scottish clan societies from Melbourne to Toronto can feel part of a vertically murderous (and therefore glamorous) aristocratic family tradition: 'we offended MacLeods, sprung from King Godred Crovan, suffocated in an enormous cave on the Isle of Eigg all those offending Macdonalds, the scions of King Somerled'.

Lord Montagu (like so many other prominent Englishmen) is a concealed Scotsman, a Stewart disguised as a Douglas-Scott-Montagu for reasons of lolly, but in fact the direct male-line descendant of the same Earl of Lennox of 1499 referred to in my last paragraph. But as he only got his present house at

the Reformation, and it is in England, this book is fundamentally a comparison between the post-Reformation English
landed peerage and their opposite numbers on the Continent,
which can now less often (as newspaper headlines used to inform
us in my youth) be 'cut off from England by fog'.

Iain Moncreiffe of that Ilk

Easter Moncreiffe
Perthshire

Preface

Lord Arran, one of the most outspoken of modern hereditary peers and an Irish earl who sits in the House of Lords as an English baron, says, 'We are the only aristocracy in Europe that anyone gives a damn for'. I am looking at the nobilities of five European countries in the light of this common assumption, and I am examining their records to see why, if the English peers have acquired some special instinct for survival, this should have been. The countries chosen range from Russia, where the order of nobility came to a sudden and tragic end at the revolution, to Spain where noblemen still hold the biggest fortunes and certainly the longest titles in Europe. I shall also be looking at France, Italy and Austria, which occupy a kind of mid-way position. There, the nobility retain their titles and much of their social prestige, but hold only a fraction of their former lands and enjoy no automatic political influence. I must admit at once that I feel the English peerage has survived more completely than these European counterparts, and most of the reasons for this are spelt out at length in the pages which follow. One or two general points can well be raised here.

The English peerage had, until the twentieth century, the superb security and self-confidence which came from membership of the smallest and most exclusive nobility in Europe, backed by the solid guarantee of extensive landed estates. They had no need to spend all their spare cash on sumptuous displays of conspicuous consumption, keeping up with the Cecils and the Cavendishes – as did the insecure Neapolitan counts of eighteenth-century Italy where titles were two a penny – but could invest in coal mines, experimental crops and canals. Nor did they need to cling obsessively to every small mark on their status, like the poor Spanish hidalgo, who had only his honour and his pedigree to console him for the emptiness of his larder. The English peer, secure in his elevated station, could devote a

25

good part of his time to public affairs, and develop that concern for the national interest which is one of the greatest glories in the history of the English peerage. He could afford to be flexible, confident that neither penury nor ignominy would follow from making judicious concessions.

The English peerage had always remained closely linked to agriculture, for centuries the major British industry, and never developed into the claustrophobic hothouse world epitomised by Versailles. In the eighteenth century the English court, dominated by dowdy and sometimes unprepossessing German kings, was not a Mecca for the fashionable, and the ambitious had ample opportunity during the carefully timed parliamentary recesses to withdraw to their estates. The countryside was safe enough to make possible a more agreeable life than that of the Russian or Spanish outback, at the mercy of robber barons, and the famous English love of bloodsports was always strong enough to lure the peers from London.

The peers have always been indubitably English. Unlike the fashionable Russian nobles, to take an extreme case, who prided themselves on speaking only French and English and considered it 'good form' to have their laundering done in Paris or London, English peers have generally been the epitome of the Englishman, frequently marked out by curious and endearing eccentricities, but squarely English and proud of it. Much of their popularity sprang from this simple characteristic.

Finally, the English peers, like all successful people, have been lucky. They have been lucky in their geographical location, especially in the twentieth century when wars and the special stresses they inflict on continental powers have brought social revolution on the continent. The Russians, the Hungarians, the Austrians and the Germans were all transformed by the revolutionary stresses of continental war. But perhaps most of all, the English peerage has been lucky in its monarchy. Peers have always been, from their earliest origins, closely connected with kings, 'the by-product of kings' in Sir Iain Moncreiffe's phrase. It is significant that, of all the countries dealt with, England is the only one to have a monarchy still in working order. In spite of the somewhat classless image of the modern

26

British monarchy, most people, as my public opinion survey shows, still closely identify the two groups, the aristocracy and the royal family. The English peerage has been helped to survive because the monarchy has survived – and perhaps vice versa? – and the monarchy has survived because, at least since Queen Victoria, it has never descended to the weakness and the ineptitude of the last Czar of all the Russias.

But is the luck of the English peerage going to last? Peers have managed to hold on to the vestiges of political power and have learnt to use it flexibly. As my interviews with a few of my colleagues in the Upper House show, they are at least as open-minded and adaptable in their views as any other sample of the population. The remaining political power of the peerage was recently under examination. Many peers believe that those who inherit their titles should not automatically enjoy a vote in the Upper House, regardless of their contribution to public life. Almost all peers, and here I include myself, assume that in this age rank alone carries little weight. But perhaps we have all, peers, journalists and politicians alike, over-estimated the egalitarian current of the times. My public opinion survey suggests that a surprising amount of respect and even affection for the hereditary peerage still exists. Indeed, exactly half of those interviewed think that hereditary peers should automatically continue to sit and to vote in the Lords.

In any event, the role of peers in parliament seems likely to change at some time in the future. It is only to be hoped that Lord Snow's forebodings about House of Lords reform, will not be fulfilled. 'You will lose the aristocracy completely if it doesn't work,' he said. 'We know that from other countries. The French and Italian aristocracies have absolutely no function except a rather bizarre snobbery.'

But even if the hereditary peers ceased to sit in the Upper House altogether, which isn't envisaged by either of the two main parties at the moment, there is no doubt that they would continue to work hard outside Westminster. English peers have demonstrated time and again in the past hundred years that they are strong, tough people, who start life with enormous natural advantages, and are well able to compete effectively in diverse human activities from show business to ceramics. Many

27

of them will undoubtedly survive and prosper in whatever walk of life they may choose. Who knows, many more of them may exploit their centuries of inherited political experience, and make their way back into public life through the House of Commons.

Chapter One

French Nobility

The French nobility have seldom practised moderation. During the last five centuries of their turbulent history, they have been at various times the most powerful, the most witty, the most enlightened and cleverest nobility in Europe. For two hundred years they set the pace in fashion, conversation and manners, and managed to make most of their European counterparts seem by comparison parochial if not boorish. In politics they have been less successful. The intransigence of some and the carefree adoption of explosive ideas and slogans by others helped to provoke the revolution, the greatest aristocratic disaster before the Russian calamity of 1917 and one from which the French nobility has never recovered. Instead of the steady, phlegmatic adaptation to new circumstances which is the story of the British peerage, the French nobility have plunged from the heights of grandeur to the depths of degradation, not just once but several times, and their history is one of the wild fluctuations of fortune. 'Nothing except in excess' might be their collective motto.

The medieval French nobility derived its position from the 'terre' or fief: there were no personal titles as in modern Britain. There were originally only two classes in France, the nobles being those who owned the land, the roturiers or non-nobles those who tilled it. There was no land without the seigneur, no seigneur without the land. The nobles were exempt from most taxes, but provided military service. It has been estimated, from very approximate figures, that two thirds of the[1] nobility were killed in battle, and whole families became extinct. In France, as in England, the nobility emerged from the middle ages as blood-stained warlords. Their lives centred on killing and wounding, but it was not entirely savage existence – the honourable professions of chivalry managed, perhaps more effectively

29

than the Geneva Convention has done, to set a limit to bestial excesses in combat. Similarly the life in the castles, from which the nobility ruled the provinces with the help of private armies of retainers, was not all brawling, drunkenness and lack of privacy. The ideal of courtly love and the deference due to a lady had some civilising influence, and in Burgundy at least the nobility helped to create a courtly society as sophisticated as any in Europe. But by the end of the fifteenth century a society which relied on chivalry and courtly love for its claim to refinement was already old-fashioned. In the Italian peninsula a new concept of polite society and a new philosophy of the gentleman was being developed which was to influence European nobility for centuries. It was the blending of French and Italian ideas at this point which laid the foundations of that French pre-eminence in the civilised arts which lasted until the revolution.

Once again, war and refinement were strangely intertwined. It is paradoxical that King Charles VIII's invasion of Italy in 1495, which let loose thirty years of carnage, should have been so great a civilising influence on the French nobility, as scores of their number sought fame and fortune in that beckoning country. Italy was at the peak of her cultural Renaissance and successive French kings and their courtiers were dazzled by the architecture of Milan and Florence, so different from their rude northern towns, and by the wealth of painting, sculpture and scholarship. Some of the Italian treasures were brought back to France as the spoils of war, and Italian influence soon made itself felt in the new luxurious hunting lodges which the nobility were building along the Loire. The traditional design of French castles combined with the sophisticated elevation and greater comfort of the Italian palaces to produce some of the world's most perfect buildings, a magnificent contribution made to architecture by the French nobility.

It was the civility of Italian life which impressed the most. Sophistication of a kind had existed in their medieval castles, but the polished manners and educated tastes of the Italian courts seemed of a different world. When Francis I (1515-1547) became a convert to the Italian fashions in his turn, demanding these accomplishments at his court, a generation of noblemen devoured Castiglione's *Book of the Courtier,* the best-selling handbook of etiquette, which prescribed the qualities of a gentleman for the aristocrats of western Europe. A gentleman was cultivated as well as athletic, with a knowledge of the classics as well as a grace and skill at riding and fencing, a man of taste as well as strength and courage. He gave visible evidence of good breeding with a versatility which showed him to be good – but not quite good enough to be professional – at everything. Above all, he must never seem to be trying. Nonchalance was the hallmark of a nobleman and the French nobility worked hard to achieve it. In time, they would far outstrip their masters and set the European standards of noble behaviour.

The arrival of Catherine de Medici from Italy in 1533 for her marriage to the Dauphin completed the transformation; she brought in her retinue a band of Italian chefs and a new implement for the table, the fork, which between them laid the foundations of French cuisine. The French nobleman was also to be a gourmet.

What the French nobility gained in polish in the first half of the sixteenth century, they were on their way to losing in power. The French kings of this period, like their Tudor contemporaries, found pretensions threatening. Like family relationships everywhere, the cousinhood of kings and nobles had its stressful moments. Kings were rarely convinced of their nobles' unswerving loyalty and in cases of treason they were generally the first suspects. In every European country, kings sought ways of clipping their nobles' power, until, much later, the French revolution presented them both with a common threat – the people.

Louis XII made a start on the process which in France was completed by Louis XIV. He no longer allowed nobles to raise taxes in their provinces without his permission, and often interfered with their conduct of seigniorial justice. Francis I adopted a technique which had a brilliant future – he tempted whichever noblemen he could to remain at court under the royal eye, acting almost as palace servants, their time harmlessly consumed in performing an elaborate court ceremonial.

The suppression of the nobles was very incomplete in the sixteenth century, and the successive reigns of Catherine de

Medici's weak-minded sons, and the outbreak of the religious wars which accompanied them, gave the nobility a golden opportunity to make up the lost ground. The greatest of their number had the income and standing of minor kings. The Duc de Guise, closely related to the royal family by marriage, owned estates worth 53,000 *livres* a year as well as holding numerous titles. His brother Charles, Cardinal of Lorraine, was even richer. The cardinal was Duke of Rheims and Chevreuse, Bishop of Metz, Bishop of Verdun and holder of eleven abbacies. The Guise family possessed vast secular and ecclesiastical patronage, and the cardinal even operated his own network of private agents, which made him one of the best-informed men in Europe. The chief Protestant rival of the Guise family was Louis, Prince de Condé, of the house of Bourbon, a great landowner in western France who was, like his leading opponents, related to the monarchy. Falling into line behind one of the grandees, the lesser nobility seized the opportunity afforded by the wars to pay off old private scores and enrich themselves. Both sides terrorised their areas. 'I have often heard my mother say,' wrote a Huguenot later, 'that just before I was born, she several times had the greatest difficulty to save herself from being drowned like others of all ages and sexes by a great lord of the country, a persecutor of religion. He had them thrown into a river close by his house, saying that he would make them drink out of his big saucer.'[2] Ravaging bands of noble retainers, based on the fortified castles still in the hands of the nobility, destroyed crops and interrupted communications.

The victory at the end of the wars of the Bourbon Henri IV, nephew of the Prince de Condé was the beginning of the end of their high-handedness. As a protestant who converted to Catholicism and granted toleration to Huguenots, he put a stop to lawlessness masquerading as piety.

What he began, Richelieu and Louis XIV completed, and the absolute power of the Bourbon kings was built on the submission of the aristocracy. Henri IV was less successful at converting his nobles into progressive landlords. The agricultural textbook, *Théâtre d'agriculture et mesnage de champs,* which the King promoted as part of his reconstruction programme, fell on deaf ears as far as the nobility were concerned. Most of the nobility were much more concerned about hunting rights and feudal dues than about scientific farming.

Richelieu, the powerful cardinal who virtually ruled France for eighteen years, took up the struggle with the nobility where Henri IV had left off. In 1626 he ordered that all fortresses not essential to the defence of the realm should be destroyed, and with them went some of the danger of the overmighty subject. Duelling, a costly and compulsive noble diversion, was forbidden on pain of death; and a young nobleman of the great family of Montmorency, who had already killed twenty-two men in duels and had the temerity to fight another under Richelieu's very window in the Palais Royale, was sentenced to death.

The cardinal made sufficient progress to allow the Crown to survive the war of the Fronde, when the nobility took advantage of the minority of Louis XIV to stage their last bid for independence. Noblemen led revolts in their provinces, the Duc de La Rochefoucauld in Poitou, the Duc de Bouillon in Turenne, the Comte de Tavannes in Burgundy, and even made treasonable plans for a Spanish invasion to support them. The Queen Mother and the infant king were forced to flee from Paris on two occasions, and the memory of that humiliation was to make Louis XIV, in maturity, reduce his nobility to decorative impotence.

The great new palace at Versailles was built to be a cage where the high nobility would be imprisoned on display, their time consumed in ceremonial, their ambition devoted to questions of precedence, who should hand the offertory bag round in chapel or hand the king the royal shirt in the morning, rather than treason and revolt. The turbulence which had once destroyed the peace of the countryside now troubled the palatial galleries and even threatened to disturb the royal devotions; quarrels about precedence always seemed at their worst in chapel, and in 1704, for instance, the king was obliged to exclude from the Good Friday service the quarrelsome dukes and princes who could not agree which protocol should prevail.

The régime at Versailles, for all its surface splendour, was anything but soft. The King once said that the mark of a man of quality was his indifference to cold, heat, hunger and thirst; and this was no idle talking-point. A nobleman needed an iron

B   33

constitution to survive in that spartan environment, where comfort was ruthlessly sacrificed to appearances, where draughty windows, and smoky fires were ignored as long as the façade was impressive, and where court doctors seemed bent on destroying rather than preserving life. Only short spells of recuperation from the exhausting routine were allowed, when noblemen retired briefly to take the waters at Vichy, Cauterets or Bombon-l'Archambault, and while away the time with illicit love-affairs started in the pump-room.

It has always puzzled me why the nobility, so proud, independent, and sometimes intelligent, should have been so readily prepared to become mere palace servants, prepared to wait for hours in the Gallery of Mirrors for a quick glimpse of their sovereign on his way from the royal bedroom to the chapel, and hypnotised into believing that pleasing the king in however trivial a way was the supreme objective of life. Part of the answer seems to lie in the French love of fashion. Louis XIV managed to establish that Versailles alone was smart; even Paris was not the place for a man who cared about his image, while the provinces were dowdy and ridiculous. Noblemen were exiled to their estates as a punishment. The king played on that obsession with status, which is seen at its most extreme in the Duc de Saint-Simon, the snobbish chronicler of the world of Versailles, who wrote :

'The most cherished and the liveliest passion that I experience, is that for my dignity and rank. I care far less about my personal fortune, and it would be a transport of delight that I would sacrifice the present and the future, if only I could enhance my dignity.'[3]

Enhancing one's dignity was impossible in the provinces, nor could a nobleman obtain the generous pensions and court offices essential to men whose estates seldom produced the revenues of their English counterparts. The larger income to be drawn from English estates made their owners less susceptible to the blandishments of court life, in any case much less stylish in England than in France, and this had great repercussions on their respective future developments. The painful dilemma facing the great French nobleman of Louis XIV's time was neatly summed up by La Bruyère :

'A nobleman, if he lives at home in his province, lives free but without substance; if he lives at court, he is taken care of, but enslaved.'[4]

Few of those elevated enough to have the chance hesitated to choose enslavement and their descendants paid the price for their choice up to the revolution. Perhaps they have never ceased paying. The capacity to rule withered with disuse, instead of being refurbished anew in every generation as in England, and too many noblemen became unable to exercise judgement on anything but protocol. When an opportunity did arise for them to show leadership, after Louis XIV's death, they made a mess of it with their irresponsibility and petty squabbles. Until the revolution their descendants enjoyed privileges but were excluded from power, and their grandsons, in the last days of the old regime, were to cast longing eyes on England, where peers had virtually no privileges but enjoyed great power, and virtually ran the country. The Comte de Ségur declared that : 'The brilliant but frivolous life of our nobility, at court and in town, could no longer satisfy our pride, when we thought of the dignity and independence of a peer in England, of a member of the House of Commons.'[5]

In Louis XIV's day at least, the life at court had minor compensations. This was a society which set the highest international standards of behaviour, aped and envied by clumsy German princelings, by rough English peers more at ease in the hunting field than the drawing-room, and by crude Russians who all came to France to put some gloss on their manners. All over Europe, noblemen recommended their sons to copy French behaviour and study French habits when the grand tour took them to this centre of enlightenment. It was about this time that French became the international language of diplomacy, which it remained until the Second World War.

Lord Chesterfield wrote to his son :

'What a number of sins does the cheerful, easy good-breeding of the French frequently cover. Many of them want common sense, many more common learning; but, in general, they make up so much, by their manner, for these defects that, frequently, they pass undiscovered. I have often said, and do think, that a Frenchman who, with a fund of virtue, learning, and good sense,

35

has the manners and good breeding of his country, is the perfection of human nature.'[6]

At course, politeness was taken to great lengths, as courtiers took their cue from Louis XIV, who must have been one of the politest men who ever lived. The Duc de Saint-Simon described how he found the Duc de Coislin with a broken-down carriage somewhere between Fontainebleau and Versailles, offered him a lift but found the offer was refused in case the Duc deprived a maid-servant of her seat on the coach.

The Arts flourished under noble patronage. Molière and Racine wrote plays for their entertainment, the Royal Gobelin manufacture produced exquisite tapestries for their walls, and Watteau painted pictures for their chateaux, dream-like compositions of gay picnics in magic parks where it never rains, to act as a background to festivities and pageantries of court society.

The French nobility imposed its standards, not only on foreign peers, but on the new moneyed recruits who worked their way into the ranks with comparative ease. The acquisition of nobility was not just a snobbish ambition, but a good investment, since it brought exemption from most taxes. By the seventeenth century there were personal titles as well as those derived from the land, and there were three main ways of acquiring nobility for those not born to the rank. The first was by receipt of a knighthood conferred by the king for public services, civil or military. The possession of seigniorial estates, which not infrequently came onto the market, also entitled the holder to a title after a certain length of time had elapsed. The third method was by holding certain offices, mainly legal, which brought nobility with them. Louis XIV financed his wars partly by the sale of these offices and their attendant privileges, and the 'noblesse de robe' grew accordingly. During his reign in particular, when expensive royal ambitions stimulated the market, men of money but inferior birth could obtain a title more easily in France than in England. The marriages between the old families and the new men who had entered at this favourable moment, laid the basis of the greater French aristocracy of the eighteenth century, and the old families set the tone.

Apart from the legitimate new recruits to the nobility, there were a vast number of self-elevated imposters, sporting spurious and convoluted family trees designed to gain entry to society and evade the tax collector. Periodic 'recherches' into noble credentials never entirely succeeded in eliminating them.

But new recruits, even legitimate ones, were not automatically on a par with the oldest families. The Honours of Court, the right to ride in the king's carriage, to hunt in the royal forests, and to have their wives presented at court, were confined to those who could show unbroken noble descent from 1400. Pages in the royal stables had to prove noble descent from 1500. Aspirants to the Royal School for Ladies at St. Cyr had to prove 140 years of noble descent. Consequently, the court nobility were only a fraction of the whole. Outside in the provinces, the poor and unfashionable nobility, not necessarily titled, lived a very different life. The so-called feudal privileges were a drawback rather than an advantage to efficient agriculture and much less profitable than the privileges enjoyed by the commercial classes, while the fallow field system condemned the bulk of the French nobility to poverty by the English standards of the time. After the mid-eighteenth century feudal dues produced very little more than the cost of enforcing them. In the country before the revolution very little capital was sunk into the land of France in comparison with England. There were among the court nobility men as rich as English dukes, but the English agriculturalist, Arthur Young, who toured France in the 1780s, came across noblemen struggling to bring up families on twenty-six pounds a year, and others engaged on the back-breaking labour of ploughing their own fields. Many were too poor to own a carriage and, if they were able to spend the winter in a neighbouring town, had to make do with cheap lodgings. There were even some, according to a proverb of the time, forced to stay in bed while their breeches were mended. The average income was certainly much lower than that of the untitled English gentry.

Their poverty was not always their fault, and was seldom the result of wild extravagance. Arthur Young remarked that, 'where one gentleman of small property in the provinces of France runs out his fortune, there are ten such in England that do it.'

Many were genuinely interested in getting the best possible returns from their land, and studied reports of the latest methods.

Arthur Young said that he had never had such a practical lesson in farming as from the aristocratic young Madame de Luneville who farmed her land profitably and understood her crops. But for most the feudal system and a chronic shortage of capital prevented the kind of agricultural improvement patronised by peers in England.

Few of them were prepared to make up for their losses in trade. The poorer they were, the more they clung to their noble lineage, their superiority to vulgar commerce and their honorary privileges: the right of noblemen to carry a sword, to be sprinkled with holy water apart from the rest of the congregation, to enjoy a monopoly of army commissions, and to have the church draped in black when a death occurred in their families. Without these distinctions, they would be nothing but poor yeoman farmers. It was the poor provincial nobility, not Les Grands, who were a rigid and conservative group before 1789. In France, as in Spain, poverty and noble status was a dangerous combination, producing intransigence and insecurity. Part of the flexibility of the British peerage was due to the virtual absence of such figures until the twentieth century. There were in England, of course, noble rakes who went through their patrimony in six glorious months; but large numbers of poverty-stricken peers, never.

The great court nobility, on the other hand, had often as big an income as their English counterparts. Their estates, which they seldom visited or investigated, were rarely efficiently run or highly profitable but they had long found more agreeable sources of income. Marriage with rich heiresses had, since the reign of Louis XIV, been an accepted way of diverting the new commercial fortunes to their pockets, and came to be heavily relied on as a source of income. Duclos commented that, 'there are few fortunes that do not find their way into the distingushed families . . . without the commerce which has grown up between pride and necessity most of the noble houses would fall into misery and in consequence into obscurity.'[8]

Nor did Les Grands share their inferiors' contempt for commerce, so long as it was on a sufficiently large scale; big financial transactions were quite respectable, only petty money-grubbing was sordid. This philosophy was, incidentally, to have a long international run amongst the titled classes, reappearing among other places in the Britain of Sir Iain Moncreiffe's childhood, when a gentleman who did go in for money-making was expected to make a lot. Some of the great French nobility made very much indeed. In the Franche-Comté, the Comte de Rosen, the Prince of Montbéliard and the Comte d'Autrey all had substantial interests in the iron industry. The Comte d'Esseville intrigued for the concession of the ironworks in the king's duchy of Chateauroux in 1771. The Prince de Carignan drew 120,000 *livres* a year, as much as a Duke's income in England, from the roulette tables in the gaming house which he owned in Paris.

It was perhaps the impact of money and the changes which it brought which gave so many of the high nobility their extraordinary receptiveness to new ideas. Wit and learning had long been esteemed in France more highly than anywhere else, and as the great scholars of the century, many of them born into the estate of the nobility, became more challenging and provocative, criticising privilege and authority, preaching fraternity and brotherly love, many of the nobility were happy to follow them. Voltaire was lionised by high society. Servants probably first heard of the fashion for equality from behind their masters' chairs, and it no doubt profoundly upset their sense of propriety. The new fashion only too often spread from the top downwards, directly promoted by the admonitions of the master of the house. 'The man I esteem the most is the most honest man, without asking what his birth is,' said the Maréchal de Casteja, rebuking a snobbish land agent, who had refused to eat with the servants.[9] One wonders whether the Maréchal was prepared to follow his philosophy to its logical conclusion, or whether he even realised what that conclusion was. Thoughtless radicalism was just as dangerous as thoughtless conservatism. The fashion for equality in France was quite different from the slow adaptability to new circumstances which has been the glory of the English peerage. The one was all theory, starry-eyed idealism for some, the latest fad for others, the insouciant adoption of slogans whose real significance was never grasped. The other was a patient, realistic adaptation to the facts of life. Englishmen found the political conversation of the French salons little to their tastes. Horace Walpole, son of the first Earl of

39

Orford, who visited Paris in 1765, was disconcerted to find that his aristocratic friends, unlike their London counterparts, were continually preoccupied with problems of philosophy and politics, and with what they describe as 'the abuses of the régime'. 'They might be growing wise,' he grumbled, 'but the intermediate passage is dullness.'

With the new and fashionable egalitarianism, there went a vogue for sensibility and sympathy, admirable qualities in themselves but often adopted with that abandonment which is a recurrent feature of the French nobility. Miss Edith Sichel has described one such episode, more ludicrous than most :

'A young nobleman was driving his coach from Paris to a ball at Versailles. On his road he met some peasants bearing a litter. The rain was pouring; he was clad in laces and satins, but nothing daunted, and without asking a question, he proceeded to try to alleviate Human Suffering. For an hour he stood there, the storm beating on his powdered head, without producing the slightest effect. Amazed at this, he at last enquired the nature of the patient's illness. *'Ah monsieur,'* replied one of the peasants, *'vous pensiez que c'était un malade. C'est un cadavre!'*[10]

This was living in cloud cuckoo land, the same dream world which made swooning and convulsions fashionable, encouraged ladies of gentle nurture to collapse on poets' graves, and led noblewomen to dress up as shepherdesses in blue and pink satin, indulging in moonlight operas and Watteau picnics in woody groves transplanted for the occasion. There may perhaps have been heartless noblemen like the Marquis de Saint-Evremonde in Dickens' *A Tale of Two Cities,* running down children with their carriages, seducing their peasants' daughters and murdering their protesting brothers, but in an extraordinary number of cases quite the reverse of such callousness applied – the heart was dictating to the head.

The appeal of liberty was strongest to the young and it was enthusiasm for the cause, as well as a desire for revenge on England, which led young noblemen like the Marquis de Lafayette, the Vicomte de Noailles and the Comte de Ségur, to scheme and plan for a chance to fight in the American revolutionary armies. The democratic behaviour of the Americans deeply impressed them. Lafayette wrote that :

'The manners of this people are simple, honest, dignified; they belong to a country where every cranny resounds with the lovely name of Liberty. Although there are immense fortunes here, I defy anybody to find the slightest difference in the respective manners of richer and poorer to each other.'[11]

The success of the American revolution was hailed with delight in liberal circles, blind to the possible implications of their doctrines and carried away by slogans whose real significance they somehow failed to grasp. The Comte de Ségur later wrote:

'With respect to us, the young French nobility, we felt no regret for the past, no anxiety for the future, and gaily trod a soil bedecked with flowers which hid a precipice from our sight. Lighthearted critics of old fashions, of the feudal pride of our ancestors, and of their solemn behaviour, whatever partook of tradition appeared to us ridiculous and troublesome. The gravity of ancient doctrines was irksome to us. In the same way we were drawn to and entertained by the attractive philosophy of Voltaire; and, without searching into that professed by graver writers, we admired it as bearing the stamp of courage and of resistance to arbitrary power.'[12]

While the American revolution encouraged habits of sloppy thinking, of admirable and generous sentiments without a practical programme, the cost it imposed on the already shaky French economy brought revolution a step nearer. For the country's bankruptcy which played so big a part in the revolution the nobility must bear some of the blame. Of Louis XVI's thirty-six ministers all except one were noble, and none succeeded in solving the problem. Their best efforts were thwarted by the court nobility, who resisted economies. Eleven million pounds were spent annually on courtiers, mistresses and placemen, but Turgot's efforts to suppress useless and expensive court offices led to his dismissal from the post of Minister of Finance, engineered by Les Grands in 1776. The high nobility had voiced the noisiest demand to join the American war, which strained the economy almost to breaking point. The defeat of France at Britain's hand in 1763 still rankled in many noble circles. Honour demanded that this humiliation be avenged at the earliest possible moment, and honour, in the words of Montesquieu, was 'the child and father of the nobility'.

41

The elderly, the conservative and the responsible, who did not share the new vogue for liberty and equality, were not aware of any danger. The Comte de Ségur, whose father, as Minister of War, held a key post in the government, wrote:

'The heads of the ancient families of the nobility, believing themselves as unshakeable as the monarchy itself, slumbered in perfect security upon a volcano. The discharge of the duties of their offices, promotions, royal indifference or royal favours, and the nomination or dismissal of ministers, engrossed all their attention, were the sole motives of their actions, and the only subjects of their conversation.'[13]

Secure in their illusions, the nobility lived out the last days of the ancient regime when, in spite of new money and interminable talk of reform in the salons, they enjoyed the *'douceur de vivre'* in Talleyrand's famous phrase, which no class in France would ever experience again, when the wittiest and most articulate nobility in Europe, enjoying the best the world had to offer in intellect, comfort, elegance, food and the arts, displayed for the last time their great expertise at the art of living.

It was the Marquis de Lafayette, hero of the American war and a believer in some kind of constitutional monarchy, who drew up a formal protest, inveighing against the extravagances of the Court and the misery which heavy taxation brought to the peasant, proposing the abolition of useless expenses and the calling of the Estates General. On 4th August, 1789, one young noble after another, many inspired like Lafayette by unselfish but vague ideas, rose from their seats in the First Estate to renounce their privileges for the sake of Fraternity. The Vicomte de Noailles' resolution to do away with all feudal rights, tithes and taxes, was enthusiastically carried. Lafayette immediately dropped the aristocratic prefix 'de' from his name. Others had the coats of arms on their carriages painted out and dropped their mottoes.

Amongst the poorer nobility, many resisted losing the few distinctions which they had in life, including the right to sit separately from the third estate, and court advisers began to panic as the third estate grew out of control. After the fall of the Bastille, the more hysterical among the nobility, led by the king's brothers, began the flight across the border. This kind of irresponsible panic was absolutely disastrous at such a delicate moment. The Duc d'Audiffret-Pasquier later condemned the frivolous motives which caused the emigration, careless of the way such action jeopardised the king :

'In the years 89, 90 and 91, emigration was for some a question of escaping from danger; for a very small number, a genuine enthusiasm; for many a point of honour, to be accepted without argument; for the great majority, the fashionable thing to do; while for all or nearly all of them it meant hope sustained by the craziest correspondence and the intrigues of a few ambitious men bent upon making their fortune. Such were the motives that led to this mass emigration, so confident to begin with, so much to be pitied later on, most of whom bore with courage and resignation their misfortunes in foreign lands.'[14]

The emigration played into the hands of men more extreme than most noblemen. The bourgeoisie of the third estate, joined by sympathetic nobles, seized the initiative, and openly defied the crown. On 19th June, 1790, hereditary nobility, titles and coats of arms were abolished. The aristocratic order in France was wiped out, and nobility everywhere in Europe began its gigantic about-turn. Monarchy, which for centuries had seemed the main challenge to noble authority, now became its most precious ally against the much more alarming threat from the other direction – radicalism.

Most of the emigrés counted on a quick return. A few formed armed bands on the border, in the territory of the Elector of Trèves, but most were happy just to sit it out, whiling away the time until their inevitable return with amusing themselves. The early emigrés came from the least sensible sections of French society. Extravagant while the money lasted, they put up prices wherever they went. Many were haughty and insolent, others frivolous and irresponsible, and all fed exaggerated tales of their misfortunes to the press.

The emigration made much more difficult the survival of the king and liberal aristocrats, and helped to provoke increasingly extreme measures against the code of their class. In 1792 primogeniture was abolished, in 1793 illegitimate children were granted equal shares with legitimate ones in estates, and in 1794 all nobility were exiled from Paris. The liberals had lost control.

43

Lafayette, who had served during the first years of the revolution, and had declared in 1791 that 'as a lover of Liberty and Equality, I enjoy the change which has placed all citizens on one level',[15] was declared a traitor.

After the king's execution, emigré hopes began to fade. Scattered now from Switzerland to England, from Livonia to Philadelphia, and constantly moved on by local authorities, they settled down to a long wait. Jewellery and other possessions soon vanished, sold at usually cut prices to dealers who were quick to advertise 'best prices for French diamonds', but most emigrés eventually faced their dilemma with courage and resourcefulness. Adversity brought out the best in them. Noblemen gave lessons, for a trifle, in languages, chess, fencing or dancing. Noblewomen, who until the revolution had scarcely known how to handle money, organised sewing circles and opened restaurants. The Comtesse de Guéry, an exile in London, discovered an unsuspected talent for making ice-cream, soon considered to be the best in the capital, and her café was patronised by the Prince of Wales and the Royal Dukes. The Comte de Caumont learnt the trade of bookbinding, and his work is now highly prized by bibliophiles. The Marquis de Bouille, more conventional, wrote his memoirs, the recourse of countless noblemen down on their luck in the centuries to come.

The French nobility were the first to display that resourcefulness in adversity which has since become an international feature of European aristocrats. From emigré Russian counts running flourishing nightclubs in the Paris of the 1920s, to a modern English peer like Lord Lichfield helping to pay off arrears of death duties by a career in fashion design, aristocrats have been disproportionately able to compete if forced to make the effort. There must clearly be built-in advantages to an aristocratic upbringing, advantages of environment and perhaps of heredity, which build confidence and foster a fighting spirit which rarely goes under. The French nobility has seldom seemed so admirable as it seemed in exile.

Even in the direst poverty, standards did not entirely slip. Good conversation and good manners were still cultivated, and in Protestant countries hard earned money was scratched together to build Catholic chapels. Imitation salons were held in the evenings, and gifts of prayer books exchanged. There were still limits to the jobs considered permissible. When a Chevalier of the Order of St. Louis became a servant, the indignity was felt to be too great; a court-martial, convened by senior officers of the order in London, solemnly heard mass and declared that, since the state of servitude was inconsistent with the dignity of the order, he be stripped of his distinction.

Less happily, ardent monarchists and reformers kept up a running feud in exile; only occasionally were disputes forgotten. When the Duc de La Châtre, an ultra-royalist, met the Comte de Narbonne, a constitutional monarchist also in exile in England, he said:

'You have ruined everything with your constitution. You are the primary cause of all our misfortunes. Well, there it is, now let us all die of hunger gaily together.'[16]

The emigrés, although they made more noise in the world than the rest, were in fact only a tiny proportion of the French nobility. Out of nearly half a million nobles at the revolution, only sixteen thousand left the country. Most of the rest lived as quietly and unobtrusively as possible while the Terror, which killed 1150 of their order, was at its height. But there can have been few noble families that did not number emigrés among their relatives and friends, and this fact alone put their property and even their lives at risk. Not only was emigré property confiscated, but that of their relatives was sequestered until any inheritance likely to go to fugitives was deducted. Wives of emigrés, however devoted, found it prudent to petition for a civil divorce.

The land held by the aristocracy, though shrunk to something like half, was not entirely confiscated, and amongst the remaining nobility there were many whose surviving estates received attention unequalled after years of neglect. The memoirs of Léontine, daughter of the Marquis de Villeneuve, who grew up quietly at the chateau of Hauterive near Castres in the years after the revolution, give a curious picture of this submerged world. The chateau had been pillaged and only the scantiest furniture – a monogrammed armchair and a great bed with faded draperies – survived amongst the cheap chintz curtains and bare brick floors. The Marquis managed the estates himself, and was

45

invariably in the saddle by dawn, waking the servants, allocating work for the day and making his rounds of the property. Here too, as with the exiles, something of the old standards was salvaged. At dinner time, the Marquis changed his clothes, joined his wife and his mother in the drawing-room, and often entertained a few friends – a modest luxury they still permitted themselves. A returning emigré, however boring, was always made welcome.

There must have been thousands of families, living just such a life with one foot in the farmyard and one foot in the salon, and their estates, free now from the fetters of feudalism, were better run than ever before.

After the fall of Robespierre, the first of a handful of intrepid emigrés insinuated themselves back in France and by 1799 when Napoleon became First Consul, there were groups of former exiles living discreetly throughout the country, able from time to time to meet together to enjoy a little of the old life. Pasquier, who had been in prison and in hiding, was able to renew his acquaintance with several society women he had known before the revolution, and later wrote :

'We discussed politics at home and abroad, in the past and in the present, the nature and value of different constitutions, the religious needs of the new society; we argued about classical literature and the great masters of the century of Louis XIV, as well as about the literary revival.'[17]

It took more than a revolution to destroy society's delight in good conversation.

The more pliable of the returning exiles were soon tempted by Napoleon's conciliatory noises to take up office under him in a state once again becoming hierarchical. Altruistic reasons could always be found to quieten the consciences of those anxious to emerge from obscurity. Pasquier, who was amongst them, spoke of the 'necessity of aiding and supporting any government that showed itself to be animated by a sincere desire to restore order'. We recognise across the years the authentic voice of the collaborator. To take such a step provoked bitter opposition from family and friends and was never forgotten.

The 'turncoats' were prominent among those favoured when in 1806 the Emperor revived the institution of nobility. This was to be a new order, consisting only of personal titles deriving from the Emperor and granted to those who had served him in the army and administration. By the end of the Empire 31 dukes, 388 counts, 1,090 barons and about 1500 knights had been created – far larger than the contemporary English peerage – and endowed with fine chateaux in the Ile de France and entailed estates from the Emperor's private domain or from foreign conquests.

This was a service nobility, headed by the generals of the Imperial army, whose titles fittingly reflected Napoleon's great victories. Marshal Soult became Duc de Dalmatie, Marshal Kellermann Duc de Valmy, and Marshal Ney Prince de la Moskowa. Bernadotte eventually became King of Sweden, Murat King of Naples. Many of the new notables were self-made men who had risen by their own talents in the most fluid army in Europe; Ney was the son of a cooper, Lefevre of a miller, and Murat of an innkeeper. Before appearing at court and living in the grand style, they really needed some kind of finishing school, and emigrés were soon whiling away the long evenings in exile mocking their pretensions, ludicrously combined with muddy boots, doubtful linen and camp manners.

The Emperor was anxious that this mint-new nobility should be fused with the old whenever possible. Any aristocrat who supported his government, whether actually in office or not, was given a title, although invariably a new one which he owed unequivocally to the Emperor. Pasquier, who supervised this operation as Procurer-General to the Council of Seals and Titles, found that this policy brought much heart-burning:

'Amongst those who were upset in this way, there was much talk of a Madame de Montmorency, a lady-in-waiting to the Empress. . . . She had been made a countess, whereas she wished to be only a baroness, because this was the title she had borne in 1789 and was the one that had always been preferred by the eldest sons of the family of Montmorency, jealous of preserving the title of first baron in Christendom which had belonged to them from time immemorial. Napoleon firmly rejected her demand, and referring to a certain flightiness in her youth, told her, "You are not a good enough Christian for me to endorse such a claim."[18]

47

The Emperor and the new nobility set the tone of a society which was very different from the old. Heavily organised functions, of almost military precision that suggested 'reviews with ladies taking part' as the Comte de Saint-Aulaire remarked, were now the order of the day. There was a surface glitter and parade of wealth at the grand festivities, with rows of women smothered in flowers, diamonds and waving feathers, generals in uniform covered in gold braid, and ministers all richly dressed, their breasts plastered with the stars and ribbons offered by a conquered Europe. But there was little of the poise, easy manners and natural elegance of the ancient regime, and stilted punctilio killed much chance of relaxation or enjoyment. At the ball given in 1806 on the marriage of the Emperor's step-daughter Hortense to the King of Holland, the guests were parked in two ballrooms, the Galerie de Diane and the Galerie des Maréchaux, according to the colour of their tickets, and were not allowed to move from one to the other. For most of the evening they were not allowed to dance, but were confined to watching quadrilles performed by sixteen selected ladies and sixteen chamberlains. 'I have known many monarchs,' commented the Comtesse de Boigne, 'but none of them treated the public so cavalierly.'[19]

The energies repressed at the stiff official receptions broke out riotously in the great private houses where wild practical jokes were all the rage. At Lucien Buonaparte's house at Plessis-Chamant, for instance, people let their hair down by squirting water on unsuspecting guests, or slipping a live fox between the sheets of their beds. Literary salons did not really flourish in this atmosphere, and most of the great writers and intellectuals stood aloof. Snobs and adventurers, rather than philosophers, swelled the receptions.

The organised character of official entertaining, with its regular explosions of magnificence, lasted until the end, but as the military situation became more precarious, society seemed more and more to be hastily encamped between two campaigns, and those who had much to lose tried to ensure themselves against the Emperor's overthrow, and the return of a Bourbon king.

The Charter issued by Louis XVIII, who returned to the throne of his brother in 1814, contained the conciliatory article that 'the titles of the old nobility will be restored; those of the new will be retained'. The Imperial nobility had at least accustomed France to hereditary distinctions once more, and made much easier the resumption of old titles at the restoration. But the two noble groups were not exactly on good terms. The old nobility, whose sufferings were magnified in restrospect, were intoxicated with the revival of the old court, and could barely bring themselves to utter the odious official titles of Buonaparte's upstarts. Marshal Ney, the Prince de la Moskowa, often found his wife in tears at being persistently referred to under her maiden name of 'Mademoiselle Aiguié'.

The two groups were never completely assimilated. In Marcel Proust's *Remembrance of Things Past,* which delicately explores the nuances of society nearly a hundred years later, the Prince de Borodino, whose title derived from Napoleon, was not received in the salons of the old nobility, who regarded him, not as a true gentleman, but as the grandson of an upstart. When service in the army necessarily brought the two groups together, observers had no difficulty in distinguishing in their respective manners and behaviour, the difference that existed between the two aristocracies.

Men of old family who had compromised their honour by coming to terms with the Emperor were not forgiven, and they and their descendants were referred to as the 'touched-up nobility'. However, it must be pointed out that respect was more forthcoming by the old aristocracy towards those whose ancestors had shown genuine military valour.

The restored nobility found it hard to behave with moderation, and the dark hints and veiled allusions which they dropped in the early, intoxicated days of their return, did their popular esteem untold harm. Pasquier, who made an official tour of the country in late 1814, having managed skilfully to transfer his allegiance to the new king, reported with alarm the distrust which the aristocracy was arousing:

'Amongst these old noble families there are certainly some who, by their imprudent language even more than by their deeds, encourage the suspicion and fears that we should be striving to dispel. To say that, since the Restoration, the nobility has lost more than it has gained in public opinion is sad, but it is nonetheless true. As a result of the criminal acts of violence committed by the Revolutionary party, people were prepared to feel sorry for the aristocracy, even to like them. But directly they believed that they were prepared to abuse their power, the position changed.'[20]

Threatening as they might seem to some, the nobility were in nothing like as strong a position as their ancestors. Many confiscated estates were never restored: too many bourgeois landlords who had done well out of the revolution firmly blocked that path. Not all were landless, of course. Many families had never emigrated and managed to keep out of trouble; others had friends who had, collusively, bought their estates on their behalf. Fifty years later the Marquis d'Aligre was amongst the five biggest landowners in Europe. Lands that survived were now held absolutely without the crippling restrictions of the feudal system to block progressive measures and noblemen, more often than their bourgeois counterparts, were to pioneer modern methods. But the nobility as a whole did not enjoy anything like that solid stake in the land which was one of the great features of the English peerage.

This difference had great significance. French society was for a century to be more rural and agricultural than English society, but the French nobility was much more out of touch, without that almost instinctive understanding of the thoughts and feelings of the illiterate countrymen, which was one of the strengths of the English peerage. The French nobility was all bloom and no root, and the lack of communication across the classes meant that, from time to time, the fierce hatred of aristocrats, stimulated by the Terror, broke out again with a virulence never seen in England.

Their comparatively landless position had financial repercussions as well, especially as royal subsidies were not as forthcoming as they have been. The royal bounty, which had once flowed into the pockets of the old nobility, was not often handed out by Louis XVIII, naturally selfish and tight-fisted and in any case subjected to a strict annual budget. Even the royal favourites who had stood by him through everything could not rely on the king to pay their debts. The great offices in Church and State, which had once been their near monopoly – all the

50

bishops and most of the abbots had been noble in 1789 – were no longer automatically theirs.

It was not much consolation that the constitution set up a Chamber of Peers modelled on the English House of Lords, an institution which was unnatural in France. It was an artificial situation to have peers, not necessarily distinguished by virtue, merit or experience, and without the economic weight of their English models. A duke, to qualify for his seat, had to be able to settle an income of £1,200 on his son and heir; a baron £400. These were trivial sums compared with England, where £10,000 a year was considered the minimum necessary to equip a man for the peerage. There were other drawbacks at least as serious as the lack of a big stake in the land. The new French peers had little of the political nous of the British, brought up from birth to play a part in public life, and usually serving an apprenticeship in the House of Commons as member for a family borough before taking their seat in the Lords. Few of the French peers had parliamentary gifts striking enough to make up for the priceless inheritance and experience which their British equals enjoyed.

Parliamentary life was an understandably strange experience in which peers were not yet at their ease. But even the court, which had once seemed so brilliant, was nothing like its former self. Most of the court favourites were old, even decrepit members of the old nobility who had suffered exile with the royal family. Caricaturists loved to depict them as strange old dowagers and broken down nobles with nothing left but their titles. Bourgeois habits had crept into even the most elevated families, and a dinner guest noted gloomily that the great Duke of Montmorency used napkin rings. But poverty, among men of ancient lineage, was now taken as a sign of honourable fidelity to the Crown, and an aristocrat never hesitated to admit his difficulty if he was too poor to own a carriage.

The revolution had been a traumatic experience, and many of those who had suffered found solace in religion. Piety, a striking feature of the returning emigrés, became an inescapable require-ment of good breeding. Priests figured prominently in the home life of the high aristocracy. Here they would still rub shoulders with intellectuals, and even venture into the literary salons which lionised Chateaubriand and later Victor Hugo, but the more earnest atmosphere which the priests represented extinguished the wit and finesse of earlier days. Conversation was not as free-ranging as it had been, and radical ideas were no longer tolerated, let alone fashionable. The novelist Stendhal wrote of the salons of the old nobility (*Scarlet and Black*):

'So long as you do not speak lightly of God, or of the clergy, or of the King, or of the men in power, or of the artists patronised by the Court, or of anything established, so long as you do not say anything good . . . of Rousseau or Voltaire, or of the opposition press, or of anything that allowed itself the liberty of a little freedom of speech, so long above all, as you did not talk politics, you could discuss anything you pleased with freedom.'

The nobility never recovered from the revolution, which threw them badly off balance. Understandable but exaggerated brooding on their losses, intrigues and pressure to recover their lost lands, a fanatical devotion to the Church which had sustained them in exile, all made them a dissatisfied and dangerous group. It was not just King Charles X, Louis XVIII's successor, who had learnt nothing and forgotten nothing[21] – this was also true of far too many of the old nobility who clustered round him. Their immoderate policies, ceaselessly demanding restoration of their old position and that of the Church, and encouraging the king to exert his authority, helped to provoke the revolution which sent Charles X into exile in 1830.

The 1830 revolution abruptly shattered the illusions of the old nobility. For fifteen years they had almost persuaded themselves that time would restore to them the position of their ancestors. Now another great crisis of conscience confronted them, and a new rift opened up in the already fractured ranks of the nobility, between those loyal to Charles X, the legitimate king, last royal relic of the pre-revolution court, and his cousin Louis Philippe, a man of almost bourgeois habits from the younger, Orléans, branch of the royal house which had supported the revolution.

Some of the peers had little trouble in adjusting their allegiance, among them the aged Lafayette, the Duc de Broglie, and the inevitable Pasquier, who had already served Louis XVI, Napoleon, and Louis XVIII, and whose new loyalty brought him the Presidency of the new Chamber of Peers, and, fourteen years later, the dukedom of Audiffret-Pasquier. In the Chamber of Peers, which survived although it was not hereditary, the survivors were joined by men of varying distinction promoted for services to the regime or society – Marshal Bugeaud, one of the generals victorious in Algeria, who became Duc D'Isly, Victor Hugo who became a Vicomte as a gesture to the Arts, and the chemist Gay-Lussac.

Most of the old nobility refused to compromise, and clustered together in haughty disapproval in the Faubourg St Germain or retired to their surviving country estates. They were profoundly demoralised by what was, for some of them, the second catastrophe within a lifetime, bringing with it what was virtually a second exile. 'The emigré of the interior,' it has been said, 'became a familiar figure; sulky, hostile, living in a world of dreams and resentments. He was idle unless he had enough land to occupy him, and enough energy or intelligence to farm it. Few were as lucky as an officer of the Guards who married a woman of the Macintosh family and founded, in Clermont-Ferrand, a little rubber business that became, in due course, the great firm of Michelin.'[22]

Some even resigned their army commissions. The royalist officer of the interior, unemployed and increasingly embittered, was a familiar figure in most provincial capitals, joining from time to time the dispirited deputations which made their way to London's Belgrave Square to reaffirm their loyalty to Charles X, or his grandson and successor 'Henri V'.

It was galling that Paris which so many of them boycotted should again become the favourite haunt of the nobility of Europe. German princes and English noblemen settled there, rubbing shoulders with Russian grand dukes. But it was perhaps some consolation that the new Chamber of Peers in France enjoyed even less prestige than the old one, and, in the 1840s produced a series of scandals which exploded among old and new nobility alike and seriously compromised the regime.

At the beginning of 1847 two new members of the Chamber of Peers, President Teste and General Cubières, were found guilty of fraud and corruption. Shortly afterwards scandal hit the old nobility in the person of the Duc de Choiseul-Praslin.

Victor Hugo, who as a peer of France had access to inside information, described the incident as follows:

'The Duc de Choiseul-Praslin had married the daughter of Marshal Sébastiani in 1824, when he was nineteen and his bride sixteen. The marriage appeared to be a happy one until the arrival in the Praslin's house of a governess, Mademoiselle Deluzy, who became the Duke's mistress. Sébastiani threatened to obtain a separation and thus ruin his son-in-law unless Mademoiselle Deluzy was dismissed; and Praslin obeyed. But on 18th August, 1847, the Duchess was found stabbed to death. The Duke was promptly arrested, and on the 20th was transferred to the Luxembourg, where he died on the 24th: a phial which had contained arsenic was found in his possession.'[23]

The interesting thing about the Praslin affair was how quickly it fanned the hostility to aristocrats which had flickered beneath the surface of French life since the revolution. Rumours spread that the Duke's suicide was faked, that the Chamber of Peers had connived at his escape and that he was in fact living in luxury in London with his mistress. Public opinion swung savagely against the peers, aggravating the bitterness which was already felt by the poor at a time of economic crisis and widespread poverty. Hard words were thrown at the English peers during the 'hungry forties' – especially by the middle classes – but there were few hostile scenes in England like that created by the Duc de Montpensier's fête, a splendid and magnificent occasion when more than four thousand guests were entertained in satin and silk-lined tents. As Victor Hugo described it:

'Yesterday, from the Tuileries to the Barrière du Trône, a triple row of onlookers lined the quays, the streets, and the Faubourg Sainte-Antoine as the carriages of the guests passed by. Every few moments this crowd hurled at the gilded and bedizened persons in their carriages shouts of disgust and hate. It was like a cloud of hatred around that transient splendour.'[24]

Booing, spitting and mud-slinging were an ominous reminder of 1789. The French nobility were once again paying the price for their history and their isolation.

The Duc d'Audiffret-Pasquier, now retired from public life, blamed his own class for the revolution of 1848, which sent Louis Philippe in his turn into exile. Mournfully reminiscing on the events of the last year of the reign, he lamented later to Victor Hugo :

'*Nostra culpa, nostra culpa, nostra maxima culpa!* What a year 1847 was. How far 1847 led up to 1848! Take just our Chamber of Peers for instance – Teste and Cubières condemned for corruption. The word "fraud" attached to the epaulets of a general, and the word "theft" to the robe of a President. And then the Comte Bresson cuts his throat. The Prince of Echmühl stabs his mistress, an old whore who wasn't worth as much as a kick. The Comte Mortier tries to kill his children. The Duc de Praslin murders his wife. Isn't there the hand fate in all this? The upper class of society has shocked the lower. . . . It is with that sort of thing, gossip, chatter, horrible talk, that the rotten old world was undermined.'[25]

The return of a republic, most hated of all constitutions to most noblemen, led many of their order to lie low for the time, longing to take a stand against a despised regime, hoping and scheming that out of the early disorder would emerge a royalist restoration, but fearing greatly another reign of terror at their expense. When the 'strong man' who emerged from the chaos of 1848 proved to be not a Bourbon but another Buonaparte, the disappointment of many aristocrats was doubly deep.

Napoleon III, like his uncle, anxious for a nobility to grace the splendours of the new Imperial court, produced a new episode in the saga of 'box and cox' which is the history of the French nobility since the revolution. The Napoleonic creations, forced to endure calculated snubs from the old families for nearly forty years, were now triumphant. Princess Mathilde, the first Napoleon's niece, and Count Walewski, his illegitimate son, were now second only to the Emperor. Most of the legitimist royalists maintained as before their sullen opposition, cherishing their pedigrees and consoling themselves with the exploits of distant ancestors. Only on the rarest of occasions were they prepared to drop their exclusive pretensions.

Society of the Second Empire displayed a surface glitter which had not been seen in France since the first Napoleon. A flashy splendour marked the season in Paris, the season in Biarritz, and the great hunting season at Compiègne. To the Spanish and Austrian nobility, used to the more subtle display of rank, more exclusive company, and less obvious opulence, the whole thing seemed rather vulgar.

The common denominator of the new society was money. Everything seemed to be up for sale. Among the new creations were men who made their fortune in the new economic boom. The daughter of the financier and railway speculator, Jules Isaac Mirès, became Princesse de Polignac. New sources of income became vital to maintain the costly display essential for a place in society, and railway stock became as respectable as rents as a means of support. Noblemen of illustrious names, like the Comte de Ségur and the Vicomte de Noailles, sat as directors on the boards of railways. Society readily opened its doors to the well-heeled, even to Jews. The cultivated Jew, Charles Haas, the model for Proust's Swann, whose stockbroker father had left him a considerable fortune, was admitted to that exclusive club, the Cercle de la rue Royale. The ultimate tribute paid to money came in 1862, when the Emperor paid a visit to Baron James de Rothschild at his chateau of Ferrières, more like a state visit between two sovereigns than the condescension of emperor to subject. The second empire, like the first, did not provide an environment conducive to the arts. As far as the Empire had any links with literature they were provided by Princess Mathilde, of the Imperial family, who entertained Sainte-Beuve. Intellectuals were critical of a capitalistic atmosphere which seemed philistine, and men like Sainte-Beuve who joined the ranks were little esteemed. But what the new nobility failed to do for the arts, it made up for in sport. The Jockey Club, the most prestigious social group in Paris and the social arbiter of the times, organised the increasingly important sport of horse-racing. Longchamps and Chantilly became as fashionable as Ascot and as eminent as Newmarket. In 1865 Gladiateur, bred and trained in France, had a triumphant season in England, carrying off both the Derby and the St Leger.

The new nobility provided the most spectacular sights of the second Empire, but these curious aristocrats of Europe who flocked to the city driving their carriages down the Champs Elysées or riding in the Bois de Boulogne, also played their part in its fall. Prince Pierre Buonaparte, tried but acquitted for the murder of a journalist, in 1870, reminded opposition journalists only too conveniently of the Duc de Praslin. But it was the Duc de Gramont, perhaps the most incompetent foreign minister France has ever had, a grand seigneur with limited brains and even more limited vocabulary, who bore the heaviest responsibility. It was Grammont who insisted, at a time when the Emperor, though not the Empress, was pacific, on transforming a minor dispute with Prussia into a matter of life and death in which France's honour was irretrievably involved. In the disastrous war which followed, the Empire was the first casualty.

At first, the battering at the hands of Prussia and the humiliation only equalled in 1940 seemed the prelude to a triumphant royalist return, not the beginning of the end of an official aristocracy in France. When a majority of royalists were returned to the new national assembly, this seemed a great triumph for the old nobility. The bulk of them were still legitimists; a few had gone over to Louis Philippe, a few more to Napoleon, but most had cherished their loyalty to 'Henri V', boycotting the vulgar glamour of the second empire, sulking in their chateaux and in hired rooms in provincial towns. But if they had not lost the taste for power, they had lost the capacity for judgement and when their great chance came they muffed it. Riddled with prejudices and grudges, hating the Orléanists even more than the Imperialists, not above thoughts of revenge for their forty long years in the wilderness, they, combined with the stubbornness and unreality of their king, defeated the royalist cause.

An aristocracy without a king must always have something of an air of unreality, just as a king without a nobility would be left in strange and lonely isolation. The two must be complementary. The French nobility, destined to live out the rest of their existence under a republic, without a centre to unify them, apart from the Jockey Club, and without an official function in the state, splintered more sharply than before into unreconcilable groups, often living in the unreal and aimless world described so vividly by Marcel Proust. Few had much remaining stake in the land. In 1885 there were fewer than one thousand estates of more than 1,000 acres in France. A few were returned to the Chamber of Deputies as royalists in opposition, but none took any part in the business of governing. Only in money matters had they really adjusted to their times. Here the old nobility

were quick to emulate the Imperialists. The Duc de La Rochefoucauld who, as President of the Jockey Club, was the acknow-
ledged leader of the upper crust, drew his income from Pom-
meroy champagne and Singer sewing machines. Heiresses
were eagerly competed for amongst the oldest of French families,
and an heiress who was even moderately attractive might well
receive a proposal from each of the unmarried dukes in turn.
Among the more successful in this particular line was Count
Boni de Castellane, a member of the Chamber of Deputies, and
married to the somewhat dour American heiress, Anna Gould.
But religion was still, on occasion, more powerful than the commercial instinct. On the advice of the priests, many aristocratic
families invested in the Union Générale, a Catholic bank
founded with the blessing of the pope; at the collapse of the
bank in 1882 many aristocratic families suffered heavily, and
the disaster, blamed on the Jews, helped to raise to white heat
the already existing anti-semitism in old noble circles. It is
ironical that there is in fact a considerable amount of Jewish
blood in some of the great historic families.

There were of course some men of broad sympathies, enlightened views and distinction amongst their number – Comte
Robert de Montesquiou wrote complicated symbolist poetry
which was highly regarded; the Comte de Vogüé, novelist and
Academician, wrote studies of the great Russian novelists which
first brought Turgenev, Tolstoy and Dostoevsky to serious notice
in France. But far too many were like Comte Aimery de la
Rochefoucauld, noted for the 'almost fossil-like rigidity of his
aristocratic prejudices', who salved his indignation over sloppy
protocol at a dinner party by walking home with a friend and
talking about rank. The Count looked down on the Duc de
Luynes, Chamberlain to the current Pretender to the throne,
as a man whose family 'were mere nobodies in the year
1000'.[26]

Such ludicrous snobbery was brought on by the particular
insecurity and boredom of French high society. By contrast, the
tenth Duke of Devonshire, the English contemporary of Comte
Aimery, who owned nearly 200,000 acres and three times refused
the office of Prime Minister, had no need to concern himself
with establishing his pedigree. The Marquess of Salisbury, British

Prime Minister 'since God knows when,' in Churchill's phrase, could afford to be the shabbiest man in London society, and was merely amused when turned away from the Monte Carlo Casino for his unsuitable attire. The rest of the English peerage, though less eminent, were able to relax and be themselves. While Queen Victoria lived, at least, their stake in politics, land and society seemed relatively secure.

The French had no such confidence, and enjoyed little influence in public life to give purpose to their lives. The bored and idle young man was a familiar figure in late Victorian London society – where would the plays of Oscar Wilde be without him? – but few English households can have been quite as aimless and narrow-minded as that of the Duc de Luynes. The Englishman George Wyndham, who visited the duke's chateau at Dampierre, was dismayed at the deadness underlying the surface chatter, the absence of books, the conversation which faded as soon as it left the subject of sport. The host and his friends struck him as 'children arrested in intelligence, who hate Jews, Americans, the present, the past two centuries, the future and the fine arts'.[27]

The Dreyfus affair, the hysterical and violent upheaval over the guilt or innocence of a Jewish army officer convicted of treason, provided a rallying cry for almost all the old nobility, a cause into which they could pour the accumulated frustrations of a lifetime. It seemed to many the last chance to restore the old values, religion, the army and patriotism, to expose the rottenness of International Jewry and even, out of the turmoil, to procure the collapse of the hated republic and the return of the Bourbons. To achieve these ends, even social sacrifices were not too much to ask. At the first public meeting of the National Anti-Semitic League, the Duc d'Uzès, the Duc de Luynes, Prince Poniatowski and the Comte de Breteuil happily rubbed shoulders with workers from butchers' shops and slaughterhouses. The decision to award Dreyfus a retrial led to one of the most curious episodes in the turbulent history of the French nobility. Baron Fernand de Christiani, a tall blond man with a blond moustache, and wearing a white carnation and a white cravat, publicly assaulted the President of France at Auteuil races, delivering a hefty blow on the head with a heavy cane.

His English equivalent would have put down a question in the House.

The Dreyfus affair discredited both the old nobility and the institution they venerated – the Catholic Church. Condemned to recognise at last the permanence of a republic, their fierce devotion to succeeding pretenders has faded, although there is still great affection for the Comte de Paris. But even in adversity they have led the way internationally. For nearly fifty years the chief example in Europe of a displaced nobility, they were joined in 1918 by the Austrians and Germans, endowed with titles whose significance, like theirs was now purely private; while the Russians faced an emigration which recalled the great calamity of 1789.

The old nobility remained well into the twentieth century a select one. The titled imposters, who have had such a long run in France, still flourished, protected ever since 1835 by the law which deprived the nobility of any redress against usurpers; but social ridicule and the exclusiveness of the old families made France less comfortable for them than elsewhere. In 1936 the Genealogists' Magazine noted severely :

'Those who, having made money, take to themselves a title, generally migrate to countries like England, where it is said they "love a lord", or to America where they adore them, where a venal and complacent Press publishes their doings.... The title and honours of one of the most illustrious and historic French families of the sixteenth century are now held by a butcher in America, whose only affinity is the shedding of blood.'[28]

The old aloofness of the genuine nobility had broken down somewhat since the last war under the impact of the mass media, but the French nobleman still remains for the most part less accessible than his English counterpart. Only a small circle still participate in that civilised living which has been one of the continuing and distinctive characteristics of their order.

Chapter Two

Spanish Nobility

'We who are as good as you swear to you, who are no better than we, to accept you as our King and sovereign lord, provided you observe all our estates and laws; and if not, no.'[1] The Aragonese nobles' grudging oath of fealty to their sovereign breathes the proud spirit which for centuries Europeans associated with a Spanish nobleman. God and time, not any king, had made a Spanish grandee.

In fact, the infidels seem to have had more of a hand in shaping the mould than the Almighty. The eight centuries of struggle against the Moors gave the Spanish nobility those distinctive qualities which it has hardly lost until this day : its pride, appetite for religion and fierce passion of the spirit. The small Christian kings of the reconquest relied heavily on noble support for their holy crusade, and the newly conquered lands of the South, granted as rewards for their efforts, formed the basis of the great noble estates of Southern Spain. The counts of the South had always before their eyes the possibility of turning their counties into independent kingdoms – the counts of Portugal showed the way. The military orders of Alcantara, Calatrava and Santiago, formed in the twelfth century, brought land and troops under their control and reinforced their solidarity as a class, just as their decorated uniforms and privileges would set apart their noble members far into the future, when the reconquest was ancient history, and a ceremonial sword the nearest the knights came to active service.

The crusading spirit had a long life in Spain. The military virtues, pride, valour and partisanship were perpetuated into the centuries ahead when the political virtues, flexibility, compromise and the common touch, would have been more appropriate.

61

The fierce and quarrelsome independence of the nobles was slightly curbed when Castile and Aragon were united in the fifteenth century. The military orders were brought under royal control. When Queen Isabella learnt of the death of the Grand Master of Santiago in 1476, she rode hard for three days, the last part in torrents of rain, to ensure that the knights of the order should elect her husband as their new grand master. The Inquisition was a useful threat to hold over the heads of a turbulent nobility – nearly all of them had Arab or Jewish blood hidden somewhere in their pedigrees. To complete the process, the aristocracy were discouraged from living on their estates, where permanent occupation and poor communications gave them influence, and some castles were systematically destroyed to make them permanently uninhabitable. Thus early on the local ties which have for centuries provided much of the strength of the English peerage were snapped. It is still rare to find a large Spanish landowner who lives on his estate.

The nobility were steadily impregnated with Castilian values – Castilian horror of change, rigidity and social stratification. But it was the voyages of Columbus and the winning of undreamt of wealth in the new empire of Mexico and Peru which most transformed them. Gold and silver, flowing into Spain unearned, like the prize from some gigantic sweepstake, profoundly affected the attitudes of the nobility. Money and wealth became separated in their minds from labour, effort and production. Spain came too quickly unprepared into her inheritance, and her good luck aggravated the most impractical aspects of Castilian character – pride, belief in miracles, and contempt for work, outside the honourable service of the state.

The disdain for commerce originated in the difference between service to the Nation and service to oneself. It was unthinkable that the head of the Nation, its first servant the king, should engage personally in profitable commerce for his own benefit. His duty lay in the administration of justice, in ensuring law and order in peace and victory in war, and in forming a bridge between Church and State. The great nobles were originally kinsmen of the sovereign, performing similar functions on a lesser scale, and for men of rank, down to the humblest hidalgo, to participate in trade was considered a betrayal of their class. Traces of this idea could be found in every European country, but nowhere was it ever so pronounced as in Spain, where the conquest of the Indies reinforced its strength. What other nations called 'the Spanish disease', the disdain for labour as degrading, took an unshakeable hold. Over the centuries Spain was to pay a heavy price for stumbling on the richest Empire in the world. In 1900 the Secretary of the Association of Catalan Industrialists analysed his country's difficulties like this: 'If we can get the privileged classes to work, that is the whole problem.'[2]

In the course of the sixteenth century, the great nobility were gradually excluded from real power. The Emperor Charles V wrote to his son Philip, then a young man learning the job of kingship:

'You must avoid placing [the Duke of Alba] and other grandees very intimately in the interior government because he and others will exert every means to gain your goodwill, which will afterwards cost you dear. I believe that he will not hesitate to tempt you even by means of women, and I beg you most especially to avoid this.'[3]

In the early days, Philip used the Duke only in harmless ceremonial capacities: for instance, he and the Duchess accompanied Philip to England for the royal marriage to Queen Mary, when the free and easy manners of the English court scandalised the Duchess. She much resented being kissed on the mouth by the Earl of Derby at their first meeting. Later on, the Duke of Alba, perhaps the finest soldier of his generation and one of the outstanding figures of the age, was given a number of vital posts, but in the European Empire, not in Spain itself.

The Duke illustrates much of the best side of the sixteenth-century nobility, still a vigorous group whose arteries had not yet hardened. Alba came from a long line of fighting men; his father had been killed in battle against the Turks when the boy was three. Although ruthless and sometimes cruel as a commander, and blunt to the point of rudeness to his sovereign, he was a talented general whose loyalty was never in doubt. Although much of his life was spent in military camps and on battlefields, he was not an uncultivated man: he had a good knowledge of Latin and Greek, kept in regular correspondence

63

with Erasmus the distinguished scholar, and in 1573 received two paintings from Titian. His descendant, the seventeenth Duke, later wrote, 'All this is a proof that the atmosphere of noble houses was not so indifferent to culture as some of their detractors claim when they picture them as occupied solely with fighting, sporting and feasting.'[4]

Fighting was, all the same, the chief occupation of his class. Apart from Alba, the Duke of Medina Celi, as Viceroy of Naples, and the Duke of Medina Sidonia, a conscientious administrator on land, but inefficient and unhappy at sea as commander of the Armada, were given vital assignments, neither of them in fact fulfilled very creditably. What is more, noblemen could still be found serving as privates in the Spanish infantry, and officers and common soldiers still messed together. Rigid social distinctions had not yet hardened. But by the end of the century many more noblemen than ever before were looking for less exciting employment than the life of even an officer in the army. Municipal offices, which offered good pay for a minimal amount of work, were increasingly snapped up by the nobility. Court offices they had long looked on as their special preserve – now they crowded as well into government sinecures and local offices. Position was the tribute which the state owed to rank.

As governors and magistrates, the Spanish nobility were not disinterested public servants. The influential classes of every European country had their share of graft, but nowhere was incorruptibility so hard to find as in Spain, while public spiritedness became more common in England than anywhere else. Shakespeare gives several examples of the crooked courtier, ready to plead the suit of anyone with money to cross his palm; he does not, as does Cervantes, who died on the same day, always assume that the governor and the magistrate are the born enemies of the weak and the poor, that they belong body and soul to the first person who takes the trouble to bribe them, and that self-interest dictates their every move. 'In a few days I shall leave for my governorship to which I go very anxious to make money,' writes Sancho Panza trustingly to his wife, 'and I am told that all new governors go in the same frame of mind.'[5] Perhaps it was the absence of any personal link with other classes, or regular contact with tenants and labourers, which accounts for this striking difference. In any event, corruption was to have a particularly long history in Spain, and to provide plots for some of the best grand operas of the eighteenth and nineteenth centuries.

Inefficiency was added to venality as the seventeenth century wore on. The gentlemanly ideal, with its emphasis on leisure, made for delays and confusion in the administration, and by the middle of the century the low state of public service figures prominently in the reports of Venetian ambassadors. Pietro Basadonna, ambassador in Madrid from 1649-1653, reported that:

'One must put away entirely the common idea that the Spaniards are prudent, and understand that there is no nation in the world more ignorant of good government, or more inclined to destruction; indeed, it is only when one has seen how execrably they manage their private affairs that one finds it possible to believe all that one is told of public affairs.'[6]

In obedience to the as yet undiscovered Parkinson's Law, noble expenditure rose to meet the income available. Another Venetian ambassador noted that:

'Officials' salaries absorb large sums of money. There is not a person scarcely who does not live on the king or who, if he lacked a salary from him, could maintain himself on his own income, whilst the chief nobles, supported at court by remunerative posts, have entirely abandoned their own properties.'[7]

Foreign travellers began to make those sanctimonious criticisms of the idleness of the nobility that appear in almost every travelogue until the twentieth century. Carlo Ruzzini, travelling in Spain in the 1690s, noted that, 'the nobles never visit their estates, which for that reason are ruined, and in order to dress themselves they have to sponge on the king.'[8]

When, in 1700, the last of the Habsburgs, the weak and epileptic Charles II, was succeeded by the grandson of Louis XIV, the great nobility were well on the way to becoming decorated court pensioners, and the new king, schooled in his grandfather's methods at Versailles, was bound to encourage the trend. He, no more than his royal predecessors, was likely to trust them with real power, especially since they had been both unreliable and incompetent during the War of the Succession which ended in 1713. The loyalty of the grandees to the new royal house was suspect : at the height of the war, even the more favourably inclined had merely retired to their estates to await the outcome of events. Louis XIV advised his grandson to 'preserve all the external prerogatives of their rank, and at the same time exclude them from a knowledge of all matters which might add to their credit',[9]

The grandees, with their consciousness of rank bordering on obsession, were soon outmanoeuvred. While the really powerful offices of state were falling into the hands of Frenchmen and Italians, lesser nobility and lawyers, the grandees were preoccupied with their claim to rank equal with the French princes of the blood. When the new king granted the peers of France the same rights as the grandees, the Duke of Argos saw fit to remind him, in a long and formal document, of the exclusive privileges and standing of his elevated class. Their prerogatives included the right to keep on their hats and be seated in the royal presence; to be called 'Cousin' by the sovereign; to have a private bodyguard wherever they went; to be arrested only by the sovereign's personal order; to hitch four mules to their carriages in Madrid and to be escorted by four torch-bearers. The Duke of Argos was exiled for his temerity, and Philip V debased the title of grandee with lavish new creations. The old families could only privately nurse their exclusiveness, reserving the intimate appellation 'tu' for those of the old blood. It was the absence of real power or responsibility which encouraged this preoccupation with the more trifling manifestations of rank.

The rank below the grandees, the titulos, were also swelled by new creations to the point where, by the end of the eighteenth century, wits delighted to point out that there was hardly a river, village or field in Spain that had not given its name to a title. The titles of baron, viscount, count or marquis were granted as favours to subjects who had performed some usually quite menial service for their king. The title of Marqués de Réal Transporte (Marquis of the Royal Transport) was bestowed in 1760 upon Gutierre de Heira for safely conducting the royal family from Naples to Barcelona on the ship 'Phoenix'. A title of this sort was granted almost every week during the

eighteenth century, but the titulos were still a small group compared with the rank below them, the hidalgos, or ordinary
nobility, who numbered half a million according to the 1787
census.

The status of hidalgo varied greatly from province to province.
In the Basque provinces all the male population claimed this
rank, as a relic of their ancestors' part in the reconquest. In the
South and centre, less than one per cent were entitled to it. Most
hidalgos had inherited their position, but new hidalgos, called
hidalgos de privilegio, could be created by the king. Then there
were special categories: the Hidalgos de Goteras were recognised
only in the village where they lived; the Hidalgo de Bragneta
won his rank for siring seven successive male children, an honour
hard won by any standards. The Hidalgo de Cuatro Costados
based his claim on the nobility of all four grandparents, and
helped to keep the genealogists prosperous.

Few hidalgos were rich, but they nearly all regarded manual
labour as a disgrace. Only the muscular Asturians could be
found earning their living in menial jobs. The rest preferred
to receive alms or even to beg rather than disgrace their station
by working. The poor hidalgo, obsessed with rank and honour,
was the favourite target of generations of jokers. Impoverished
nobility soon excites ridicule, especially when the nobleman tries
to salve his penury in satisfied contemplation of his family tree.
Satirists said that even the most insignificant hidalgo had his
coat of arms panelled in colossal dimensions over the door, on
the windows, and over the fireplace of his house, and em-
broidered on the hats and stockings of his servants, though his
larder was empty. He was generally pictured as refusing to
receive a stranger in his home, without making detailed enquiries into the visitor's pedigree. He was said to acquire a
library merely for the pleasure of placing his escutcheon on each
volume. His genealogical tree was placed conspicuously in his
salon. 'How nourishing indeed,' a wit commented, 'was the
crust of black bread eaten beneath the genealogical tree!'[10]

It was easy to scoff, but the poor hidalgo was not just a figure
of fun. He was prepared to suffer cold, hunger, pain and dis-
comfort if he could live with honour. And for all the obsession
with rank which the hidalgo exemplifies, Spain was one of the

67

few places in the world where a duke could converse with a peasant without condescension from the one, or servility from the other. Everyone, whatever his rank, had a natural dignity.

But foreign travellers, as well as fellow countrymen, gave the nobility a bad press. While the poor hidalgos were satirised as rank-obsessed paupers, the grandees were usually pilloried as absentee landlords, tied body and soul to the tedious routine of court life. It is true that the visit of a grandee to his estates was a great event in local history : the villagers would fête their señor like visiting royalty, with loyal addresses, processions and church services. The grandees found country life intolerably tedious. They had none of the love of country sports so dear to the English peers; in spite of royal example they did not hunt or, until the end of the nineteenth century, shoot. Banditry made country roads dangerous, and isolated country houses of the English type unthinkable. The Spanish nobility had not for centuries enjoyed the priceless advantage, taken for granted by the English peers, of direct experience of agricultural problems, or personal contact with tenants and peasants. They lived in an artificial world, following the court in its mathematically timed moves from royal residence to royal residence. Stiff and intricate ceremonial, endlessly repeated and planned down to the tiniest gesture, emphasised the gulf between king and nobles, and created that gloomy convent atmosphere which made Madrid a hardship post for intelligent ambassadors. 'I do not conceive it possible for any great city to be duller or less agreeable than Madrid,' complained William Eden, the British Ambassador. 'Its cleanliness is its only virtue, in every other respect it is an execrable place. . . . The society is formal and the reverse of gay.'[11]

The estates of the grandees were often neglected. Their tenants were unknown to them, and the lord was unaware that stewards often demanded a second rent for their own benefit. Some landlords cultivated their land directly through their stewards, using seasonal labour forces, but in any event it was a point of honour not to challenge their accounts. Such money-grubbing suspicion was beneath the dignity of a nobleman. The wholesale embezzlement which resulted profoundly shocked visiting Englishmen, used to the personal supervision of even

the dukes over their estates. Joseph Townshend, the rector of
Pewsey in Wiltshire, wrote in his journal when he travelled in
Spain in 1786 :

'It is difficult to estimate what with good management would
be the revenue of these great lords. Such a property as the Duke
of Alba's, producing under administration eighty thousand
pounds a year; what would it not yield, if let out to substantial
farmers. If, whilst they plough, and sow, and reap, and thrash,
and sell, and eat, and drink, upon the duke's account, he
received such an income, what would it be if every inch of land
were made productive, and if that produce were expended with
economy? With such vast possessions well managed, he might
live on splendour little inferior to the greatest sovereign of
Europe. But instead of this, devoured by the servants, they are
most of them in debt, and, under the feeling of poverty, live
exceedingly retired, scarcely venturing at any time to give a
dinner to their friends.'[12]

The grandees had neither the incentives nor the attitudes
which went to make improving landlords in England. Most of
their lands were held by an entail even stricter than the English
one, and included movable property. The tenant for life merely
had the income from the estate, but had little chance of borrowing money on its security, and had little encouragement to improve it, especially when he had no direct heir, for some reason
a frequent affliction in Spain. Spare money was more likely to
be devoted to improving the prospects of the younger children
or, even more likely, on that conspicuous consumption which was
a vital part of living up to one's station. Large retinues of
liveried servants were as much a mark of nobility as unpaid
bills. Joseph Townshend related with wonder the size of the
great households :

'The Marqués de Peñafiel, who is married to the young
Duchess of Benavente, and is at once Duke of Osuna, of Arcos,
of Vejar, of Candia, etc., with an income of about fifty thousand pounds sterling, employed, when I was at Madrid, twenty-
nine accountants, including his two secretaries, and I understood
he has since increased their number; beside these, he has an
advocate, and a family physician, for whom, with his principal
secretary and his treasurer, he keeps four carriages.

69

'The Duke of Medina Celi has thirty accountants in Madrid, besides vast establishments on his estates, more especially in Catalonia, most of which belongs to him, and in the province of Andalusia, where he has extensive property. His son, the Marqués de Cogolludo, who has a separate establishment, informed me, that he himself paid, only at Madrid, thirty thousand réals a month, or near four thousand pounds a year in stipends to his servants.'

Servants' wages drained away what might have been used for investment, but even in spite of this, the capitalist outlook, of increased investment bringing increased returns, was foreign to the attitudes of the great nobility. Even lower down the aristocratic scale, agriculture was not found interesting, nor country life agreeable. In the South, the lesser nobility concentrated in the few fashionable noble towns, where their social life centred on the Maestranza, the horse-breeding and equestrian club, which organised bull fights and provided pretty uniforms for its members. The clubs perpetuated their members' sense of caste, preventing suits for criminal action against their members, their wives or their servants.

But not all the lesser nobility were town-dwelling rentiers. In the small towns of Castile and the North, the hidalgos necessarily lived close to their land. They had their seats on the parish council, and their municipal offices. In many areas of the north the minor nobility were actually interested in local affairs and in agricultural improvements. The smaller nobility of the Basque and Asturian provinces were often devoted to their districts, and widely known as good landlords. Economic societies – an invention of the Basques – were founded to interest the gentry in economic progress, and distributed new information, and promoted the ideal of the improving landlord, always occupied with the welfare of his village. The Marqués de Peñaflora was one of the best nobles of this type. As mayor of his town in the Basque provinces, he used his influence to start an academy to debate different topics each night of the week. An enthusiastic amateur scientist, he became a leading light in the Royal Society of the Basque provinces. He even formulated a plan of agricultural reform, based on one isolated copy of the proceedings of the Dublin Society, which happened to have come into his possession. But even in the North, men of Peña-flora's calibre were rare, and the extensive privileges of the noble class helped to prevent the kind of innovations which he sponsored.

Everywhere in Spain, seigniorial rights helped the nobility to survive on uneconomic holdings. Frequently monopolies like the baking of bread, milling of flour, and almost medieval claims to tributes and services supported the existence of the greater nobility. These feudal rights had originated as feudal obligations binding on the lord, compelling him to sink capital into his villages by providing such necessities as mills. Thus seigniorial rights were varied and complex – some were disguised rent payments, some came from the sale or grant of municipal offices, and some came from judicial rights. Taken together, they supplied much of the prestige and income of the aristocracy. The exemption from taxes, enjoyed by all the nobility except the hidalgos, was another valuable asset, although all title holders had to make a payment to the Crown on coming into their inheritance. Even if reduced to bankruptcy and crime, the noble-man was protected from disgrace. An edict of 1781 provided that 'nobles arrested as vagabonds and evildoers should be sent to the army with the qualification of distinguished soldiers'.

By the end of the eighteenth century the greater nobility were showing signs of decadence. In politics, they had lost any commanding position they once had. Compared with their pre-decessors, they were not a cultivated group. A few adventurous men had corresponded with Voltaire and Rousseau; the Duchess of Alba and her circle patronised Goya, but these few were swamped by a prevailing indifference to the arts which would have been unthinkable in contemporary France. 'In many of the houses you find good pictures collected by their ancestors,' commented Townshend, 'but, as for the present generation, they seem to have little taste for the polite arts: their time and attention appear to be lost in trifles.'

The nobility, like every other class, were presented with a great challenge when Napoleon invaded Spain in 1808. They did not, on the whole, rise to the occasion. The local nobility with real roots in their localities did become resistance leaders and were accepted as local patriots. The Marqués de Santa Cruz led the resistance junta of Oviedo province. But too many of the nobility were identified with a foreign court, too involved in devious attempts to insure themselves whatever happened, to inspire confidence. Some of the resistance bands made it a rule that gentlemen should be excluded, since men of property could not be trusted to behave with disinterest. 'Has a grandee ever liberated a village?' was the cry.

The suspect patriotism of the Spanish propertied classes provides a glaring contrast with England, where, well into the twentieth century, the conviction prevailed that those with a stake in the country should be the first to fight in her defence. The Duke of Wellington, whose distinguished contribution to the liberation of Spain from the Napoleonic armies won him a Spanish title and estates, was a firm believer in the superior fighting quality of the British upper classes.

The nineteenth century, with all the upheavals it brought to Spain, presented the aristocracy with the biggest challenge of all. Gradually their feudal rights and privileges were whittled away. In 1811 a series of laws removed their seigniorial jurisdictions, and after 1820 disentailing laws removed the legal protection for intact estates. In 1837 a new constitution, with a limited monarchy, a system of elections, and upper and lower chambers, was set up. With their inflexible history, there was little chance that the Spanish nobility would adapt to the new conditions and adopt the democratic virtues. Nearly all Spanish landowners belonged to the extreme right, and few were anxious for the new constitutional experiment to work as intended. Instead, the nobility were pushed more closely than ever before into alliance with the Church. In 1835, when most of the Church's property was confiscated, the Church itself, in previous centuries often the protector of the poor, became increasingly the partisan of the rich.

The aristocracy could not reconcile itself to free elections. The caciques, agents who arranged the elections to ensure the return of the approved candidates, were great powers in the provinces of Spain from 1840 until 1917. In all except the North, caciques were almost invariably landowners, who used their influence to secure tax evasion for themselves and their friends, and charge their enemies double. The rich often managed to escape virtually

all tax demands. The old failure to provide disinterested government, and the new refusal to allow the vote to be freely exercised, widened the divisions between the classes in Spain. Public-
spirited aristocrats were rare. The Marqués de Pontejas was
from 1835–1837 an exemplary mayor of Madrid, who paved
the streets of the city and had gutters laid. At the end of the
century the Marqués de Cabrinana exposed the corruption of
the Madrid Urban Council, only to find to his cost how little
his peers appreciated such activities : he narrowly missed assas-
sination, was condemned for libel, and almost the whole of the
aristocracy cut him.

The greater nobility were still absentees, remote and unknown
figures in their villages. The grandees, who had been steadily
accumulating titles by inter-marriage, lived in a world of their
own, and their style of living could still occasionally dazzle the
world. The purple mantle of the grandee represented a pride
unique in Europe, beside whose pretensions the claims of mere
English dukes paled into insignificance.

The twelfth Duke of Osuna, who in 1844 inherited the
greatest fortune in Spain, devoted the rest of his life solely to
living up to his elevated station. Osuna took the expected life
style of a European nobleman to the extremest lengths of cari-
cature. Noblemen everywhere took pride in their position : the
duke's passport bore thirty-four titles, a modest selection only,
and he was in the habit of writing on his beautifully engraved
visiting cards, 'The grandee of the grandees of Spain'. The form
of address which correspondents were instructed to use included
the phrase, 'God bless the important life of Your Excellency'.
Some noblemen everywhere, even in England, believed in style :
the Duke was a great dandy, who never wore a pair of gloves
more than once, owned 366 pairs of trousers, and disdained to
take back the valuable pearl studs which often fell from his
shirts. Most of the European nobility at least paid lip service to
the arts : Osuna was a patron on the most lavish of scales. He
inherited the finest private library in Europe, kept up a full
orchestra, choir and nine chaplains, was deluged with dedications, and casually handed out silver studs or gold cigarette cases
to poets who brought him their verses. Noblemen everywhere
were expected to be generous, 'to spend like a nobleman' was

a saying current in many languages, and meanness, even in an aristocrat genuinely hard up, was despised. Osuna was extravagant on the grandest of grand scales. In 1856, as envoy extraordinary to Russia, he dazzled St Petersburg and, word had it, ended a dinner party with the grand gesture of throwing a gold dinner service into the river Neva, to the considerable amazement of several dozen guests.[13]

Osuna had a sad end. Obese and deaf, he was left at the end without an heir. Flagrantly cheated all his life, he left his patrimony in the hands of creditors. His life had been all display and adventure, waste and extravagance, an obsession with the urge to do things properly whatever the cost. But when it came to style he had no rivals. Even today, the Spanish grandee who puts himself out to impress can leave the rest of us European nobility standing.

The lesser Spanish nobility were, perhaps fortunately, unable to rise to these frenzied displays of grandeur, and could no longer afford to be entirely socially exclusive. There were in the nineteenth century many new creations to swell their ranks, but the new aristocracy quickly adopted the outlook and attitudes of the old. In Madrid, the aristocratic salon set the tone for all the 'respectable classes', in their devotion to the Church, their charitable work, and resistance to 'progress'.

The gulf between the classes, instead of narrowing as in England, appeared to widen at the end of the century. Too many Spaniards looked on the aristocracy as a class of parasites, combining outdated attitudes with a veneer of foreign manners.

The aristocracy still upheld the traditional Catholic values which gave it its unique flavour. The Marqués de Villavieja, a Mexican-born nobleman of Spanish blood, stayed for the first time in 1883 in a Spanish noble household, the Madrid home of the Duke of Fernan-Nuñez. He commented:

'The homes of the Spanish aristocracy were kept with all the magnificence and tradition peculiar to cultured Spain. There was however a curious mixture of pomp and primitive simplicity. Rigorous maintaining of etiquette and old ceremonial went hand in hand with a peculiar naturalness and bonhomie totally different from what is met with in other countries. There was, too, a patriarchal atmosphere about the daily life; the master of the house exercised absolute sovereignty, yet there was no feeling that the younger members of the family were suppressed.'[14]

The greater nobility, for all their traditional ways, became increasingly attracted by English sports and English habits, in the period when King Edward VII, as Prince of Wales, set the tone for the upper set of Europe. As early as the 1840s, the eleventh Duke of Osuna had set up a racing stable of English thoroughbreds, with jockeys, grooms and trainers in the English style. Thirty years later, the Marqués de Villavieja took his friend, the sixteenth Duke of Alba, to Scotland for the first time, for the shooting. He later wrote :

'The new aspect of life in Great Britain suited him to such a degree that he insisted on sharing all the moors I took in the following years. He even made me promise always to telegraph to him on the first of every August to let him know where we could meet on the twelfth, and so keen was he on shooting in Scotland that he would give up any other engagement in order to join me on the said date, no matter where in the world he was staying.'

The peculiarly English sports were taken up with enthusiasm by Alphonso XIII, the last Spanish king. When he started polo in 1908, a new way of life began in Madrid, and relations between the Spanish aristocracy and the rest of the sporting world became closer than ever before. Until the fall of the monarchy in 1931 the Spanish polo teams were masters of any on the continent, but the vogue for this most exclusive of sports did nothing to close the gulf which divided Spain itself.

English clothes, English words, and even occasionally education at an English Catholic school, began to creep into aristocratic life, and with it there went occasionally a certain nostalgia for the calm of English country house life, so foreign to the Spanish tradition. As the classes in Spain moved nearer to a head-on collision, that timeless security which was the reward of England's more adaptable peerage, had a certain appeal. The Marqués de Villavieja wrote rather wistfully that :

'The incomprehensible comfort and well-being of an English country house, the feeling of unshakeable security in the midst of a troubled world, is something extraordinarily soothing.'

75

In spite of the pro-German sympathies of most Spanish aristocrats in two world wars, some traces of this Anglophilia
remained. The seventeenth Duke of Alba, educated in England
at Beaumont and an enthusiastic polo-player, was Spanish
ambassador in London during the second world war. His more
chauvinistic critics liked to declare that Britain had two spokes-
men for her interests, one in the British embassy in Madrid, and
the other in the Spanish embassy in London.

While the monarchy lasted in Spain, the divisions amongst
the classes were never bridged. Alphonso XIII, for all his virtues,
was not a popular figure, and the court and old aristocracy
were threatened by the declining prestige of the Crown. Many
of them, especially the ladies, were involved in good works which
were admirable, but seldom brought popularity. In the 1890s
a charitable movement, inspired by the ideas of Concepción
Arenal, a Galician who had made her name as a prison
reformer, had many aristocratic supporters. Organisations, staf-
fed by titled ladies, ran committees against white slavery, helped
the orphaned and the illegitimate, and encouraged devotion.
The Marqués de Comillas financed and organised the workers'
pilgrimage to Rome in 1894. But none of this helped to reconcile the aristocracy and the intransigently hostile socialists and
anarchists, who were beginning to sway the towns against them.
Religion was more a dividing line than a uniting force by this
time, and aristocratic ladies who organised boycotts of anti-
clerical ministers only added fuel to the flames.

The aristocracy had little support from the intellectuals. Unlike England and France, artists and writers in Spain were not
welcomed at aristocratic gatherings. The Marqués de
Villavieja, who admitted his own dislike for reading and music,
wrote :

'In Madrid it was a rare thing for a society lady to keep
a real salon where scientists, writers and artists could find good
listeners and encouragement. This delightful French form of
social intercourse did not seem to appeal very greatly to the
Spaniards who ruled the Madrid society. They loved more than
anything their tertulias, where everybody could talk to his heart's
content, and had no particular patience for any deeper
conversation.'

There were, of course, distinguished exceptions to this general indifference. The seventeenth Duke of Alba, one of the outstanding personalities and great talkers of the twentieth century, had, by his death in 1953, made his mark in many different fields. He was a progressive landowner, a governor of the Bank of Spain, and held the ministries of education and foreign affairs. He was a director of the Réal Academia de la Historia, one of the most distinguished historical bodies in the world, and was a generous patron of writers and painters. He had a mind always open to innovations: he owned one of the first motorcars in Spain, and helped to stimulate the enthusiasm of King Alphonso for motoring, much as my own father did that of King Edward VII at the beginning of this century. Indeed one of the world's first true sports cars, the 1911 Hispano-Suiza, was named the 'Alphonso'. Alba was an aristocrat to his finger-tips, but his particular kind of versatility was only too rare amongst his contemporaries.

Remote from the industrial workers in the towns, and from the intellectuals in the cities, the aristocracy could look for little popularity from the Spanish peasantry. The grandees were still absentee landlords as their forebears had been. Even the Duke of Alba, who had a good reputation as a landlord, used to visit his ancestral estates equipped with lorries and tents, as if he were making an expedition to the heart of Africa. In Andalusia about one third of the great estates were still in the hands of the descendants of the reconquista nobles and, at a time when the peasantry had a standard of living amongst the lowest in Europe, it was often resented that too many landlords cultivated only the best land, leaving the rest fallow, or used good land for sport. Near Seville 75,000 acres of the very best land were devoted to bull-breeding, although this was less unpopular than the great shooting estates, bull-fighting being a priority for most Spaniards of all classes. The average aristocrat had still not learnt that necessary self-interest which was also, in England, the national interest.

It is worthwhile to compare the record of Spanish landowners, before the improvements of the last fifteen years, with that of the Dukes of Wellington, whose 2,500 acre estate near Granada was granted to the first Duke in 1812, along with the title of Duque de Ciudad Rodrigo, and another estate since sold, for his part in the defeat of Napoleon. The Wellington estate used to be called the finest agricultural property in Granada, and has always set an example of good husbandry and estate management. It has always been run by an English agent – in reality, a squire, agent and farm manager rolled into one – and progressive methods have always been tried. In the middle of the nineteenth century a number of English ploughs were introduced, and an English ploughman named Giles went out to demonstrate their use. Giles was buried in the churchyard and his descendants, now completely Spanish, still live in the village. More recently, the Duke's estate pioneered a cheap and effective method of irrigation, using heavy plastic sheeting as a lining for earth reservoirs. But for a regrettably long time, Spanish aristocrats rarely equalled this kind of progressive farming and personal interest.

It would of course be quite unjust to blame the aristocracy entirely for the disaster of the civil war. Just as every class and every interest suffered in that appalling calamity, so every class had played its part in bringing it about. But the land problem was an important contributory cause, as was the inflexibility of the nobility, so unlike that supreme adaptability which has done so much to prevent revolution in England.

In 1931, when the monarchy fell, the Spanish nobility were an isolated class, remote from the life of the country, semi-foreign and unpopular. When the elections produced the republican vote which brought the monarchy to an end, the aristocracy were confused and uncertain. The grandees for the most part kept silent, hoping perhaps, as the Russians had done before them, that the sacrifice of the monarch would appease their own critics. The Duke of Almenara Alta, President of the Nobles' Club, appealed to the upper classes to increase their Monarchist campaign in the coming municipal elections. The grandees of Spain, he declared, had 'the firm intention of serving the king to the point, if need be, of sacrifice'.[15] The Duque de Miranda gallantly and faithfully followed the king into exile, but the aristocracy as a whole, it has been written 'observed the fall of the monarchy as they might have watched a bad film.'[16] Not all of them were unmoved by the spectacle. The Marqués de

Villavieja wrote, 'the fall of the monarchy gave me a greater shock than any fall from a polo pony'.

When the republic was declared, many aristocrats shut up their town houses and left the country in droves, in protest against the new regime. Their history, and that bitterness which affected all parties in Spain, made them an early target. In 1932 the estates of the grandees were forfeited without any right of appeal. Compensation was to be paid only on the basis of submitted tax returns, a shrewdly calculated measure to keep payments to the absolute minimum. Titles of nobility were abolished, and postmen forbidden to deliver mail to people so addressed. Remaining aristocrats or their sympathisers were purged from the civil service, and the names of streets which commemorated an aristocratic past were changed. Not surprisingly, the Amnesty bill of 1933, which returned the property of the grandees, did little to assuage the fear and panic of the titled classes.

Some aristocrats fought with distinction in the civil war. The Duke of Seville was a distinguished nationalist general; and the Duke of Peñaranda, brother of the Duke of Alba, was just one of a number of noblemen who stayed in the country in her deepest trouble and paid with their lives. Others served as envoys and propagandists for General Franco. But many left the war to be fought out by others, while they awaited the issue in the comfort of Biarritz, their views almost irrelevant. In their absence, several of the Madrid palaces were looted, and some of the collections of pictures destroyed by republicans, or in the bombing of the city.

After the war, most landowners had their estates returned to them, although some land was kept back for colonisation by the peasants. These small holdings in fact face great disadvantages caused by lack of equipment and necessary capital. In the period since the war, a few of the large estates have been broken up, some mansions converted into luxury hotels, and most inefficient landlords weeded out. Others have of their own accord made up for centuries of neglect by their predecessors, modernising their lands and improving the lot of the tenants. American methods of husbandry are having considerable influence on agriculture, especially in the hotter parts of the country, and the standard of estate administration has improved enormously. One of the most lucrative new developments has been organising partridge shooting for rich Americans. A few badly run estates survive, and it is still rare to find a Spanish landowner who lives on the spot, but most of the big properties are now run on similar lines to others in Western Europe, and it is possible to find estates as efficient and up-to-date as any in the world.

After the civil war, aristocrats began again to play their part in governing the country. Count Jordana, a prominent nationalist general who had been General Franco's Vice-President of Council during the war, became Foreign Minister in 1942 and did much to commend the new regime to foreign ambassadors. Other noblemen served in Spanish embassies: in fact, since the war the Spanish embassy in London has invariably been occupied by an aristocrat, although not necessarily from an ancient family. But while many aristocrats have been loyal supporters of General Franco, others recognise their first commitment to be to the royal family. The Count of Barcelona, son of Alphonso XIII and called by his supporters King Juan III, maintains a court in exile in his sprawling white villa in the Portuguese resort of Estoril, and fifteen grandees take turns in coming over from Spain to act as his lords in waiting. Most aristocrats welcome the royal restoration which will succeed General Franco, although some regret that Don Juan's son, Prince Juan Carlos, specially groomed by General Franco, will occupy the throne instead of his father.

This difficulty apart, the position of the Spanish nobility is a happy one. In modern times the fortune of European nobilities has been closely linked to that of their monarchs. The Spanish nobility is unique in facing a future which looks even more promising than the present.

The Spanish aristocracy has had a chequered and not always creditable history. It has never, at least until very recent times, developed the close landed links, the public spirit or the political experience which have been the pride of the English peerage. But in one respect at least, it has a claim to rank with the English – it has survived, and survived in a style which has become virtually extinct elsewhere. The wedding in 1947 of the

Duchess of Alba to Don Luis Martinez de Iruja y Artazcoz was the last great feudal wedding in Europe, when the bride wore jewellery worth £300,000, and three thousand guests were royally entertained. The bride was created Duchess of Montoro on her twenty-first birthday by her father, the late Duke, in accordance with Spanish custom whereby a noble can confer his other titles at will on sons, daughers, or even distant relatives. The Duchess now holds seven dukedoms, fourteen marquisates, nineteen countships and one of the largest fortunes in Europe, while her husband, in line with normal Spanish practice, bears the courtesy title of Duke of Alba. In the 1970s, when so many of their European counterparts have been reduced to obscurity, the Spanish nobility have performed no mean feat in remaining in possession of the biggest estates and most euphonious titles on the continent.

Chapter Three

Austrian Nobility

The Austrian nobility, always socially exclusive, had strikingly cosmopolitan origins. The nobility of the old Hapsburg lands were greatly affected by the flair of that extraordinary family for advantageous marriages, which spread its rule around Europe. The Emperor Maximilian I's marriage to Mary of Burgundy brought the Netherlands under Habsburg rule and the Burgundian etiquette to their court. During the reign of the Emperor Charles V (1519-1556), whose rule stretched from Spain and Italy to the Netherlands, Spanish and Italian families were transplanted to the Austrian court, and elaborate Spanish ceremonial adopted in Vienna. The Hoyos, who came from Spain in 1520, were the founders of one noble family prominent in Austrian high society well into the twentieth century. In 1593, when Austria was under attack from the Turks, a number of Spanish, Italian and Walloon adventurers joined the Austrian army, and the more successful, rewarded with patents of nobility, added their foreign names to the already heterogeneous nobility.

The old families who had been in Austria even before the Habsburgs, kept however a very honoured place. They were called the Twelve Apostle families and held – by tacit approval of everybody who counted – various important posts in Church and State. Among these families were the Liechtensteins, Starhembergs, Trauns and Studenbergs, to name just a few who still exist in the country.

This cosmopolitan nobility came to dominate the society of a great multi-racial Empire and to enjoy the special splendour of Vienna, a great East European super-capital, the focus of nearly a dozen nationalities. They were to be an Imperial nobility more truly than the British ever were. But in the end they were to fall victims of their elevated status, when the great multi-racial Empire broke up under the strains of nationalism and war.

In the sixteenth century the Austrian nobility no less than the Hungarian – who also came under Habsburg rule but kept special characteristics of their own* – plumed themselves on being the bulwark of Christendom. But they were in fact no more high-minded than their English counterparts when the Reformation provided a convenient cloak for an opposition movement against the Habsburgs. Independence of the ruling house had long been an ambition latent especially among the old nobility, who regarded the Habsburgs as foreigners, and the Reformation brought the impulse to the surface. By the end of the sixteenth century there were only five Catholic noble families left in the Archduchy of Austria proper, seven in Carinthia and one in Styria; and with Protestantism came a fierce independence of their sovereign, and a proud, aggressive spirit. Their castles, donjons and mansions dominated the countryside; from these bastions, in the courtyard of which a moderate sized village might often have stood, with fountains and cisterns comparable with the great works of the Romans, the Protestant lords ruled like petty kings.

The nobles were fiery envangelists for their faith. Protestant ladies took up missionary work among their Catholic counterparts, while their menfolk sometimes adopted drastic methods of conversion. The Protestant lord of Hofkirchen treacherously murdered his Catholic host, Nicholas von Bucheim, under the pretext of a friendly visit. Even Protestants admitted that many nobles were not ornaments to the faith. The Protestant physician Florian Crucius wrote in 1619 that, 'there are among them great numbers of traitors who, under the cloak of the gospel, are mere downright Epicureans, not caring for any religion but for that which panders to their palates and their lusts.'[1]

The Thirty Years' War brought ample retribution. The Emperor Ferdinand the Catholic reconverted Austria to Catholicism by force, and in 1627 Protestant landowners in the newly reconquered Bohemia were given four months in which to see the light or leave their estates and emigrate. Many Czech

*This chapter deals with the nobility of Austria only, unless specifically stated otherwise.

83

families were driven into exile and thousands of acres changed hands as loyal German families like the Schwarzenbergs or successful generals of the war claimed the confiscated estates awarded to them as spoil. Most Czech aristocrats were ousted, only eight old families surviving, with their titles confirmed but their lives now re-oriented towards Vienna. In Austria itself the Protestant nobility suffered almost as badly. In the Archduchy only thirteen old noble families remained in possession. These included one or two Protestant families who tactfully did not parade their religion and did not openly oppose the Habsburgs. But the luck and skill of the Zinzendorfs, a great family who succeeded in remaining Protestant and holding high imperial appointments right up to their extinction in the late eighteenth century, were very rare. Another new aristocracy supplanted most of the Protestants. Large areas of Vienna, seized from Protestant nobles or Protestant merchants, changed hands, and in their place a new nobility began building those baroque palaces which gave the capital its distinctive character. Another band of foreign soldiers who served the Habsburg cause in Germany were incorporated in noble society, among them successful adventurers from Italy, Spain, the Netherlands, England and Ireland. Walter Leslie, a Scottish gentleman of baronial family who rose to the military rank of Field-Marshal-General and held the political post of Vice-President of the Hofkriegsrat, received large estates in Bohemia, married into the old nobility, kept one of the most splendid houses in Vienna and received the highest distinction of the Empire, the Order of the Golden Fleece. This order which originated in Burgundy, is the only order comparable to the Garter.

The old Catholic nobility, the few Protestants who had survived, and the new title-holders were soon joined by a number of returning exiles, penitent converts to the old faith when it became clear that, in Austria at least, Catholicism was triumphant. The returning exiles reclaimed what they could of their estates, and many of them soon became the most bigoted partisans of their new religion.

The Habsburgs gained little glory and lost considerable influence in the Thirty Years' War, but for all their losses in Germany, they had one solid gain in Austria. The Austrian

84

nobility was never again in a position of such threatening independence. They had lost the first round in the contest between
monarchy and nobility, in theory 'cousins', but in practice rivals
for power in every European country. The Emperor's overall
authority was established, and an army of Jesuits moved in to
enforce, not just devotion to the faith, but a rigid uniformity
and order. As confessors to noble families and later as masters
of a boarding school for noble boys established by the Empress
Maria Theresa, they did their best to instil the habit of
obedience and extinguish dangerous free thought. The freedom
to be different, a much cherished class privilege of the British
aristocracy, was squashed.

The aristocracy were left with formidable privileges intact.
They monopolised the numerous offices at court, the places in
the privy council, and the higher commands in the army. They
alone had the right to hold seigniorial estates, their members
monopolised bishoprics, and they had special penalties at law
appropriate to their rank. It was legally an offence not to
address a nobleman as 'Your Excellency'. Special schools
and convents for the nobility, and the setting aside of an area
like the Prater or pleasure garden in Vienna exclusively for
their use, encouraged their pride and sense of caste.

The Austrian nobility long remained among the most rank-
conscious in Europe, and the system whereby titles descended
to all sons and to their sons reinforced their sense of separate-
ness; the nobility was instantly recognisable by the fact that they
all had titles, unlike England, where a duke's grandson might be
plain Mister. Marriages outside the nobility, or even between
high and low nobility, were not just frowned on : a bride from
outside the high nobility could not share her husband's rank.

It was the Austrian nobles' rank consciousness, almost Spanish
in its intensity, which struck my kinswoman, Lady Mary Wortley
Montagu, who visited Vienna in 1716, en route for Istanbul.
Lady Mary, a witty member of the international set, reported
to a friend in London : 'They are never lively but upon points
of ceremony. Tis not long since two coaches meeting in a narrow
street at night, the Ladys in them, not being able to adjust the
Ceremonial of which should go back, sat there with equal
Galantry till 2 in the morning, and were both so fully determin'd

to dye upon the spot rather than yeild in a point of that importance that the street would never have been clear'd till their
Deaths if the Emperor had not sent his Guards to part 'em; and
even then they refus'd to stir till the Expedient was found out of
takeing them both out in chairs exactly at the same moment,
after which it was with some difficulty the pas was decided
between the two coachmen, no lesse tenacious of their Ranke
than the Ladys.'[2]

Pride of rank showed itself most clearly in the carefully
arranged marriages which took place early, thirteen being a
not uncommon age for the bride. The Emperor's permission had
to be obtained for the match – no mere formality – and pedigree
counted above all else. 'Happy are the shee's that can number
among their Ancestors Counts of the Empire,' wrote Lady Mary
Wortley Montagu. 'They have neither occasion for Beauty,
money, or good Conduct to get them Lovers and Husbands.'

Lovers were as numerous as husbands, as Lady Mary reported
to her friend Lady Rich:

'. . . that perplexing word Reputation has quite another meaning here than what you give it at London, and getting a Lover
is so far from loseing, that 'tis properly getting reputation. . . .
I have not seen any such Prudes as to pretend fidelity to their
husbands, who are certainly the best natur'd set of people in
the World, and they look upon their Wive's Galants as
favourably as they do upon their Deputys that take the troublesome part of their busynesse off their hands, tho they have not
the lesse to do, for they are generally deputys in another place
themselves. In one word, 'tis the establish'd custom for every
Lady to have two husbands, one that bears the Name, and
another that performs the Dutys; and these engagements are so
well known, that it would be a downright affront and publickly
resented if you invited a Woman of Quality to dinner without
at the same time inviting her two attendants of Lover and
Husband, between whom she allways sits in state with great
gravity.'

The joke was that these liaisons, originally affairs of the heart
which solaced the victims of a loveless marriage, had become
just as calculating as formal wedlock. Lady Mary reported that
a lady attached more weight to the rank of her lover than that

of her husband, and liaisons involved complicated financial settlements :

'These sub-marriages generally last 20 years together, and the lady often commands the poor Lover's estate even to the utter ruin of his family, tho they are as seldom begun by passion as other matches. But a man makes but an ill figure that is not in some commerce of this Nature, and a Woman looks out for a Lover as soon as she's marry'd as part of her equipage, without which she would not be gentile; and the first article of the Treaty is establishing the pension, which remains to the Lady when the Galant should prove inconstant . . . I really know several Women of the first Quality whose pensions are as well known as their annual rents, and yet nobody esteems them the lesse. On the contrary, their Descretion would be call'd in Question if they should be suspected to be mistresses for nothing, and a great part of their Emulation consists in trying who shall get most.'

Some of this should perhaps be taken with a pinch of salt, Lady Mary's habit of blithe exaggeration accounting for a good deal of her popularity at the time and since. In any case, aristocratic morality underwent something of a transformation in the course of the next one hundred years. Casanova describes in his memoires the obstacles which the Empress Maria Theresa's moralistic regime put in his path.

Whatever the doubt about aristocratic morality, the economic position of their order is beyond dispute. The nobility's main source of wealth lay in its landed estates. These were not quite as extensive as those of the Hungarian magnates, who sometimes had estates as big as small kingdoms. The Esterházy family, the greatest of them all, owned at one time nearly seven million Hungarian acres. But, except for the sovereign, no other class in Austria could even begin to compete with their wealth. Their great estates, worked by serf labour, were held together by a system of strict entail which nearly always prevented estates from being mortgaged or sold outside the family. In terms of sheer acreage, the Austrian nobility compared favourably with the English, but the feudal system and the comparative conservatism and poverty of the area made the practice of progressive farming more difficult than in England. Wherever possible noblemen,

like their English peers, pioneered new methods. In 1666 Sieg-
fried Christoph von Breuner used sawing machines on his
estate. Noblemen in Upper Austria cultivated tobacco from
around 1659 until 1729, when the Emperor monopolised the
business. Others tried farming silk worms by planting mulberry
trees and built silk-producing factories.

Commercial ventures suffered from competition from
Bohemia, but in this field too noblemen, the so-called mer-
cantilists, were prepared to venture into new enterprises. In 1650
Count Kurz organised a textile factory in Horn. The Kufsteins
produced powder which they sold almost exclusively to the Army
during the Thirty Years War. Count Albrecht Zinzendorf
obtained the right to produce scythes in 1661. At the same time
the Hoyos started timber selling on a big scale, trying unsuccessfully to get a monopoly to sell their wood to the iron mines in
Styria.

It is clear that a substantial number of noblemen had energy
and business sense which were clearly beneficial to the economy;
but the chief claim of their class to European fame was in quite
another field, that of patronage of music. The other arts had
comparatively little support; some nobles had large collections
of pictures, among them the Princes Liechtenstein, who sported
one of the biggest galleries north of the Alps, but writers and poets
were not encouraged much, and certainly not invited to aristocratic gatherings. Music was different – and the Austrian nobility
is chiefly remembered for patronage of composers of some of the
most glorious music ever written.

Patronage of music did not mean, certainly at the beginning,
keeping company with composers. Joseph Haydn spent the
greater part of his working life as household musician to the
noble Hungarian family of Esterhàzy. As feudal dependant to
several generations of this family, he wore livery, dined with
the servants and carefully fulfilled the terms of his contract 'that
he, Joseph Haydn, will daily appear in the ante-chamber before
and after noon, whether here in Vienna or on the country estates,
and ask to be admitted to receive renewed orders from His Serene
Highness as to whether there should be music'.[3]

Mozart, for a time more fortunate, was actually petted by
archduchesses and grandees, admirers of the perfect divertimenti

he wrote for summer evenings in country mansions. He had as patroness during his most creative period Countess Wilhelmine Thun, a charming, musical and cultured lady, but he was less content than Haydn to accept a menial role, and was ultimately given a pauper's funeral.

The nobility provided one of Beethoven's main sources of income. His third symphony, the Eroica, had its first public performance in the heavy baroque palace of Prince Lobkowicz in Vienna. The prince bought the score, his private orchestra gave the performance, and music lovers of all classes were admitted to the concert. But Beethoven, even more than Mozart, reacted against aristocratic patronage. The man who, in mature years, 'found the world despicable', was calculatedly rude to aristocrats who made up the fashionable audiences flocking to his concerts. They in their turn were excited by his music and, at first, intrigued by the novelty of his truculence. 'My nobility,' said Beethoven pointing to his head and heart, 'is *here* and *here*.'[4]

Beethoven marked the turning point. The great musical tradition which aristocrats had done so much for, never again had the wholehearted support of the high aristocracy. After Beethoven, native musicians were neglected by high society; and after 1815 Italian opera was the aristocratic passion. The highlight of the musical year was the three months' season of Italian opera, with Italian conductors and singers. Even the regular director of the Viennese opera, Nicolai, could hardly make ends meet, and Schubert did not bother to cultivate even those few patrons that remained.

By this time the aristocracy were on the defensive again. In the course of the eighteenth century they faced the second round of the conflict with the monarchy, and this time they started from a much weaker position. From the Middle Ages onwards, special ceremonial occasions had been devised to emphasise their subjection to the Crown. The Landmarschall every year summoned noblemen to gather in their carriages outside Vienna to await the Emperor; they entered the town driving behind their sovereign and were forbidden to delay him with their petitions inside the walls. To this purely ceremonial subjection had been added their very substantial loss of independence after the Thirty Years' War. The Empress Maria Theresa took the process a stage further. She borrowed the well-tried techniques of Louis XIV and played every trick in her hand to keep the nobility at court, under her eye, well beyond the customary ceremonial appearance. Meanwhile in the provinces, her officials helped to limit the power of the landlords over their tenants, and it was decreed that, in any case of litigation between them, the burden of proof should be thrown upon the landlord and the benefit of any doubt given to the tenant.

The Empress's son, the impetuous reformer Joseph II, went much further than his mother had contemplated, and was personally much more critical of the nobility than ever she had been. He refused to acknowledge the unsupported claims of mere birth – a curious attitude for the heir of all the Habsburgs – and tried to weaken feudal privilege. The privilege of corporate standing, by which for two hundred years only established nobles could hold seignioral estates, was abolished. The ancient rights of some families to levy tolls and customs by land and water on their estates were ended, and the imposition of forced labour was confined to certain fixed limits.

In his dealing with the Hungarian nobility, more independent than the Austrian, Joseph II spelt out the kind of nobility which he thought he would like to create in his dominions, one displaying that sense of responsibility which he admired in the English peerage. His ideas in practice cut across some of the dearly held traditions of his territories. The Hungarians had enjoyed tax exemptions in return for military service in the armies. When the existence of a standing army no longer made military service obligatory, Joseph tried to make the nobility liable to taxation, and spelt out to the Chancellor of Hungary his idea of what nobility really meant :

'The privileges and liberties of a nobility or a nation, in all countries and republics of the world, do not consist in the nobles contributing nothing to the public burdens; on the contrary, they, for instance in England and Holland, pay more than others; but their privileges consist solely in this, that they themselves submit to bear the burdens requisite for the general welfare and that when an increase of taxes is demanded by circumstances, they take the lead by voluntarily granting them.'[5]

The Emperor clearly perceived the essential character of the

English peerage, whose voluntary voting of land taxes was the clearest sign of their essential public spirit as a class. But that public spirit was the product of very special circumstances, and although Joseph II could take away his nobility's full immunity from taxation, he could not create a comparable sense of responsibility at will.

In other small ways, he was able to alter the aristocratic environment. In Vienna, the Prater, or pleasure garden, previously the special preserve of noble carriages, was thrown open to ordinary pedestrians. To discourage noble rakes from seducing burghers' daughters, a statute declared that illegitimate children should be heirs-at-law equally with legitimate ones to the estates of their fathers. This move, also adopted by the French after the revolution, was shrewdly aimed: the distinction between legitimacy and illegitimacy is fundamental to any institution like monarchy or nobility which depends upon inheritance.

Joseph II also appointed commoners to bishoprics, previously an aristocratic preserve, and a noblewoman, widow of a general, who wrote to him asking for a high army post for her undistinguished son, received the crushing reply:

'I do not see the obligation of a monarch to give a place to one of his subjects because he is a nobleman. I really pity you, madam, for having a son who is neither fit to be an officer nor a statesman nor a priest; in short, who is nothing but a nobleman.'[6]

All citizens were given equality before the law, and distinctions of rank were to be ignored when giving sentence. Count Podstatsky Liechtenstein, who had forged bank-notes, was sentenced to sweep the streets like any common convict, dressed in coarse brown cloth, with cropped hair and in chains. But the Emperor's well-meant efforts to break down social barriers between the high aristocracy and the bourgeoisie had no success – no Emperor could take away their social exclusiveness.

Joseph reduced the prestige of mere titles by greatly swelling the number of the so-called 'bagatelle nobility'. For most of the eighteenth century, it was possible for officials of the court, even down to valets, horse-breakers and dancing masters to receive ennoblement, although this did not necessarily include a title.

91

The Habsburgs were notoriously fond of their servants – in 1702 the valet of the Emperor Leopold I, John Baptist Locatelli, was made a baron, and the precedent was followed by several succeeding rulers. Junior officials, especially postmasters charged with the delicate task of intercepting mail, and lower army officers also swelled the bagatelle nobility, which became so widespread that in Joseph II's reign every respectable man was addressed as 'Herr von', the von being not only the sign of a noble family but of the right to use a coronet. The higher territorial aristocracy, of course, merely withdrew still further behind an impregnable social barrier, the international sign of a nobility on the defensive.

Joseph II granted letters of nobility, not just to court servants, but to successful businessmen, manufacturers, bankers, merchants and publishers. Two bankers, Joseph John Nepomuch Fuchs and John Friess, were even promoted to the high rank of count, but the astonishment of the Viennese was greatest when he created Jewish barons, such as the banker Joseph Arnstein, whose wife was in high favour. Joseph also granted titles to those prepared to pay for them.

This mass of mint-new noblemen reacted in the familiar, Italian way, with lavish squandering of money to underline their status, but the access of monied titles did little to change the character of the high aristocracy. They remained obstinately blue-blooded, their society limited to an exclusive circle and their marriages confined to those with the right quarters. The disdain of old nobility for new was common to every European country but it had a specially long run in Austria, and was reflected, often humorously, in opera. Baron Ochs, in the Viennese pastiche, *Der Rosenkavalier,* comments ironically on the newly created von Faninal, 'on the patent of whose nobility the ink is scarcely dry'.

It was the older, high Austrian nobility, mixing in Vienna with the great nobles of Hungary, Galicia and North Italy, which impressed the diplomats of Europe at the Congress of Vienna (1814–1815), busy settling the new frontiers of Europe during the daytime, and negotiating more temporary arrangements at night. The nobility's linguistic versatility – including German, French, Italian and sometimes English in their range –

their luxurious hospitality, and the concentration in one city of the town houses of magnates drawn from almost all over central Europe, gave this society its particular prestige, and it never again after the Congress had as good an opportunity for displaying its brilliance to advantage.

In the eighteen twenties and thirties, while the Austrian Prince Metternich preserved throughout Europe the aristocratic order now threatened, not from above by kings but from below by radicals and republicans, the high aristocracy existed remote from the rest of society, enjoying exclusively the pleasures of the grandest capital in Europe.

Each May they took the traditional Prater drive down the two-mile-long Hauptallee, appearing before the eyes of the curious common people in gleaming carriages with carefully groomed horses and liveried footmen, before returning to their narrow Viennese palaces, with carved stone coats-of-arms on their façades. On their country estates, which they visited each year from the fifteenth of June until the third of November, giant battues were the favourite sport of the day. Mrs Frances Trollope, mother of the English novelist, who visited Vienna in 1837, wrote that: 'The passion for shooting, or the chase as it is more nobly called, is if possible stronger here than with us; it pervades all ages and all ranks, all tempers and all professions and nowhere in the world can this amusement be enjoyed in greater perfection than in Austria, Hungary and Bohemia. The enormous tracts of land possessed by the nobles in all these countries, offer such fields for sport as can hardly be equalled elsewhere, for the game is strictly preserved, and there is choice of ground without stint or end . . .'[7]

Mrs Trollope, although undistinguished by any long pedigree, was an ardent admirer of aristocratic society, and her value as a propagandist enabled her to penetrate the exclusive high society. She observed that the high aristocracy never alluded in any way to the circle of banker barons, mainly Jewish, whose society with its balls, dinners and masquerades was a close imitation of their own. Occasionally a great nobleman, driven by the need for a loan, would find it prudent to attend a function of the 'bourgeois aristocracy', but he would on no account refer to it afterwards, or acknowledge any of its members when accompanied by a lady of his own class. In this respect, the Austrian nobleman treated the banker baron as the French aristocrat did the demi-mondaine.

The rigid exclusion of the famous and the eminent, so different from the lion-hunting aristocracies of England and France, was more of a surprise to the carefully observant Mrs Trollope : 'One does not here, as in Paris or London, perpetually encounter, by some lucky unexpected accident, people whom one has known for years by reputation . . . It is, I think, to the fixedness of the one, and the variability of the other sets, that the great difference between the tone of society in Vienna, and that of more mutable capitals may be traced. If with us there is a stronger and more animated collision of intellect, at Vienna there is less risk of meeting within the arena of good society those whose more fitting place is without it. An habitué in the set which constitutes good company here, even though a stranger, may venture to enter into conversation with his neighbour, without any awkward doubts and fears as to the prudence or propriety of attempting the adventure . . . Should some un-initiated visitor in a London or Paris salon, on the contrary, venture upon familiar conversation with any one or every one he happened to meet there, he might find himself in com-munion with the first poet in existence, or the first boxer; he might be exchanging civilities with a mighty silly peer of the realm, or with the peer's elegant, eloquent, and much more illustrious banker. He might be listening to the powerful language of a methodist parson, a profound philosopher or a tragic actor; and would be equally likely to have made his experiment on the noble of twenty descents or the parvenu of yesterday.'

Wide social contacts brought inestimable political advantages to the English peers, who also enjoyed a solid base in country life; and the political inadequacies of the bulk of the Austrians was no doubt connected with their narrow social horizons. The reactions against the excesses of the French revolution and its aftermath lasted longer and penetrated deeper in Austria than in England. All European nobility faced a terrifying new threat: the centuries-old efforts of kings to curb their 'overmighty subjects' seemed mildness itself compared with the bloody attacks of radicals from below. Faced with a common enemy,

94

the Austrian monarchy and nobility closed their ranks, and the high nobility won back some of the privileges lost under Joseph II. On the whole they became much less prepared than their English counterparts to make concessions to change. But a few exceptional members of the lower nobility were more receptive, and began to marshal their influence in the local diets, and Lower Austria Estates, to urge reforms. Among their number was Freiherr von Schmerling, Count Montecuccoli and Count Colloredo-Mansfeld. Von Moering, a distinguished officer on the General Staff, produced under a pseudonym a volume called *The Sybilline Book of Austria* which made a scathing attack on existing society. The regime placed no trust in any but the privileged nobility, he complained, and treated the masses simply as beasts of burden. It was a handful of aristocrats of Von Moering's stamp who first brought liberal ideas out into the open, and helped prepare the way for the revolution of 1848, which drove the Emperor from his capital, Prince Metternich into exile, and several large landowners from their estates.

The reaction which followed, as the new young Emperor Franz Joseph won back control, was mainly the work of members of the high aristocracy. The only major gain of the revolutionary demands was the abolition of the Robot, the system by which tenants had to put in a fixed amount of work with their own teams of animals on the landlords' lands. The real beneficiaries of this rebel demand, however, were the great landlords. With the compensation money for the loss of their forced labour – and the Schwarzenberg family alone received 1,870,000 florins – the landlords could well afford to hire good free labour, much more effective than before. Many landlords converted themselves into great capitalists, able to invest in new agricultural machinery, new saw-mills and sugar-beet factories, and working their estates more economically than ever before. The old Spanish prejudices against commercial enterprise were greatly weakened, and a few noblemen branched out as entrepreneurs and industrialists, mining coal, manufacturing paper and investing in spas and hotels. In any event, very wealthy aristocrats, with large and flourishing estates, lasted out the monarchy.

From the 1848 revolution until the first world war, aristocrats increasingly invested in stocks and shares. In 1873 a slump brought with it a scandal which heavily affected members of the first society, those with the requisite quartier for admittance to the court. The historian Josef Redlich attended in December 1912 a luncheon made up almost entirely of the crême de la crême, where all the men and even some of the ladies were talking incessantly about their investments on the Stock Exchange. Redlich commented severely that this was 'a strange form of the degeneration of our high aristocracy',[8] but it was in reality a healthy sign. The high aristocracy was becoming an even more integral part of the economic life of the country. But unfortunately their economic enterprise was not always matched by much political sense as a class.

Prince Felix Schwarzenberg, the first Prime Minister after the 1848 revolution, was an Austrian aristocrat in the Hollywood style, slim, pale and arrogantly aloof. It is ironical that he, of all people, should have been so hostile to his own class as a political power. He blamed the high aristocracy with their irresponsibility and political incompetence, for the outbreak of the 1848 revolution. He considered them a divisive force in the Empire, and quite incapable of the political sense which he, like his Italian contemporary Count Cavour, admired in the English peerage. Schwarzenberg devised a constitution which excluded them as a class from government on the grounds that:

'I consider it impossible to instil into our aristocracy true vitality and much-needed resilience, because to this end not only respectable individuals are called for, but also a politically trained, well organised and courageous class. This class we completely lack. I do not know of more than a dozen men of our class in the entire Monarchy who could in the present circumstances serve profitably in an upper chamber. . . .'[9]

In fact Schwarzenberg's proposed constitution was never implemented, but the Prince succeeded in giving the new young Emperor a shared distrust of his class, and destroying that special solidarity of king and nobles which the French revolution had created. Franz Joseph always insisted that the highest careers in the Imperial service, with certain exceptions, were open to all the talents. The high nobility were repeatedly incensed by his Majesty's predilection for clever politicians of no family. Their last chance to recover aristocratic control came in 1861 with the October Diploma, a new constitution based on aristocratic control in the provinces. When they made a mess of this, demonstrating again their essential self-interest, they had shot their bolt. Individual aristocrats were influential until the very end of the reign, but the high aristocracy could not exert combined pressure to further their own class interests. Only certain posts in the diplomatic service and the administration were left of their once formidable monopoly. Here, they still stood some of their ground. As late as the turn of the century, an eminent professor of common law at the University of Vienna failed a student of ancient lineage during the decisive examination qualifying for the higher Civil Service with the remark, 'I know it won't prevent your being made Governor of Upper Austria, Count, but at least I can delay it for a year'.[10]

Socially, the high aristocracy were as exclusive as ever, widely credited with pronouncements like that of Field-Marshal Windisch-Grätz : 'Mankind begins with the barons'; and set apart by their distinctive speech, a modified form of the Vienna dialect, abounding in deliberately ungrammatical forms which grated on purist ears. They lived in a society confined to those with sixteen quarterings, where the obligatory answer to an insult to one's honour was still the duel. The banker aristocracy, and Jewish millionaires, the builders of most of the large new residences in Vienna, were still beyond the pale; but Baron Maurice de Hirsch, a rich Jew of the third generation, had the golden opportunity of repaying a lifetime of snubs. In 1890 he had the pleasure of entertaining the Prince of Wales, and a party of aristocratic friends, at a house-party on his estates, an occasion which was celebrated with the slaughter of partridges on an awe-inspiring scale. An average of ten guns killed twenty thousand partridges in ten days. The Prince of Wales, who as 'first gentleman' of Europe enjoyed immense social prestige, had advanced English views about rank, and was delighted to teach the exclusive Austrian nobility a lesson.

The plutocrats and banker barons had taken over what remained of the tradition of musical patronage. The high aristocracy, descendants of the patrons of Haydn and Mozart, had now little but contempt for the few eccentrics among their

number who continued the old ways. Nora, Countess Wydenbruck, who was just old enough to catch the unrepeatable
flavour of high society life in Vienna before the Great War,
recalled that :

'Aunt Misa had a small but lovely voice and was a true
musician. Her salon was a musical centre where one could meet
and hear the Rose Quartet, Bruno Walter, Marie Gutther-
Schoder and Eric Korngold. But Viennese society had changed
since the great days of Beethoven, and people said, "Poor Misa
likes to surround herself with jugglers".'[11]

At least this attitude gave an envious bourgeoisie the chance
to plume itself upon superior brains. Ilsa Barea, born and bred
in middle-class Vienna, recalled that :

'A mother might say to her daughter, as I have heard it said
myself : "You really could marry a count", meaning that she
was pretty or charming enough for it, and hastily add : "But
he'd be too stupid for you".'

But visiting aristocrats, with no particular axe to grind, were
equally unimpressed by the intelligence of Austrian high society.
Consuela Vanderbilt, Duchess of Marlborough had, with her
experience of American millionaires and English dukes, a broad
standard of comparison. She visited Vienna in 1904 and later
wrote :

'In 1904 Vienna was still an eighteenth-century capital. It
has an antique elegance and an archaic respect for tradition and
birth. The beau monde was still that of the rich and well born
. . . Breeding gives a distinction perhaps beyond its value. A
thoroughbred, be it among animals or men, is generally more
physically favoured, and aristocratic Austrians I met looked
like greyhounds, with their long lean bodies and small heads.
A polished education tends to bestow a certain ease of manner,
and this these Viennese possessed to an eminent degree. It sometimes helped one to forget that they were as a rule more
educated than intelligent. It was, I thought, a pity that they
could express their thoughts in so many different languages when
they had so few thoughts to express.'[12]

The Duchess's compatriot, Theodore Roosevelt, was more
dazzled by the most accomplished social manners in Europe.
When asked, on his return from an extensive European tour,

what type of person he found most congenial, he replied, 'The Austrian gentleman'.[13]

Those aristocrats with real talent and the desire to develop it had to contend with more prejudice than usual for any European aristocrat who, even today, can easily be labelled a dilettante. Schnitzler's novel, *The Road into the Open,* a carefully documented picture of Viennese society just after the turn of the century, portrays a young aristocrat whose attempt to gain recognition as a serious professional musician is constantly baulked by the attitude which dismisses noblemen as amateur.

It was the army where aristocrats were most at home. High Austrian society was largely made up of officers who never wore civilian clothes, except when out shooting. Countess Wydenbruck wrote that, 'the army was a world in itself, a world in which the peculiar Austrian charm, that mixture of ancien regime courtliness and slightly cynical wit could be found in its most unadulterated form.' It was probably the close links between high society and the army which encouraged the war-mongering unhappily common in high society before the Great War. Joseph Redlich, a diligent recorder of the sayings of the titled, recorded in his diary on 11th July 1913 a talk with Alice Countess Hoyos. The Countess, born an English commoner and without a drop of Austrian blood herself, was married into the ancient family of Spanish origin whose male members had a long tradition of service in the army. She declared that, if the Foreign Minister had been a man, he would have intervened in the war between Serbia and Bulgaria, even at the risk of war with Russia. On 26th July, 1914, the Countess's daughter-in-law greeted Redlich with inexpressible delight when he brought confirmation of the war with Serbia. It was the beginning of the war which would sweep away her world.

There were others, headed by Count Tisza, the Hungarian Prime Minister, who were bitterly opposed to the war – just as many noble families were opposed to Hitler in 1938 – but were powerless to prevent it. The death of Franz Joseph in 1916, after a reign of sixty-eight years, was another nail in the coffin of the old way of life. Although he had ruled through professional bureaucrats and politicians, and mixed little with high society, he had kept their loyalty to the end. From the beginning his successor, the Emperor Karl, held no such ties. The Empress, a foreign princess of Bourbon-Parma, was unkindly associated with Austria's enemies, and the high aristocracy looked askance at his Majesty's democratic habit of shaking hands with every soldier he decorated. When Karl, the last of the Hapsburgs, abdicated on 11th November, 1918, as his Empire fell apart under the strains of nationalism and military defeat, he was deserted by all but a few faithful courtiers. Although there was little personal sympathy between them, although the nobility could survive the fall of their sovereign, the abdication was bound to be an inestimable blow to the nobility as a class. The Austrian nobility were to learn, like the French and Russians before them, the folly of lukewarm attachment to the Crown.

The new republic brought the aristocracy as a class little benefit. The laws of entail which secured the permanence of intact estates were abolished, and thousands of acres changed hands as big estates were widely broken up, and replaced by small owner farmers. The Austrian nobility were less lucky than the Hungarian, some of whom were able to keep their estates intact until the Russian occupation of Eastern Europe at the end of the Second World War, and who showed during their twenty years respite a resilience and adaptability undeserving of their abrupt end.

The town houses and palaces of Vienna did not escape the fate of the Austrian country estates after the First World War. From 1922 onwards an ambitious programme of working-class housing, health schemes and adult education was financed by heavy taxes on property in the city. This virtually eliminated private incomes from house rents, and forced all but the richest of large house-owners to sell up. Aristocrats more than ever before took to supplementing their reduced incomes by reckless speculation on the stock exchange, not realising the precariousness of the early gains after the war. In 1923 came the disastrous inflation leading to collapse of the currency. Countess Wydenbruck was just one of a host of aristocrats whose inheritance and savings were wiped out :

'The fortune my father had left me melted away like snow in the Spring; stocks and shares, gilt-edged securities and the war loan in which I had invested much of his capital, had

100

become worthless. I realised – too late – the folly of not having invested in real estate.'

The Countess was reduced to selling her jewellery and the silver dishes which had figured prominently in her father's diplomatic entertaining. Others of her class, the owners still of castles and chateaux, began to take in paying guests, a state of affairs which produced Czernin's witticism in *This Salzburg:* ' "Meine Gräfin" [my lady] is not the literal translation of "my landlady".'[14]

Frustrated on all fronts, many aristocrats joined the right-wing, semi-military organisation, the Heimwehr, a private army which joined battle with its Socialist counterpart, broke strikes and sacked the new workers' flats in Vienna. The motives which prompted them are not perhaps hard to understand – a sense of grievance at their losses, anxiety about the growth of militant Socialism, and frustration at the weakness of the new democratic republic. But although right-wing, few aristocrats supported the Nazis. Prince Ernst Rudiger von Starhemberg, the powerfully built aristocrat who led the Heimwehr, became the greatest enemy of the Nazis in Austria. After the 1938 Anschluss, which united Gemany and Austria under Nazi domination, he went into exile and ended by fighting with the Free French against Hitler in the Second World War. The hostility of Austrian nobles, combined with the attempt on his life by the German Count von Stauffenberg, made Hitler determine to eliminate the aristocracies of Austria and Germany after the war. Their opposition to Nazism at least was a worthy cause for Austrian nobility, who had not always in the past shown political sense.

Since the Second World War, the Austrian nobility had been once again joined by many of the Czech, Polish and Hungarian nobility, once united with them under Habsburg rule, now refugees from Communist rule in Eastern Europe. The Austrians themselves, although more fortunate, have never ceased to suffer from the fall of the monarchy. The present Habsburg claimant, now allowed back into Austria, commands many of their loyalties, and still confers the ancient Order of the Golden Fleece. Some aristocrats still feel obliged to ask his permission for marriage. But a pretender to a throne, no matter how deep the personal loyalty he commands, can never fill the role of a reigning monarch, and in Austria, as in France, Spain and Italy, the nobility have found no adequate substitute for the focus of loyalty to a sovereign.

Nevertheless, the present-day Austrian nobility, particularly the younger ones, are showing a healthy resilience and a willingness to come to terms with the 20th century. For instance, the young Prince Charles Schwarzenberg has profitably developed not only the great Schwarzenberg Palais in Vienna, but also his country estates in a manner worthy of the best estate owner in England. There are signs that his example is being followed by many others. Certainly Austria can claim to have the only influential aristocracy today which borders on Communist Europe.

Chapter Four

Italian Nobility

Until the unification of Italy one hundred years ago, the Florentine, Roman, Neapolitan and Venetian aristocracies each perpetuated their own special characteristics as leading citizens of separate states. The difference between the merchant princes of Venice, at their peak as proud, rich and secure as any noblemen in Europe, and the poverty-stricken, backward Sicilian nobleman preoccupied with honour and the blood feud, loomed as large as that between any other European states. But in some respects the aristocracies of the peninsula shared a common history, geography and experience. Almost all participated in that remarkable outburst of human energy, the Renaissance, and all, except the Neapolitan, were the product of an unusual blending of the upper and middle classes, of aristocrat and bourgeois. The patricians of Northern Italy were unlike the nobility of anywhere else in Europe, and it is tragic that so much of their vigour, versatility and enlightenment were lost in the centuries after the Renaissance.

The typical nobleman of the Middle Ages had been a robber baron, uncouth, hardly literate, and savage, clinging to rocky fortresses like Urbino, Rimini and Orvieto. Their kind were not eliminated during the great flowering of the Renaissance: the blood-stained feuds of noble families which provided Shakespeare with the plot of Romeo and Juliet were common in most parts of the peninsula, where killing was a common noble practice in the fifteenth and sixteenth centuries. But this group were rivalled by another aristocracy of the lowland commercial centres. From the twelfth century onwards, noblemen, bishops and burghers lived together in the walled cities of the north, developing and sharing great wealth, enjoying a leisure which brought them into contact, and acquiring similar tastes. It was a new kind of society which emerged in Florence, Milan and Venice, combining aristocratic and bourgeois attitudes to a sometimes quite baffling degree.

For centuries the aristocratic life in Europe necessarily implied abundance, a superfluity of material goods to permit living in style, untroubled by the task of breadwinning; it implied leisure to enjoy a pleasurable life, and it implied that work, what there was of it, should be service to the state rather than service to oneself. The aristocratic virtues were honour, dignity, style and generosity. The bourgeois life implied regular effort to maintain a satisfactory standard of living, and the bourgeois virtues were thrift, diligence and sobriety. In the north Italian cities, the élite managed to combine these characteristics. The great men of Florence, though usually untitled and with a diligence which was wholly bourgeois, were essentially aristocrats in social standing, prestige and culture; the great merchant princes of Venice combined the sharpest business sense in Europe with a pride of pedigree at least as strong as that of a grandee of Spain.

By the fifteenth century what gave this confusing bourgeois aristocracy that essential and obvious distinctiveness which all aristocracies must have, was its culture and education. Wealthy merchants, city noblemen or successful mercenary soldiers cultivated a knowledge of the classics and an ease of manner which made them immediately recognisable as gentlemen.

It was natural that the scholars and philosophers of the peninsula, who mixed on an equal footing with merchant princes and city nobles, should look for a new definition of nobility more fitting to the uncharted world which was developing around them. Pedigree alone, although always immensely prized, was clearly insufficient on its own to satisfy some of the most enquiring minds in Europe, fascinated by the idea of nobility, and ready to challenge some of its most sacred assumptions. Dante, in *The Divine Comedy*, considered that a long pedigree combined with personal worth constituted nobility – noble origin was only a mantle from which time was always cutting something away, unless the wearer constantly added to it by his own qualities. Dante, like the current Marquess of Hertford, found quite senseless the conventional belief, still with us, that the older the title, and the further removed from the actual winner of the distinction, the greater the prestige. Others questioned the equally sacrosant association between aristocrats and blood sports. One hundred and fifty years after Dante, the Florentine humanist Poggio openly ridiculed the old-fashioned, philistine idea of a nobleman who was only a man of action. He wrote:

'A man is all the farther removed from true nobility, the longer his forefathers have plied the trade of brigands. The taste for hawking and hunting savours no more of nobility than the nests and lairs of the hunted creatures of spikenard. The cultivation of the soil, as practised by the ancients, would be much nobler than this senseless wandering through the hills and woods, by which men make themselves liker to the brutes than to reasonable creatures.'[1]

It was left for Baldassare Castiglione, himself the offspring of a poor but noble family, to give in the early sixteenth century what seemed to be the last word on the subject: his *Book of the Courtier* became the bible of would-be aristocrats everywhere, and his ideal demanded the best of all worlds. The true nobleman had a long lineage and an admirable character, his perfectly trained body excelled at athletics and his distinguished mind was at home with the classics, previously the special province of scholars. Above all, he had a grace of manner which instantly identified him as a gentleman. The great men of the Italian cities, of Rome, Florence and Venice, only too often fell short of Castiglione's ideal, but in all the centres except Naples it was the model to which they aspired.

In the Republic of Florence, the brightest centre of the early Renaissance, the old feudal nobility were early on rivalled by a powerful merchant class. The merchant princes prized birth as much as anyone and in manners, dress, education and prestige they were clearly an aristocracy, whose wealth put them at least on a par with the great noblemen of Northern Europe. The Medici family, the greatest of them all, twice provided Queens of France. Indeed, I descend from Marie de Medici who was the grandmother of Charles II. The leisure activities of this society were clearly not those of tradesmen. Cosimo de Medici poured out money on buildings scattered with the Medici arms, on paintings and sculpture, and patronised

Donatello. His grandson Lorenzo spent liberally on philosophers, patronised Botticelli, and earned himself the name of The Magnificent. But even a family as eminent as the Medici were untitled, and the bourgeois world of commerce and finance was the foundation of the fortunes of all the families who kept up this aristocratic life. The Medici were not only great European bankers, but dealt in wool, silks, jewellery, plate, Flemish tapestries, classical manuscripts, and the provision of boy-sopranos for the Rome chapels. Few of the heads of the great Florentine families were mere sleeping partners in their businesses. It was not uncommon for dying parents to beg the government to fine their sons heavily if they should refuse to practise a regular profession.

Venice, another republic, had a strict and exclusive aristocracy based entirely on birth. The chief organisations of government were reserved for men whose ancestors had been members of the Great Council before 1297, and a 'studbook', the Golden Book, scrupulously preserved records of their pedigrees. The ducal families – those which had included at least one doge, such as Mocenigo and Morosini – enjoyed a specially high rank in this very hierarchical society. The blue-blooded patricians filled the kind of posts usually occupied by great noblemen of Northern Europe, and as a group they were as secure in their social and political position as the peerage in eighteenth-century England. They officered the Ventian fleets, led their countrymen in battle against the Turks, and as proconsuls they governed the outposts of Venice's widespread Mediterranean empire. Their role in this respect was only different from that of their Northern counterparts in that a rigorous spy system kept close check on their loyalty; a host of government informers reported on the least suspicion of treason, and a battery of regulations controlled their movements. They were forbidden so much as to enter the house of a foreign ambassador, on pain of death.

But the proud Venetian magnates, like the Genoese, were still a commercial aristocracy; the politically active nobility all engaged in business, and the trade of the Levant was the basis of all the largest private fortunes. Their eagerness to make money laid noblemen open occasionally to the ridicule of those of their contemporaries who still found trade and noble blood incompatible. A Veronese lawyer mocked what he called 'the knights of the age of gold' who 'every day stand in the squares and behind their counters exercising some base profession; and there are many who do not know how to put their arms on'.[2]

Not all the old families were rich. There was a party of poor nobles, dependent on the charity of their more fortunate equals, who built rows of houses for them, or made pious provision in their wills. Attempts to extract subsidies from public funds were less successful. In 1492 two poor noblemen who proposed that the state should spend 70,000 ducats for the relief of their kind were exiled for life to Nicosia. Seven years later Antonio Contarini, of one of the oldest Venetian families, complained in vain that for many years he had held no office, he had no flourishing business interests, his debts amounted to sixty ducats, and he was struggling to bring up nine children on an income of sixteen ducats a year.

Those great merchant princes who had money, whether from state office or trade or both, spent it in splendid style. As the fashion of the Renaissance spread to Venice, later than Florence and Rome, they built villas on the mainland in the new Palladian style, which was to inspire the architects of eighteenth-century England and the mansions of Virginia planters. At Maser, forty miles from Venice, for instance, the patrician Barbaro family built a sixty-six-room villa, designed by Palladio and frescoed by Veronese. The walls are decorated with a series of trompe l'oeil paintings, where imaginary doors and windows open on to a beautiful Venetian landscape. At these country villas, the entertainments of fêtes champêtres, musical evenings and recitals of Latin poetry were those of a cultivated élite. The family portraits on the walls were by the masters, Titian, Bellini and Tintoretto. In style of living, the Venetian merchant princes put to shame many noblemen, who professed to think trade a vulgar occupation.

In none of the other cities of the peninsula were merchant princes as powerful and prominent as in Florence, Genoa and Venice. In the Duchy of Milan the feudal nobility of the Lombard countryside, living on the rents of their inherited estates, prizing their pedigrees and carefully abstaining from regular work, refused to knuckle under to the merchant class of the city or even, on occasion, to the Duke himself. In 1483 the lieutenant of the Castello San Giovanni refused to open the gates of the town on the order of Duke Ludovico Sforza, claiming that he was responsible only to his feudal overlord, Count Piero dal Verme.

The old feud between Guelphs and Ghibellines, originally supporters of the medieval Popes and Holy Roman Emperors respectively, still divided the old families into two warring factions. Each side kept retinues of liveried retainers dressed in padded hose, who kept up the vendetta and rallied to the emblems of their cause. Neither side was above allying with a foreign power to help annihilate the other, and the Guelph alliance with the French in 1500 served to attract more bloodshed into an already war-torn area.

In Rome, the feuds of the ancient rival families of the Orsini, Colonna and Frangipani had also a long history. Rioting, murder, the raping of nuns and tossing of rivals into the Tiber distracted the streets of the city until Pope Alexander Borgia (1492–1503) restored the papal provinces to his control by methods even more violent than theirs. His son Cesare Borgia used the treachery of pretended friendship, strangulation and poison, to break the power of the Orsini in the papal provinces.

As might be expected, civilised manners and patronage of the arts did not always flourish among the old Roman families. Pope Pius II (1458–1464) complained that any falconer or stableboy was more welcome at the table of a Roman nobleman than a scholar. It was the popes and cardinals, sometimes but not always from noble Roman families, who were the greatest patrons of the arts in the city, although the Colonna family produced in Vittoria Colonna, Marchioness of Pescara, perhaps the most famous woman in Italy, and the friend of Michelangelo and Castiglione. They could not plead poverty as an excuse for their neglect : by the end of the sixteenth centry, great Roman noblemen not infrequently maintained households of three hundred servants, including a number of Turkish slaves.

Outside the city of Rome, a less well endowed nobility often worked hard in the administration of their estates and tried to keep out of the feuds of the great families. For all their virtues, this lesser nobility were not patrons of the arts either. Their society was sober and respectable, but a trifle boorish.

It was Naples and Sicily where the civilised idea of a Renaissance nobleman had the least effect. In Naples a large nobility, generously endowed with large estates, took little part in the administration and despised the commercial activities of the Northern merchant princes. These old feudal barons of the countryside, like those of Lombardy, were under only the loosest control, and were distracted by family feuds. In the city, the Seggi, the town nobility, were almost entirely responsible for administration, but took little of that interest in the arts which distinguished the élite of Florence and Venice.

The Italian wars, which distracted Italy for the first half of the sixteenth century and resulted in Spanish rather than French domination of the peninsula, had a profound effect on Naples. Spanish influence encouraged a passion for titles, and the increase in the numbers of nobles made high-sounding names thicker on the ground here than in almost any other part of Europe. In the seventeenth century, there were at least 119 princes, 156 dukes and 173 marquises, some of them with an income less than £2,000 a year. The distribution of titles on this scale probably had a corrupting effect, since it encouraged luxury and display among people who could not afford them, and made work appear contemptuous. Idleness and extravagance were too often taken as indispensable signs of quality. A Florentine bookseller commented scathingly on a Spanish count at the Neapolitan court: 'He had one habit which becomes a gentleman, that is at the end of the year he would have spent all his income and sometimes would have entrenched upon the next year's.'[3] Absenteeism from their estates, another Spanish habit, became common in Spanish Naples. Most of the country nobility left their estates in order to live at the court of the Viceroy.

The influence of Spain gradually spread through the rest of the peninsula in the late sixteenth and early seventeenth centuries. In Florence more and more young noblemen withdrew from trade and commerce, and had themselves adopted as knights of the prestigious Order of St Stephen, an order incompatible with bourgeois work. This was of course a trend which

109

went clean against the old Florentine tradition. Artists, too, found cultivated patrons harder to obtain.

Even in Venice, the greatest centre of the merchant princes, patrician families began to lose interest in trade, and turned to banking and land ownership as more suitable sources of a nobleman's income. The city slowly became a symbol of self-indulgence and sensuous living, a city of carnival rather than a city of commerce. Foreigners began to comment severely on the lenient upbringing of young noblemen, many of whom light-heartedly gambled away huge sums, and were the dupes or manipulators of marked cards and loaded dice :

'Fathers and mothers so idolise their children,' wrote a disapproving Frenchman, 'that they never restrain them. They soon grow accustomed to being treated like princes. That is why foreigners do not usually find honest people among these gentlemen unless they are those who have learned to live abroad, and, among these, the ones who have been to France are happily distinguishable from the rest.'[4]

Spanish influence coincided with, even if it did not entirely cause, a kind of creeping exhaustion which became more pronounced in the seventeenth century. The adoption almost everywhere of Spanish fashions of dress coincided with a decline in literature, art, politics and wealth, to all of which the nobility had once contributed.

In the eighteenth century Austria supplanted Spain as the chief power in the peninsula. By the treaty of Utrecht of 1713, Milan became an Austrian possession, and the Lombard nobles, their titles confirmed by the Emperor and incorporated in the Austrian system, now became vassals of the Habsburgs. Florence soon followed Milan under Austrian rule, while Naples was ruled as an independent kingdom by a member of the Bourbon family, with close family ties with Austria. But Austrian influence did not eradicate the very powerful effect of one hundred and fifty years of Spanish domination, and Spanish titles, Spanish attitudes and Spanish fashions remained strong in many places.

In Lombardy, one of the most cosmopolitan parts of the peninsula, French ideas and philosophy were fashionable in the eighteenth century, and salons and academies for literary and philosophical discussion, in the French style, were common. By the mid-century the salons of the Duchess Serbelloni and the Countess Borromeo were known for their French sympathies in politics as well as culture. Some of the gatherings verged on the pretentious, but the store set by scholarship led to the formation of the Trivulzio collection of manuscripts, the basis of the Trivulziana library, and the private library of the Marquis Pertusati which formed the nucleus of the Brera library.

The feudal nobility of the Lombard countryside, now vassals of the House of Habsburg and owing suit at the Emperor's court, still had large estates at their disposal. Less than one per cent of the population owned nearly half of the land of the province. The great landowners were often interested by this time in estate management and agricultural techniques. The big estates in the Po valley experimented with new rice plantations and ambitious schemes of irrigation. Unlike many parts of the peninsula, the Lombard estates were not chronically short of capital – they were held together by a strict system of primogeniture, and sometimes capital obtained through marriage with rich heiresses was put into the land. The English agriculturalist Arthur Young, who visited Italy towards the end of the century, noticed a large number of agricultural pamphlets on sale in Milan, and approved of the nobility's interest in the subject. It was, however, a little too academic, he thought. At a meeting of the Societta Patriotica there was, he says, 'a goodly company of Marchesi, Conti, Cavalieri . . . but not one close-cropped wig, or a pair of dirty breeches to give authority to the proceedings'.[5]

The younger sons of the feudal nobility had often to rely on the charity of the heir, or on their own efforts, since a strict system of primogeniture left them almost destitute of income from the family. A few entered the professions, but more popular was service in the Austrian army or diplomatic service. Some of the younger sons of the Lombard nobility made distinguished careers for themselves in this way, rising to the rank of Field-Marshal or ambassador. The Lombard Count Ludovico Belgiojoso became Austrian ambassador in London in 1769 and remained in that important post for fourteen years. Others joined the Order of the Knights of Malta, which involved performing garrison duty at Valetta, and the occasional excitement of a brush with pirates. The Church was another large employer of younger sons. The Visconti family produced in the course of the eighteenth century thirty-three nuns and twenty-nine clergy, including an Archbishop of Milan, a papal nuncio and a General of the Jesuits. But for all these opportunities, younger sons were frequently dissatisfied with a system which left them to make their own way, and several hailed the French revolution and gave Napoleon's army a rousing reception when it entered Milan in 1796. One noble even became a member of the Jacobin Club in Paris.

To these discontents were added those of the Milan patricians, whose near monopoly of civic office and magistracies was ended by reforms from Vienna, designed to eliminate their intermediate position between the Imperial court and local people. But for all the disgruntlement of younger sons and displaced patricians, noble life in Milan was luxurious, and given to a display which sometimes seemed to visitors to spill over into vulgarity. A visitor commented that, 'The character of the Milanese nobles is marked by generosity and munificence; they entertain in the most friendly manner in both town and country; in the Italian cities a foreigner is sure of a good reception, and their tables make even the French look small. However, a great many of them have not yet acquired bon ton.'[6]

Generous hospitality seems in fact to have been a rare treat in Italy, where traveller after traveller, drawn to the peninsula by its cultural heritage, and the itinerary of the grand tour, complained of meanness or stinted entertainment. So many visitors dwelt on this point because open-handedness was everywhere in Europe an expected attribute of noblemen, whose status demanded that they should appear unconcerned about money, however little they actually had. The tight-fisted Italians aroused international comment. In Piedmont, for instance, the French scholar Montesquieu exercised his French wit at the nobility's expense :

'No one eats anything in Turin : a dinner given to a foreigner is a great novelty in the town . . . The Marquis de Prie, who kept five or six Piedmontese with him for years in Flanders and Vienna, was at Turin when I was. Not one of them offered him so much as a glass of water. One day when I left for the country

112

the Marquis de Carail (the richest Lord in Piedmont) said, 'I'm
so sorry, for I wanted to ask you to dinner.'[7]

In Genoa, a less luxurious town than Venice but one whose
nobility had similar powers and functions, the same complaint
was heard, that rich noblemen were too mean to spend money
on hospitality. Montesquieu commented satirically:

'There are private individuals here with several millions. This
is because they do not spend anything, and in their beautiful
palaces there is often only one serving maid, who spins. The
lower part is full of merchandise and the upper storey is occupied
by the master. In the great houses, if you see a page, it is because
there are no lackeys. . . . They possess palaces because they can
find marble on the spot.'[8]

In Rome, where princes had up to two hundred servants and
perhaps one hundred horses in their stables, the presence of
foreign ambassadors was more conducive to hospitality, although
even here some noblemen gave orders to cut down on food
before a public ceremony. 'I'll be damned if I have yet seen
anyone offered a glass of water,' complained one visitor, no
doubt unlucky in the timing of his visit.[9]

In Venice the class of poor nobles, the Barnabotti, so called
because they had originally rented apartments in the Via San
Barnabe, lived poorly themselves, let alone entertaining others,
and lived by gambling, intrigues and miserable expedients. They
too, like some of the unendowed Lombards, adopted revolutionary slogans at the end of the century. Napoleon was not to
find them the stuff of which reliable allies are made.

Although Venice's commercial position had greatly declined by
the eighteenth century, there were still great fortunes amongst the
old families, and some enormous incomes, deriving now mainly
from property on the mainland. Although brothers and sisters
lived together as co-heirs, these fortunes were kept intact – only
one usually married, the others ending their days in convents or
monasteries. Large incomes were often devoted to conspicuous
consumption and the maintenace of swarms of liveried servants.
The Contarini and Moncenigo families kept forty to fifty servants,
and six to ten gondolas, decorated with the family coat of arms.
But even these great establishments were not lavish of hospitality.
The French traveller Charles de Brosses commented:

'I have sometimes been at a conversazione of the Procuratress Foscarini's, a house of enormous wealth, and she an extremely charming lady; as the only titbit, at 3 p.m., i.e. about eleven o'clock at night in France, twenty valets bring in, on an immense silver platter, a large sliced pumpkin known as anfouri or watermelon, a detestable dish if ever there was one. A pile of silver plates accompany it; everyone grabs at a slice, washes it down with a small cup of coffee and leaves at midnight with an empty head and belly to sup in his own house.'[10]

The Florentine nobility, much less ancient than the Venetian, were now much more liberally titled than they had once been. Citizens could obtain ennoblement by founding a commandery of the Order of St Stephen, for something over £2,000, and giving up direct participation in trade. There were still richly endowed men among their ranks. Arthur Young counted forty servants in the palace of the Marquis Riccardi, each of them with his own family and sometimes domestics of his own. The big fortunes, still based on banking or the silk and wool trade, were impressive by Italian, though not by European standards. Montesquieu noted in 1728 that the head of this same Riccardi family, the richest of them, had big domains in the Tuscan countryside and an income of more than £8,000 a year. Marquis Riccardi occupied the former Medici palace and founded the Riccardi library.

Most of the Florentine nobility, unable to aspire to these heights, lived frugally. But every effort was made to appear resplendent on festival days when dazzling clothes were brought out. Charles de Brosses noted that 'these rich clothes only appeared on important occasions and lasted all the owner's life'.[11]

The largest and in many ways the most interesting area of Italy was Naples, ruled for most of the eighteenth century by its own Bourbon kings. The income of many of the Neapolitan nobility was not large – in many cases not more than £2,000 – but every effort was made to give a magnificent impression. This numerous and far from opulent nobility were insecure in the extreme compared with the English peers, whose assured place at the top of society rested on the rarity of their titles, their seat in the Lords, their broad acres and unquestioned social prestige. While the English peers had no need to strive to impress, and could keep large portions of their capital for investment, the Neapolitan noblemen put all their goods in the shop window. Visitors were amazed at their expensive entertainments, in reception rooms usually loftier than those of London or Paris, and at their dinner parties where each guest, no matter how large the party, had a footman behind his chair. An English traveller wrote :

'No estate in England could support such a number of servants, paid and fed as English servants are; but here the wages are very moderate indeed, and the greater number of men-servants belonging to the first families give their attendance through the day only and find beds and provisions for themselves. It must be remembered, also, that few of the nobles give entertainments and those who do are said to live very sparingly; so that the whole of their revenue, whatever that may be, is exhausted on articles of show.'[12]

The splendid show did not include a display of polished manners. If the Lombard nobles had not yet, by the most exacting French standards, achieved 'bon ton', they were elegance itself compared with the Neapolitans. The Sardinian envoy in Naples reported that :

'Nowhere else in the world, I think, will you find such greed and gourmandising as among the Neopolitans, the most distinguished of whom did not blush to call out (at a party given for the Prince of Piedmont's anniversary) : "Will there be enough iced refreshments? Will supper be served?" And such questions were asked repeatedly. . . . I should have liked your Excellency to be present on this occasion, and I doubt if you would have laughed more in wonder or admiration at the spectacle of these Princes and Dukes giving a perfect imitation of the lazzaroni* during the pillaging of the dessert.'[13]

Some of these noblemen, so anxious to impress and so ignorant of sophisticated standards, combined an effervescent Latin temperament with the kind of bonhomie foreigners associated with the servant class. The Prince of San Nicandro, it was reported, was a good natured man, easy to compete with in jokes and jibes, but his plebeian speech, habits and gestures made him scarcely distinguishable from his coachman.

*Neapolitan street-loungers living by odd jobs and begging.

115

The Neapolitan state had the reputation of being the most miserably backward, inefficient and superstitious in Europe, and it is surprising with this reputation, how many noblemen of distinction it produced. Antonio Genovesi, a churchman of noble family, urged nobles to lead useful lives and become the protectors of their dependants like English peers, and his words did not always fall on deaf ears. The Prince of San Severo, for instance, was a patron of the arts, a scientist and prolific inventor in his own right. He was responsible for new methods of colouring glass and marble, for a solid crack-proof cement or stucco, and a new and superior quality paper. The printing press he set up for the publication of his own writings, formed the basis of the royal press.

Among his contemporaries, the Prince of Tatsia opened his fine private library to the public, the Prince of Noja founded a museum of antiquities, and the Duke of Maddaloni became a generous patron of the theatre, his palace serving as a club for actors and actresses. The Duke himself liked to take the stage in the role of lover. Perhaps even more important, there were some who, amidst a great deal of absenteeism and neglect, improved their estates and saw to the welfare of their peasants.

Naples was amongst the last areas of Italy to be affected by the Napoleonic invasion which began in 1796, but no part of the peninsula was allowed to escape that tremendous impact. The North was converted into the Ligurian and Cisalpine republics, based on Genoa and Milan, French armies burnt the Golden Book of the Venetian nobility and turned Venice over to Austrian rule, while Naples came under the rule of successively the brother and the brother-in-law of Napoleon. On the whole, the nobility as an order were badly weakened. In both Milan and Venice the younger or poorer of the nobility who had stood in the streets to cheer the entry of the French armies were swiftly disillusioned. Although enthusiasm for his creed may have waned, many noblemen, particularly in Lombardy, found it prudent to come to terms with the new rule after a lapse of time, when it seemed to be there to stay. In Lombardy as in France there were nobles who persuaded themselves it was their duty to support the forces of law and order.

The effects of eighteen years of French domination were

never erased, and the old powers of the feudal nobility were among the first to suffer. Feudalism was abolished, and the power of old families challenged more than ever before by those with drive, ambition, talent or luck. During the short rule of Joseph Buonaparte in Naples, the feudal rights of the barons were abolished, and the estates of absentee landlords confiscated. Everywhere the French invasion promoted the idea of one common nationhood, a development which would profoundly affect the future of the nobility.

In most areas the aristocracy did not regain anything like as strong a position as they had once held when, after 1815, the French were driven out and a ring of Austrian and semi-Austrian princes were restored. Duke Federico Confalonieri and other Milanese nobles who had been in correspondence with Piedmontese revolutionaries were brought to trial. Naples tried to resuscitate the nobility by restoring the system of entail and primogeniture, but few big estates were able to keep clear of heavy mortgages. Landlords were not often enterprising, and had not the capital to develop the land. Everywhere the old titled families retrieved their social status, but only rarely their economic position. In Rome, few old families except the Colonna and the Doria retained their former affluence. Those who had not lost money or property during the wars had often wasted their fortunes in gambling, relying on the popes to bale them out. The landlords of the Campagna, once a sober and hard-working group, now increasingly lived in Rome and farmed out their estates to wealthy merchants. Only in Tuscany was there any sign of a reinvigorated nobility interested in agricultural improvements, and only Piedmont was to produce a significant number of distinguished noblemen. In general, indifference, cheap labour and shortage of capital had a stifling effect on big estates, and few noblemen paid serious attention to commerce and industry, where the middle classes were gaining ground all the time.

With the exception of the Piedmontese, few nobles played much part in the 'Risorgimento', and few men of great possessions were listed in the secret societies fighting Austrian domination, which usually consisted of the poor and dispossessed. Piedmont was the home of an exceptionally vigorous nobility.

117

The Marquis Massimo d'Azeglio, a charming Piedmontese noble turned artist and traveller, went in 1845 to the Romagna to preach the gospel of 'faith in Piedmont and its King'. Count Cesare Balbo provided in his famous book *Italy's Hopes* the inspiration for Italy's foreign policy from 1866 onwards. Greatest of all was Count Camillo Cavour, called Milord Camillo by the democrats and hated by some of his fellow nobility for his liberalism. Cavour illustrates the best side of the Piedmontese nobility. As a younger son he had to make his own way in the world; in his first appointment as Minister of Agriculture and Commerce, he impressed colleagues by an expertise gained as administrator of the family property. The Piedmontese were the most talented nobility in the peninsula. On the whole the nobility of the new state which Cavour more than anyone helped to unite, were not in a strong position.

In hardly any areas had the nobility as a group political importance. They no longer possessed significant civil or military privileges, they were not necessarily wealthy and, unlike the English peerage, they were not brought up to the business of governing. In many areas of the South they were much too numerous to enjoy the prestige attaching to the much more exclusive English peers. In Sicily, for instance, there were sixty dukes, one hundred princes, and innumerable barons and marquises, some of them as illiterate as their grooms. Their control of the land had dropped steadily in the forty years before unification – between 1820 and 1860, the number of landowning families in Sicily rose from two thousand to twenty thousand. An observer gave in 1860 this description of the Sicilian nobility, who must have been among the most miserable in the continent :

'The Sicilian nobleman, brought up at home by a priest and allowed to herd with menials, has no companion among his equals. Thrown into the hands of a pedagogue, he merely learns to read and write, then passes into the care of a friar who teaches him his catechism and the rudiments of Latin; and he finally goes to a school of nobles, and obtains a mere smattering of Belles Lettres. Then his education finishes. Coming home at sixteen or seventeen, he throws aside his classics, betakes himself to novel reading, and sets up as a man about town.

Prevented by class prejudice from entering the army or the navy, he learns neither to command or obey; and excluded as he is from the magistracy by his legal ignorance, he neither administers justice nor enforces the laws. None of the nobility live on their estates. Most of the Sicilian towns serve for the residence of the neighbouring landlords on whose scanty outlay they depend for their subsistence. The family mansion standing on the deserted market place shows trace of former splendour in painted ceilings, gilt doors and embossed furniture. Here lost in space dwell the present possessors, ignorant of what is going on in the political world, falling gradually to the lowest level. They are destined to be supplanted by men of business and industry on a not distant day.'[14] No one has better described this period than Prince Lampedusa in *The Leopard.*

No other regional nobility had sunk as low as the Sicilian, but traces of their weaknesses could be found elsewhere. An American diplomat noted in 1860 the contempt which the Neapolitan nobility had for practical agriculture. In Venice the nobility, if too poor to own a carriage or a gondola, would hire one for the afternoon, and fix their coat of arms on the door or on the prow. The Northern nobility were on the whole more adaptable, less preoccupied with the taboos of the past, but not even in Piedmont were there larger numbers of nobles of the calibre to influence national politics. The Italian nobility were on the whole too ineffective for there to be any question of a 'House of Lords' in the new united monarchy. Count Cavour, the architect of the new state and an admirer of the English constitution who might well have favoured the idea, recognised that in the circumstances it could not seriously be considered.

The unification diminished still further the importance of the nobility as an order. The titled families of Milan and Naples resented losing the offices and patronage which they had previously controlled. Few ministers, apart from the Tuscan barons Ricasoli and Sonnino and the Sicilian Marquis of Rudini, came from the nobility. Furthermore, King Victor Emmanuel inherited the habit which had done so much to damage the prestige of the nobility in the past – his Majesty admitted that he never could refuse a cigar or a title to a gentleman, and the uncharitable commented that he was not always too careful about their being gentlemen. This Gilbert and Sullivan situation, 'when everyone is somebody, then no-one's anybody', was not really in anyone's interests. Victor Emmanuel did badly by the nobility compared with a succession of English monarchs, whose well-known reluctance to create new titles on any large scale has been one of the British Crown's great services to its peerage.

In Southern Italy, it was not just excessive numbers of largely meaningless titles, but the sheer inertia of the old ways which perpetuated much of the idleness and misery of the past. The English Countess of Warwick, who spent some months in 1903 at the villa of her sister, the Duchess of Sutherland, near Palermo, wrote home :

'What have centuries of greatness in rulers, aristocracy, genius, art, done for the country one sees today? Bad government, bad art, bad ideals, an effete and miserable aristocracy, an ignorant, depraved, servile democracy, living under conditions no better than animals and crushed by ignorance and taxation.'[15]

The nobility of Southern Italy long remained one of the unhappiest in Europe. In the North, the offspring of the old nobility merged rapidly into the rest of the population, and individuals were to play a prominent part in commerce, motoring, and the Italian film industry. But nowhere have they played that full role in almost every sphere of national life which has revealed the good fortune and the good sense of the English peerage.

Chapter Five

Russian Nobility

In 1698 the young Peter the Great set up a temporary court at John Evelyn's house at Deptford, while he studied British dockyards. When Evelyn returned to take possession, he found that the servants had been 'right nasty' about the house, the Czar had ruined his hedges by trundling a wheelbarrow through them, and damage to furnishings and furniture cost £150 to repair.[1] The Czar's court perambulated through most of Western Europe, and it was many years before European aristocrats ceased to expect rough behaviour, loutish manners and primitive habits when a Russian nobleman was announced.

The Russian nobility, drawn from vast and remote territory on the fringes of European civilisation, was something of a mystery to its western counterparts. In any case it was a most mixed society.

In Russia the Emperor was an absolute autocrat and no one held any status beneath him. A title in itself did not confer any distinction, due to the manner in which Russian titles arose and were awarded. All descendants of Rurik, who founded the Russian Realm in the 800s, bore the title of Prince together with the similar descendants of the last pagan sovereign of Lithuania, Gedimin. As Russia conquered and assimilated other nations, the title of Prince was awarded to the former Royal families coming under control and also given for services rendered. Therefore the title of Prince originally meant that one was descended in the direct male line from a dynastic family.

The Russian Empire was too distant, too culturally backward and its provinces too dangerous to figure in the Grand Tour, which helped to make society cosmopolitan in the West. Occasional travellers, more intrepid than the general run of tourists or driven by special business, sent back reports which often

121

confirmed the worst suspicions of their recipients. The Italian Count Algarotti visited in 1739 the Imperial capital of St Petersburg, where sumptuous palaces were built on a site of marsh and swamp. 'Their walls are all cracked, out of perpendicular and ready to fall,' he reported to his English correspondent, Lord Hervey. 'It has been wittily enough said that ruins make themselves in other places, but that they were built in St Petersburg.'[2]

More than half a century later, Catharine and Martha Wilmot kept a careful journal of their five years' stay in Russia. The sisters, intelligent and cultured observers, were dismayed by the superstition, lack of taste and decorum, ludicrous extravagance and lack of general conversation which even the metropolitan nobility displayed. 'When I compare Moscow with Paris or Naples in the way of amusements, rationality, or attractions,' Catharine wrote, 'the Contrast becomes laughable. . . . Their living, dress and language succeed very well; but as to manners (and now I speak of the young women particularly) they are the most abrupt, superficial and ignorant I ever happen'd to meet with in my life.'[3]

The nobility of Moscow and St Petersburg, for all their limitations, lived a sophisticated life compared with the provincial nobility, often poor and sometimes illiterate, who inhabited estates in remote areas where justice was weak and the presence of a fluid frontier often added further hazards to an uncertain life. In the North West, a report disclosed in 1767, the nobility 'suffer extreme ravages from brigands, thieves, robbers and other kinds of criminals, which stops many of them from living on their estates, for the protection of their lives from wicked torment. Those living in the provinces, either through necessity or lack of other place of refuge, are compelled to keep up three or four times the normal number of household servants.'[4]

The uncertainties of life helped to make the Russian nobility, on their own estates, the most powerful in Europe. The same lawless and precarious existence which had given the Czars despotic rule over their subjects, gave the nobility, until the emancipation of 1861, the power of despots over their serfs. The 'dark mass' of serfs, bearded, illiterate, cultivating the soil with primitive tools, could not leave their estates, after the reign of

Peter the Great (1696–1725) without their owner's consent. They could, with the minimum of restrictions, be bought and sold. The nobility, who alone had the right to own serf labour, had the power of punishing almost all offences and could, until 1809, sentence their serfs to penal servitude. In an atmosphere of fear and danger, punishments were often carried out with barbarity.

Prince Nicolas Youssoupoff, one of the most cultured noble-men of his generation, had a summary way of quelling trouble on his estate at Arkhangelskoie. When a group of serfs murdered his hated head steward by hurling him from the top of a tower, the culprits each received fifteen lashes of the knout, their nostrils were torn off, the word 'murderer' was branded on their faces with a red hot iron, and for good measure they were sent to Siberia in chains.[5]

Prince Nicolas's contemporaries kept fools, dwarfs, hunch-backs and other grotesque specimens of humanity in their house-holds for their amusement through the long winter evenings, but most were not just petty potentates who held life cheap. They managed to combine in their persons the habits of both East and West in a manner most disconcerting to foreigners. Peter the Great began that imitation of Western ways which was to give the nobility, until the revolution, its curious split personality. Peter was convinced that Russia could only compete with the West by adopting Western methods, and the sudden conversion to European manners which he imposed on his court placed a mass of pitfalls in the paths of unsuspecting noblemen. The British Ambassador to Turkey retailed the first of a series of European anecdotes at their expense :

'The Muscovite Ambassador and his retinue have appeared here so different from what they always formerly wore that ye Turks cannot tell what to make of them. They are all coutred in gold and silver lace, long perruques and, which the Turks most wonder at, without beards. Last Sunday, being at mass in Adrianople, the Ambassador and all his company did not only keep their hats off during the whole ceremony, but at ye elevation, himself and all of them pulled off their wigs. It was much taken notice of and thought an unusual act of devotion.'[6]

The greater nobility eventually mastered the intricacies of

123

European headgear, and became faithful echoes of the French aristocracy, the pattern of eighteenth-century refinement, in manners, in taste and in speech. The results were not always unappreciated. 'A Russian nobleman,' wrote Motley in 1714, 'was formerly distinguished among Foreigners by the Grossness of his Manners; whereas at present the Russians dispute with all other Nations for Politeness.'[7] The effort which went into their transformation remained considerable. Princess Catherine Dashkova, Lady-in-Waiting to the Empress Catherine II, recorded that,

'Amongst the late changes introduced at court, the French curtsy was ordered to be substituted in place of the Russian mode of salutation, which is a profound inclination of the head and body. The attempts of the old ladies to unstiffen their knees, in conformity with this innovation, were in general very unhappy, and ludicrous enough, and the Emperor had a great source of amusement in witnessing their failure.'[8]

In their new guise of cosmopolitan Europeans, the greater Russian nobility felt obliged to make at least a gesture towards patronage of the arts. As early as 1715 the palace of Prince Volkonski at Seloznez near Tula was decorated with Italian and Dutch paintings. But some of his class promoted a slavish imitation of Western models later to be associated with that other culturally deprived group, the rich Americans. Prince Nicolas Youssoupoff, for instance, a man renowned for his patronage of the arts and elegant tastes, used his wealth and influence to persuade Pope Pius VI to allow the Vatican frescoes to be copied for him by Italian artists. Similarly, in Venice, Prince Nicolas commissioned from Tiepolo, not an original work, but copies of the frescoes with which the artist had just decorated the Palazzo Labia. When it came to patronising the Arts, the Russian nobles of the time were too insecure, too conscious of their parvenu status in this field, to risk endorsing originality.

Some of their efforts crossed the dividing line between magnificence and vulgarity. Prince Nicolas was ostentatious in a way more suited to an Eastern harem than a French salon. His famous art collection included portraits of three hundred of his mistresses. In the private theatre on his Arkhangelskoie estate, his private troupe of ballet dancers were trained to strip

124

naked when the Prince shook his stick. Like converts of every kind, the Russian noble sometimes let his enthusiasm go to extremes. Another nobleman, a devotee of the opera, forbade his servants to communicate in anything but recitative.

Western culture did, of course, enrich both the life of the nobility and the artistic world of Russia as time went by. Numerous writers, among them the noble poet Pushkin, effectively combined the best of East and West. Nor was European practice always accepted uncritically. From time to time, a section of the nobility reacted against this perpetual adulation of Western ways and exalted the native traditions of the Slavs. But among the higher aristocracy at large, Western imitation was one of the most prominent characteristics until the revolution. French craftsmen, from Fabergé, the court jeweller, downwards, readily found employment; and an army of French tutors and governesses strove to imprint that foreign style which was the hallmark of good breeding.

The linguistic achievements are impressively displayed in Tolstoy's novels, where noblemen switch from French to English and from English to Russian with apparently effortless ease. But much that was artificial remained until the end, underlining one striking difference from the English peerage, whose essential Englishness accounted for much of their native popularity. The ultimate absurdity was recorded by Prince Felix Youssoupoff, the last owner of the family estates, who chronicled from exile the history of his house, under the nostalgic title of *Lost Splendour*. He wrote :

'Most of my mother's contemporaries affected to speak French only, and spoke Russian with a foreign accent. It was considered good form to have one's laundering done in London or Paris.'[9]

Like the French aristocracy whom they imitated so carefully, the Russian nobility were never anything approaching a closed caste. For all their foreign ways which separated them from the masses in outlook, habits, dress and language, the ranks of the nobility were always open to those few who had the drive to seek ennoblement. Peter the Great had offered the incentive of noble status, with its attendant privileges, the right to own serfs and to be exempt from the poll tax, to promote the

125

service of the state. His table of ranks laid down in 1722 that the attainment of a certain level in the bureaucracy, the army or the navy, carried with it hereditary nobility. In the civil service, fourteen ranks were prescribed, based on German titles. The highest eight conferred hereditary nobility, the next six personal nobility for the official but not for his children. Military rank was carefully graded to run parallel with the civil service and the Church, with varying forms of address applicable. Thus a field marshal ranked with an Imperial Chancellor and a metropolitan of the Church, the first two being addressed as 'High Excellency' and the metropolitan 'High Holiness'. Majors ranked with collegiate assessors in the civil service, both being addressed as 'High Nobility' and with an abbot in the Church, 'High Reverence'. Even a mere ensign or cornet ranked with a collegiate registrar and was styled 'Nobility'.

These fourteen grades of Peter the Great existed with few changes until the revolution of 1917 and the modes of address were strictly adhered to. Characters in Chekhov's plays are frequently addressed as 'Your Excellency', for instance Professor Serebriakov in *Uncle Vanya*, because he had been ranked with an actual State Councillor.

The emphasis on service rather than birth was a striking feature of the Russian class system. New men took precedence over noblemen of the most illustrious families in a way that astounded Lord Macartney, the British ambassador, who wrote in the 1760s:

'All nobles are equal and have precedence only according to the rank of their employment in the state: thus a common writer or common soldier, if he rises either in the civil or military, takes the place of every person whatsoever of an inferior character, though sprung from the first families of the empire.'[10]

Money was also a credential if owned in sufficiently large quantities and for long enough to blunt aristocratic dislike of raw cash. The Demidov family, originating from the Urals where mines produced in the eighteenth century a substantial proportion of all iron mined in Europe, rose from humble origins in a few generations into the highest nobility.

The sons and daughters of new hereditary nobles, and their

descendants in perpetuity, were all of noble rank, as was the case in Germany and Austria, and the nobility was consequently a rapidly growing group. Before 1600 only 738 families had been entitled to noble rank. By 1897 the figure had risen to more than a million people.

Unlike the British peerage, this numerous nobility had no access, for most of its existence, either to parliamentary experience or to real power. The old Duma, composed of nobles, was suppressed by Peter the Great when he proclaimed himself absolute monarch, and the institution revived in 1906 played only a very limited role until the revolution. Parliamentary experience, which most heirs to British peerage obtained in the House of Commons before their elevation and in the House of Lords afterwards, was outside their range. They had few of the opportunities of wielding power and responsibility which numerous British peers enjoyed in eighteenth- and nineteenth-century cabinets. Policy making and decisions were reserved for the Czar, though individuals might obtain a precarious influence.

Although their role did not involve real power, it looked for a time as though the Russian nobility might develop a professionalism unrivalled in Europe. In his anxiety for efficient state service, Peter the Great gave the Russian nobility the chance of becoming the most practically trained aristocracy in Europe. Under Peter's edict, the young nobility were forced to undergo instruction in some branch of practical knowledge, either abroad or in certain mathematical schools which the Emperor established in St Petersburg. The penalty for failing to complete the course was enforced celibacy. This being a state for which aristocrats seldom have an inclination, it is not surprising that young noblemen failed to appreciate that here was a great opportunity for relevant training at a time when their British counterparts were firmly tied to Latin and Greek.

Technical training in the armed services, in Peter's scheme, involved working one's way up from the ranks. At one time, three hundred princes from the most illustrious families were serving as privates in one Guards regiment, living in barracks, receiving a soldier's pay and food, and carrying out the menial duties expected of their lowly rank. Similarly, for those unfortunate enough to be drafted into the navy, the most detested service, a training in basic seamanship, either at Reval or in Holland, was the first requirement. Russia could, if the system had taken root, have produced an officer corps of unrivalled professionalism, and one which did something to bridge the dangerous gulf separating her people. But the overwhelming resistance to such measures soon wore down the weaker personalities of Peter the Great's successors. The onerous training for service was modified, noblemen were granted opportunities for promotion over non-nobles, and in 1762 the compulsion binding on all nobles to serve the state was ended. Numerous noblemen did, as a matter of course, continue to serve in the bureaucracy or the army, but the thorough technical training and professional attitudes were largely lost. Catherine the Great, who perpetuated the nobles' privileges, hoped that those who abandoned state service would interest themselves in economic improvements on their estates and in local government, but her hopes were disappointed. Here again, the Russian nobility were to let slip from their grasps a great opportunity.

The Russian nobility held lands ranging from the fertile soils of the Ukraine to the semi-arid areas of Central Asia. They were in touch with Western Europe, where an agricultural revolution transformed farming in the eighteenth and nineteenth centuries, and seemed in a good position to promote big advances in agriculture. This was an opportunity which most failed to seize. Whatever the attraction of other Western habits, the Russian aristocracy developed none of the flair for efficient estate management shown by the British and Prussian landowners.

Circumstances did not always help them. Unlike the British, the Russian pattern of land ownership was not based on primogeniture and estates were constantly divided and subdivided to provide portions for numerous offspring. Peter the Great's reforms, in this as in other fields, would, in the long run, have benefited the nobility. Impressed by what he had seen of the English system, he prescribed in 1714 that landed inheritance should go to one son only, to be selected by the donor. By this system he hoped that families would maintain their wealth and position, tax-collection would be easier, and younger sons would be driven to seek useful employment to support themselves. Noble resistance, however, frustrated his intentions after his death, and the new method was abolished in 1730 after only a short trial.

As a result, the average late-eighteenth-century nobleman did not have at his disposal a large number of serfs – only sixteen per cent of the nobility had more than one hundred serfs in 1777. Apart from this subdivision, the very existence of serf labour on all noble estates was a discouragement to modern and productive methods. The existence of a captive labour force, extremely conservative in outlook and more impervious to improvements than the peasants of Western Europe, was a disincentive at a time when striking advances in tools and methods were being made in Britain. If large-scale production for an outside market was to be the objective, serf labour was inferior to free hired labour and, with the subdivision of estates, most noblemen had not the capital for extensive improvements. The lack of large urban markets and of good communications, helped to stifle agricultural development. Some new advances were made in developing the potential of estates : in the second half of the eighteenth century some of the better endowed nobility were beginning to go in for a kind of manorial manufacture, taking advantage of the cheap labour available. In 1773 nobles owned sixty-six such enterprises compared with 328 merchant manufacturers. But the majority were content to continue the pattern inherited from their ancestors.

Fashion was partly to blame. More familiar with French literature and German philosophy during this period than with the techniques of improving landlords in England, the greater Russian nobility produced no counterpart of 'Turnip' Townshend, the English peer who publicised the use of turnips as a cleaning crop, an innovation which allowed the four course rotation and revolutionised livestock keeping. No Czar made agriculture fashionable, as King George III did in England. Prince Nicolas Youssoupoff, a setter of aristocratic fashion, declared of his estate : 'Arkhangelskoie is not run for profit.'

The middle and lower aristocracy, who might have been as committed to agriculture as the British gentry, aspired instead to the life of the grandees which was just out of their reach, rather than to improving their estates. Few cultivated local leadership, country sports and efficient husbandry as their real

E   129

interests dictated, while many yearned for the aristocratic salons of the capital and the sophisticated life of the princes and the counts in the international set.

Since agriculture was not considered an interest fit for gentlemen, it is not surprising that agricultural yield remained almost stationary between 1810 and 1870. As the nineteenth century wore on, the position of more and more noble landowners became precarious. By 1843 more than half of the land owned by noblemen was mortgaged to different state institutions, and many estates were also loaded with private debts. The emancipation of the serfs in 1861 aggravated their plight rather than alleviated it. Many landowners' mortgage commitments increased, and nobles' holdings continued to decline, sold out to merchants, industrialists and peasants on the make. In the two decades after emancipation they shrank by eighteen per cent in the forty provinces of European Russia.

Tolstoy's novel *Anna Karenina* which gives a vivid picture of the Russian nobility in the eighteen eighties, illustrates the attitudes which lay behind these figures. Active interest in farming was still considered eccentric, and Constantine Levin, whose enthusiasm for the subject branded him as something of a crank, was acutely aware of its lack of prestige when he came to propose matrimony.

'From her parents' standpoint, it seemed to him, he had no settled occupation or position in the world. He was thirty-two, and while his former comrades were already colonels, aides-de-camps, Bank and Railway Directors, or Heads of Government Boards, he (he knew very well what others must think of him) was merely a country squire, spending his time breeding cows, shooting snipe and erecting buildings – that is to say, a fellow without talent, who has come to no good and was only doing what in the opinion of Society good-for-nothing people always do.'[11]

Levin, for his part, found it hard to tolerate the indifference of his friends to their own estates. When one of his friends in the bureaucracy made the kind of ill-considered sale only too typical of the nobility, he vehemently attacked the ignorance which was damaging the interest of his class :

'It vexes and hurts me to see on all sides the impoverishment of the noblesse, to which I too belong and to which, in spite of the merging of the classes, I am very glad to belong. And impoverished not from extravagance. That would not matter so much : to spend like a nobleman is their business and only the noblesse know how to do it. At present the peasants round here are buying the land – that does not pain me. The squire does nothing, the peasant works and squeezes out the idler. That is as it should be and I am very glad on the peasant's account. But it hurts me to see this impoverishment as a result of – shall I call it simplicity? Here a Polish leaseholder buys for half its value the splendid estate of a lady who lives in Nice. There land that is worth ten roubles a desyatine is leased to a merchant for one rouble. And now you, without any reason, have presented that scamp with thirty thousand roubles.'

Improvidence was not entirely unknown in the late Victorian peerage, and a shark like Ernest Terah Hooley made himself a millionaire out of the fecklessness of English landowners, but bungling was never quite as widespread amongst the English peers who had more direct knowledge of their estates, and the advice of trained agents, solicitors and accountants to guide them.

Government measures to help the Russian nobility could do little when such insouciance was common. The Nobles Land Bank, set up in 1885 to lend money to the nobility on far more favourable terms than the Peasant Bank, did little to stem the sales. Some landowners, particularly in the Ukraine, retained great estates and continued their profitable business there, with large-scale units specialising in the export of grain. But in general the noble landowner was not prosperous and, as more and more estates were sold, young nobles left the land in ever increasing numbers. To be a nobleman no longer meant to be a landowner.

The nobility had done comparatively little to invest in the developing industry of Russia to compensate for their agricultural losses. By the late nineteenth century, when some of the greater English peers had made themselves almost independent of their agricultural revenues by their heavy stakes in railways, minerals, industry and real estate, the Russian nobility had been slow to seize the opportunities which even the relatively slow economic advance of Russia offered. The Russian nobility as a whole never managed to play their full part in economic enterprise. The money which some of them had acquired in the eighteenth century through the generosity of female sovereigns had been spent on luxury and personal display rather than invested. The reason here was not, as in Italy, insecurity brought on by excessive dilution of titles, but an inferiority complex vis à vis the West. St Petersburg was always straining to keep up with Paris and Vienna. There was, compared with England, little investment even in the noblemen's own lands. On the very eve of the revolution, even the most obvious resources at hand on private estates were still being neglected. Prince Felix Youssoupoff, the last of his line in possession before the revolution swept his class away, recorded :

'One of our estates on the Caucasus stretched for one hundred and twenty miles along the Caspian Sea; crude petroleum was so abundant that the soil seemed soaked with it, and the peasants used it to grease their cart wheels.'

There was more to all this than a story of lost opportunities. Just as the Russian nobility shared the odium of the Czars' rule without enjoying any real share of power, so they suffered all the unpopularity of a privileged class of landowners, without exploiting the opportunities of their position. They seem to have made the worst of all worlds.

From the time of the French revolution, when the aristocracy they had copied so assiduously were driven into exile, the more thoughtful of the Russian nobility were disturbed by the dangers underlying the Russian social system. Every generation from the French to the Russian revolutions produced its crop of reforming noblemen, driven by varying quantities of fear or social conscience. Some took comfort in the reflection that the serfs of the nobility were in general much better off than those on crown lands. Others emphasised that, like aristocrats elsewhere, their treatment of dependents was paternalistic. A peasant proverb ran : 'If there is no grain, the master will provide.' After the emancipation of the serfs, the Russian nobility liked, in the words of an 1885 manifesto, to plume itself on 'an example of generosity rare in the history of all countries and peoples'.[12] But throughout the century there were those more perceptive noblemen who realised the limitations of paternalism and the precarious position of their order.

Conscience, like fashion, came from the West. It was the Napoleonic wars which first brought doubt and self-criticism to numbers of educated noblemen, and the beginning of that liberal intelligentsia in which nobles played a part until the revolution. As one of these, Prince Volkonski, wrote :

'The campaigns of 1812-1814 brought Europe nearer to us, made us familiar with its forms of state, its public institutions, the right of its peoples. . . . By contrast with our own state life, the laughably limited rights which our people possessed, the despotism of our regime became truly present in our heart and understanding.'[13]

The upsurge of patriotic feeling which helped to drive out the French invaders of 1812, led many of the educated nobility to re-examine the idea of noblesse oblige. In the years after the wars a number of young noblemen, later prominent in the Decembrist conspiracy of 1825, formulated ideas for a new organisation of society. Colonel Pestel and Prince Serge Trubetskoy of the Union of Salvation advocated a constitutional regime and the abolition of serfdom. Nikita Muravyov, the heir to great estates, preached civil liberties and trial by jury. Under Russian conditions, these ideals could only be realised with the consent or overthrow of the Czar, and the liberal aims collapsed when the 1825 uprising failed. Everything was done to erase the memory of this episode, but the ideals which inspired it were to reappear throughout the century as a substantial minority of noblemen realised the inhumanity and the danger of the system.

In 1858 an anonymous Russian nobleman published in Paris an outspoken criticism of the self-seeking and exploitation by his class under the title of *Quelques Vérités à la Noblesse Russe*. Although he emphasised his loyalty to the Czar and his Christian principles, he did not mince his words. The nobility owed their privileges to a history of bloody rapine and treacherous self-seeking. He appealed to them to support the emancipation of the serfs, to stay on their estates and work for themselves, and to stop drawing income from oppressed labour. He warned of the dangers of resisting the inevitable advance of the peasantry :

133

'Consider how each obstacle, how each delay, is like a dam which blocks a stream, but which, when it is not opened in time, makes the water overflow, carrying along everything in its path. You put at risk all this property you hold so dear; you put at risk your existence.'

The emancipation of the peasants brought few of the changes in noble attitude which the author of this pamphlet hoped for, and the gulf between the classes yawned as widely as ever. The Populists of the eighteen seventies tried above all to bridge this gulf, to bring education and help to the peasants and to spread socialism. This movement too had its noble adherents, among them Sophie Perovskaya, the daughter of a Governor General of St Petersburg, and Prince Peter Kropotkin, the future revolutionary anarchist, who came from a distinguished family. This movement, which produced for a time the spectacle of girls of delicate nurture working fifteen hours a day in Moscow cotton factories, and young noblemen giving up promising careers to spread Socialism among the peasants, culminated in the 'mad summer' of 1874, when a famine in the Volga region produced an extraordinary response from the intelligentsia. Between two and three thousand of them literally 'went to the people', living in their villages, working by their side and sharing their tiny meals. The sacrifice was in vain. Two and a half centuries of separate development separated the Westernised upper classes from their peasant compatriots, and the peasants neither trusted nor understood their message. And the Populists, like the Decembrists before them, were crushed by the implacable hostility of the Czar.

European history suggests that the fortunes of kings and their 'cousins', the nobility, are irretrievably linked together. The Russian nobility suffered much for the blind spots of their illustrious 'relations', whose intransigence had no parallel in the English monarchy since the seventeenth century.

The nobility continued, right up to the end, to produce men of vastly more perception than their sovereigns. Count Leo Tolstoy, in his very idiosyncratic way, was totally convinced of the evils of the Russian social system. To Tolstoy, the society of his day was evil because false values were bred by the exploitation which pervaded it. The masters were degraded by their parasitism, while the peasants, crushed by ten generations of hard labour, had not the remotest chance of becoming rounded or thinking people. Tolstoy was driven by an acute social conscience to try and rid himself of the outward signs of his class. He lived and often dressed as a peasant, and learnt to make boots. He decided that property was wicked and tried unsuccessfully to get rid of his land, preaching non-violence, chastity, non-compulsion and love for mankind.

Right up to the eve of the revolution other noblemen, of lesser eminence, came to realise that they were sitting on a volcano. Prince Felix Youssoupoff, one of the most harum-scarum of the last Russian nobility whose irresponsible practical jokes were a bye-word at court, came, after his brother's death in a duel, to a critical appraisal of the world in which he lived :

'A few days later, I returned to Moscow and began my work among the poor. I started off by visiting slums where the squalor and destitution were indescribable. Most of the hovels never saw the sun; whole familes were crowded into tiny rooms, and slept on the bare ground in dampness, filth and cold.'

Prince Felix began to dream of turning the Arkhangelskoie estate into an art centre, the houses in St Petersburg and Moscow into hospitals, clinics and old people's homes, of building sanatoria on the Crimean and Caucasian estates, and of presenting his land to the peasants. His intentions were overtaken by war and revolution.

As in every other generation, Prince Felix was in a small minority of his class. Most of his contemporaries, even at the end, were unaware of danger and lived life as it came. Ladies competed for the honour of a séance, or some more intimate experience, with the unwashed Rasputin, princes and counts competed for seats at the magnificent new Diaghilev ballets which were taking Europe by storm, and exchanged expensive Fabergé gifts, such items as jewelled door-bells designed to look like boiled sweets, which momentarily relieved the boredom of an empty life. Princess Radziwill recalled from exile that, 'looseness of conduct became general, divorces numerous, and adventures of all kinds in which well-known personages figured, kept people lively and gossip busy.'[14]

There were others, like Baron Tuzenbach in Chekhov's play

The Three Sisters, who sensed the danger threatening their society, but were too supine, and perhaps overwhelmed by the sheer size of the problem, to make a move :

'The time has come,' said Tuzenbach, 'an avalanche is moving down on us, a mighty, wholesome storm is brewing, which is approaching, is already near, and soon will sweep away from our society its idleness, indifference, prejudice against work, and foul ennui.'

When that storm came, there were those nobles who hoped that the Czars, who alone had monopolised power, would suffer alone, and that the nobility would survive. In 1917 the French Ambassador noted in his diary that 'everyone consoled himself or herself with the thoughts that obviously the Russian nobility would not suffer if the Emperor, Empress, Grand Dukes, Grand Duchesses, the Church and the monasteries are ruthlessly robbed and plundered'.[15]

These were the last delusions of a noble class, removed by centuries of separation from the realities of life. Although many servants in noble households risked everything to protect their masters – and some even endured torture rather than reveal the whereabouts of the family jewels – the nobility had no firm foothold in the affection of the masses to save them when the Czars fell. Distinctions of accent, schooling and class in England were as nothing compared with the gulf which yawned between noble and peasant in Russia, and there was little encouragement for that respect and even affection for his 'betters' which made so many English countrymen conservatives. The Russian Bolsheviks were set on the removal of the nobility and the peasants were set on what remained of their land.

There were those among the nobility who regretted, not so much the errors which had produced the catastrophe, but the lack of dignity with which the nobility met their fate. Style, not substance, was the thing. Princess Catherine Radziwill lamented :

'When the hour of danger and sacrifice struck, they found themselves unable to resist the fury of the storm; they did not even die with dignity, far less confront their foes with courage and proud resignation to an undeserved fate. A more pitiful sight than that of Russian exiles dragging out their miserable

existence in foreign lands has never been seen; beside it the
French emigration at the beginning of the nineteenth century
displayed real grandeur and haughty pride in its struggle against
extinction.'

The Princess's lament is an interesting reflection of the traditional noble values, found in varying degrees throughout Europe
– pride, dignity and courage – but the real tragedy escaped her.
The Russian nobility at its best had been a talented class. For
all its lost opportunities, it had produced men of brilliance and
sensitivity, who could have contributed as much to a new Russia
as English peers were to do to twentieth-century Britain. As it
was, the Russian nobility was condemned to exile, selling their
jewellery and writing their reminiscences in Cannes, driving
taxis and running nightclubs in Paris, living on their memories
and waiting in vain for the call which would welcome them
home.

Chapter Six

English Peerage (I)

If age is the chief pride of an aristocracy, most of the English peerage cannot afford to plume itself. Compared with the Spanish descendants of the lords of the reconquest, or the Russian princes tracing their descent from Rurik who died in 879, they tend to be a group of upstarts.

The medieval barons, with their feudal tenures, their retinues of knights-at-arms, their private quarrels and their fortified castles, hardly survived the Wars of the Roses. Before the war, each great noble had been a petty king in his own area, and the Earl, the highest rank in the peerage except for the kinsmen of the king and the few marquises created after 1385, had wide responsibilities as the governor of his territory. The civil war killed off many of this old nobility. Some of the greatest names disappeared, and although their daughters sometimes transmitted the old blood to new title-holders, much of the ancient prestige had been lost. Only eighteen peers subscribed to the oath taken in Henry's VII's first parliament, and their descendants make up only a fraction of the modern peerage. In 1968 Enoch Powell gave a party at Westminster in celebration of his excellent book on the House of Lords, to which he invited all those peers whose forebears had sat in that first parliament. It was a very select party.

The small early Tudor nobility had nothing like a monopoly of the great estates of the kingdom; in many of the provinces the greatest landowner was the Church. For instance at my home, Beaulieu, the Cistercian order of monks held fourteen thousand acres, and this was small compared with the vast Church estates in the North. The dissolution of the monasteries, an early popular revolution against privilege, or perhaps an early act of nationalisation, helped to bring into being a new,

138

landed aristocracy. The *nouveaux riches,* status-hungry courtiers of Henry VIII were able to establish themselves on the land. As something like one third of the territory of England changed hands, often at knock-down prices, men like my ancestor, Thomas Wriothesley, seized the opportunity of founding a landed family, and buying a vast number of estates in Hampshire. Wriothesley, an ambitious man who had risen in the king's service by means of 'indefatigable study of the law', bought the house and site of Beaulieu Abbey from Henry VIII on 29th July 1538, and was created Baron Wriothesley in 1544 and Earl of Southampton three years later. Wriothesley was a typical *parvenu.* All over the country new men of his type were busy sinking their roots, converting monasteries into stately homes, and founding territorial families. Before long, their descendants, and mine were no exception, were as interested in ancestry and heraldry as any modern American, and would be bent on trying to prove their ancient lineage back to the army of William the Conqueror, or to the conqueror himself.

By the end of Queen Elizabeth's reign the peerage, although grown, still only numbered fifty nine, since Her Majesty was almost as reluctant to create peers as she was to spend money. Her successors more than made up for the queen's niggardliness. James I, my direct ancestor in the male line, created peerages wholesale. He made sixty new peers in just over twenty years, and in 1615 began the practice of selling the honour, the usual price being ten thousand pounds. There was, of course, much complaining from those already, if only just, established, at this invasion by the even newer rich. When Lionel Cranfield was made Earl of Middlesex, a critic commented that 'none but a poore-spirited nobility would have endured his perching on that high tree of honour, to the dishonour of the nobility, the disgrace of the gentry'.[1] Such carping was perhaps understandable, but the peerage was still in fact very small by international standards, and some of these new peers, like their Tudor predecessors, had a vigour and vitality which helped to keep the peerage red-blooded. George Calvert, for six years Secretary of State and created Lord Baltimore in 1625, sought a patent for colonisation and succeeded in founding, not just a titled house,

139

but the colony of Maryland, where the state capital is still named Baltimore after its founder.

Charles I created peerages at a slightly more moderate rate than his father, but his son, Charles II, found himself under an obligation to many of his courtiers for services they had performed during his exile and restoration, or their wives performed during his reign. For example, Edward Montagu, the commander of the fleet who took it over to the king's side at the crucial moment of the Restoration, was typical of the first category – he was created Earl of Sandwich in recognition of his sense of timing, taking his title from where the ship landed; and later this branch of the family gave its name to the snack. The number of dukedoms – the highest rank in the peerage and until then a rare honour outside the royal family – was greatly increased to pay the king's private debts. Four of the present twenty-six dukes are descended from bastard sons of Charles II : the Duke of St Albans by Nell Gwynn, the Duke of Grafton by the Duchess of Cleveland, the Duke of Richmond by the Duchess of Portsmouth, and the Duke of Buccleuch by Lucy Walters. Family tradition has it that my great-grandfather, the fifth Duke of Buccleuch, discovered among the family archives the marriage certificate of Charles II and Lucy Walters. He is supposed to have loyally presented this document, which he feared might give him some claim to the throne of England, to Queen Victoria, inviting her to throw it on the fire. It sounds a gallant gesture, but the Duke of Buccleuch, with the highest landed income of any peer of the realm at that time, had more reason than most to be content with his lot.

The Restoration peerage ranged down the scale from duke, marquis, earl, viscount to baron in the form it still retains. The peerage was a single title descending only to the eldest son or heir, unlike the system of most continental countries where the whole family was ennobled. There was in consequence no natural increase in the number of peers, which stayed constant at between one hundred and sixty and one hundred and seventy for most of the eighteenth century, compared to a quarter of a million French nobles and half a million Russians. The difference in numbers was of course widening all the time, and the possession of an English peerage was a far greater distinction

140

than noble status on the continent. Some of the greater peers, like the dukes of Bedford, Bridgewater and Devonshire, with incomes approaching forty thousand to fifty thousand pounds a year, had more money than the small independent princes of Germany or Italy; even some of the untitled country gentlemen, outside the English peerage altogether, enjoyed a more impressive education, wealth and style of living than the poorer nobility of France and Russia. The English peers had, as a result, a great sense of social security which significantly affected their attitudes: they did not feel threatened by broad social contacts or see the need to squander money on elaborate display to emphasise their high rank.

The British system, in any case, prevented rigid separation of the classes. Heirs to peerages, except in Scotland until the late eighteenth century, could and usually did sit in the House of Commons, although the higher ranking ones among them bore a subsidiary title of their house. It was confusing to foreigners that a man like Lord Malpas, for instance, Walpole's son-in-law and heir to the second Earl of Cholmondeley, was in fact a commoner. Younger sons, barring accidents to their elder brothers, and daughters, barring an elevating marriage, would remain commoners all their lives; although they themselves might bear courtesy titles, they had no such distinction to pass on to their children.

There was little social distinction between a minor peer and a major country gentleman, especially if the latter held a baronetcy, a hereditary distinction outside the peerage not entitling the holder to a seat in the House of Lords. The peer's life might centre slightly more on the metropolis than his baronet neighbour's, but in their own county they mixed on almost equal terms. In effect, society in England moved down the scale from Duke to labourer through infinitely small and subtle graduations which probably account for the English skill at assessing and adjusting to nuances of rank, and the national reputation for snobbery. 'The Englishman,' wrote Jean Rouquet in 1755, 'always has in his hands an accurate pair of scales in which he scrupulously weighs up the birth, the rank, and above all the wealth of the people he meets, in order to adjust his behaviour towards them accordingly.'[2] The national vice of snobbery was a small price to pay for the blurred class distinction in England compared to the gulf separating noble and commoner abroad. The English peerage was less of a caste.

This does not mean that it was easy to enter the peerage in the eighteenth century. Not until the twentieth century was the House of Lords an easy target for the successful businessman, anxious to round off his fortune with a title. There were in the eighteenth century a few exceptional men who reached the peerage from comparatively humble origins, but hardly any of them had made their way in trade. George Bubb Doddington, the son of an Irish fortune-hunter and apothecary, found that good fortune and a lifetime of effort were needed to secure his aim of 'making some figure in the world'. Although he had a head start – using his mother's connections to enter Parliament, inheriting an estate from his uncle and spending one hundred and forty thousand pounds on a magnificent mansion – it still took forty-six years of political intrigue, obsequious flattery of the powerful and regular desertion of his friends, to achieve the pinnacle of a barony, the lowest of the five ranks of the peerage, in 1761, the year before his death.

In theory, anyone could amass a fortune, buy the landed estate which was the necessary prerequisite of a title, and seek a peerage. In practice, few achieved it. A modest estate of ten thousand acres would cost approximately one hundred thousand pounds; and the practice of primogeniture and tying up estates by settlement and entail prevented many properties coming into the market even at that price. Only those few men in particularly lucrative positions could hope to make the transition in one generation. A succession of canny, devious and determined men might achieve it in three. It was much easier to buy a title on the black market which operated in France under the *ancien régime,* or make the way up the Russian civil service to noble rank, than to obtain a peerage in eighteenth-century England.

But once a man had achieved his coronet, he had really arrived. He then had no need to underline his status by lavish displays of conspicuous consumption, punctilious observance of etiquette, and a restricted circle of exclusively blue-blooded friends. Individuality and eccentricity, the product of security,

142

were class characteristics of the British aristocracy, and a thousand good anecdotes would be lost without them.

At the end of the century the younger Pitt, in need of rein-
forcements in the upper house, kindled new hope in the breasts
of aspiring peers. He made the largest number of new creations
of the century, increasing the size of the House by one-third.
The legend was later manufactured that peerages were hawked
round the City of London and that new blood from trade now
sullied the aristocratic stock. Disraeli, in his novel *Sybil* accused
Pitt, who lived half a century earlier, of creating 'a plebeian
aristocracy' and blending it with the patrician oligarchy. 'He
made peers of second rate squires and rich graziers. He caught
them in the alleys of Lombard Street and clutched them from
the counting-houses of Cornhill.' In fact, nearly all Pitt's new
peers came from the traditional recruiting grounds, the country
gentry, diplomacy and the law. A plebeian aristocracy did not
appear until after Disraeli's death, just after his own ennoblement.

The younger sons of peers, in their turn, did not really
'merge into the people'. Few made their way in trade and
industry. Although they ranked as commoners and helped to
bridge the gap between peers and populace, most of them had
private incomes from the family estates or from government
sinecures, which allowed them to opt for the more fashionable
and agreeable, but less financially rewarding type of career – in
the armed services or the Church, neither of which paid good
salaries at that time. Here they mixed with the offspring of
country gentlemen and the middle classes. Only the younger
sons of the poorer gentry made their way into trade.

The great distinguishing characteristics of the peerage were
not its access to new blood nor its personal links with trade,
but its lack of legal privileges. Compared to the French nobility
with their tax exemptions and feudal dues, the Russians with
their monopoly of serfs or the Spanish grandees with their
extensive freedom from arrest, the English peers were roughly
treated. They had no tax concessions, no monopoly of army
commissions and no valuable feudal rights. Their right to trial
by their peers was not necessarily a blessing. It might mean
judgement by one's enemies as much as one's friends, by one's

former fag at school as much as by one's first cousin. The House did not automatically absolve its guilty members, and the sense of solidarity was not strong enough to allow many guilty peers to escape their deserts. Lord Ferrers, for instance, was hanged at Tyburn tree in 1760 for the murder of his steward. He did not even have the consolation of a noble execution, so soothing to continental nobles, but was dispatched by the common hangman, his only privilege that of a silken halter.

Foreigners were frequently astounded at the unprivileged legal status of the great English lords, apparently so powerful and secure. Some French bourgeois were amazed to hear from a visiting Englishman that the meanest tradesman could get redress for any injury done to him by the greatest nobleman in the kingdom. 'It's not worth much to be a nobleman in your country,' they exclaimed. 'It is just not natural.'[3]

Their footing of virtual legal equality helped to ensure that the territorial aristocracy, although not easy to join, were not an unapproachable breed apart. Like aristocracies everywhere, they had their share of arrogance, pride and disdain for the 'lower orders'. They included men like the proud Duke of Somerset who, according to the traveller Celia Fiennes, 'had outriders to clear the roads of plebeians lest they should see him as they passed'.[4] They produced women like the extremely rich and eccentric Duchess of Albemarle who, vowing she would marry none but royalty, was wooed and won by my ancestor Ralph, 1st Duke of Montagu, disguised as the Emperor of China. But arrogant displays of rank were much less common in Britain than on the continent. The young bucks of London, however drunken and obstreperous, would never have dared to copy the young Parisian noblemen whom Arthur Young described, dashing their cabriolets about Paris and menacing life and limb. In London, he said approvingly, they would have been thrashed and rolled in the gutter.

Lord Chesterfield's idea of good breeding, set down at some length in his famous admonitory letters, was typical of the best kind of English peer. 'Never be proud of your rank or birth,' he told his godson, the Duke of Hamilton, 'but be as proud as you please of your character. Nothing is so contrary to true dignity as the former kind of pride. You are, it is true, of a

144

noble family, but whether of a very ancient one or not I neither know nor care, nor need you, and I dare say there are twenty fools in the House of Lords who could out-descend you in pedigree. That sort of stately pride is the standing jest of all people who can make one, but character is universally respected.'[5]

Peers did not lead an exclusive social life. They mixed as a matter of course with the country gentlemen in the county towns and in the hunting field, and patronised intellectuals and litterati in London. Lord Chesterfield valued genius more highly than rank. 'For my own part, I used to think myself in company as much above me, when I was with Mr Addison and Mr Pope, as if I had been with all the Princes in Europe,' he wrote to his son in 1749.

Nor were the British peerage unwilling to share their new country estates with a wider public. As I have described in my book *The Gilt and the Gingerbread,* the Stately Homes business is by no means a twentieth-century enterprise. In the eighteenth century there was the recognised minor Grand Tour of English country houses, and famous homes such as Holkham, Raynham, Blenheim, Wilton, Woburn, Chatsworth and Castle Howard were regularly open to the public on fixed days. Wilton even published a catalogue, and the owner of Stourhead built an inn for visitors to take refreshments. So widespread was the custom, that the Duchess of Marlborough bitterly resented Blenheim being invaded by the curious citizens of Oxford before it was even finished. The Hon. John Byng also complained at being refused admittance to Lord Guildford's house at Wroxton, and bitterly reproached the owner for not fixing a day of admission. Sometimes things even got out of hand as Lord Lyttleton's *crie de coeur* in 1778 discloses : 'Coaches full of travellers of all denominations, and troupes of holiday neighbours, are hourly chasing me from my apartment or strolling about the environs keeping me prisoner in it. The lord of the place can never call it his during the finest part of the year.' It must be admitted, however, that most of the visitors were gentlemen, and it was not the owner who benefited, but rather the servants who expected and even demanded tips.

Some houses, indeed, have always remained open, and it was

only when improved communications in the later nineteeth and early twentieth centuries brought the masses in contact with the countryside that some park gates were slammed shut. Now in 1970, after two World Wars, necessity has forced no less than four hundred private houses to be opened to the public, attracting 7 million visitors a year, this time for the benefit of the owners.

But it was sport which more than anything else spanned the classes. Racing, prize-fighting, hunting and cock-fighting had all their enthusiastic noble backers and keen plebeian followers. In the eighteenth century those sports were already well established which the Earl of Wilton was later (1868) to praise for bringing together 'people of all grades, and thus (for the time) breaking down all class barriers'.[6] Cricket, for instance, was securely established in 1774 under the aristocratic hand of peers like the Earl of Tankerville. Territorial magnates took their villagers to play each other, and high stakes and proud reputations were hazarded in these matches, and in single-wicket encounters between the champions. The Duke of Dorset enticed promising bowlers to work on his estates so that he could defeat his rival, Lord Sandwich. The famous Hambledon Club was organised by the Duke of Bolton's son, a local parson, to the high standard where it could take on the rest of England.

It was bloodsports which attracted the peers above all, and bloodsports were just one factor which helped to keep them in the country. The Hanoverian court, presided over by a series of unglamorous if not downright unprepossessing Germans, was never a Mecca for the fashionable. The ambitious looked to Parliament, whose generous recesses could have been specially designed for countrymen, and were not obliged to put in a lifetime of servitude at court. And the English countryside, even its remoter parts infested with footmen and highwaymen, was infinitely safe and alluring compared with the bandit-ridden, terrorised outback of Spain and Russia.

The English peerage was, in consequence, more rural in character than the great nobility of any other European country. Even the dukes spent more time on their own broad acres than in their elegant London houses. They were closer to agriculture than any other great nobility in Europe, and at the very least

146

roads and bridges were maintained on their estates, if only for their convenience. The majority of peers, it must be admitted, were not innovators in estate management or new farming techniques. Leading agricultural writers from the mid-eighteenth century onwards complained of lack of interest in the modern methods then being pioneered. Arthur Young, the indefatigable Secretary of the Board of Agriculture, devotes most of his pages to the improvements of the gentry and large tenant farmers. But a substantial minority of peers did play a leading part in the agricultural revolution of the century – made possible by the absence of crushing feudal restrictions – and agriculture was an interest, even a passion, far higher up the aristocratic ladder than in any continental country. In the 1720s the Duke of Somerset took a keen personal interest in his tenants' farming, and kept a notebook on matters of special interest. Sir Robert Walpole, first Earl of Orford, always opened correspondence from his steward or gamekeeper before state papers when he was prime minister. His brother-in-law, Lord Townshend, did not initiate either the cultivation of turnips as his nickname suggested, or the Norfolk four-course rotation which was already in use; but he did extend their operation on his estates, and his personal enthusiasm and great prestige made him an excellent publicist for the experimental work then being done in his county.

At Wentworth the Marquess of Rockingham kept over two thousand acres in his own hands, and was personally concerned with experiments to see how lime and manure improved turnip yield. He set up two model farms, one using Kentish methods and one those of Hertfordshire. New implements and covered drains were introduced, and a Hertfordshire farmer experienced at hoeing turnips was specially brought to the estate. Lord Howe contributed a paper on warping to the Board of Agriculture's report on the West Riding; and in 1772 Lord Sheffield founded at Lewes in Sussex a society for the 'encouragement of agriculture, manufacture and industry'.

Similar interest and enterprise were shown by the minor, provincial nobility in France, but the Versailles grandees would no doubt have shared the sentiments of the fictitious Gwendoline Fairfax, some hundred years later, who was 'glad to say

I have never seen a spade'.[7] That such fastidiousness was not encouraged amongst even the highest English aristocracy was partly due to the royal family. Jethro Tull's system of horse-hoeing husbandry was explained to George II and discussed at court. The royal mistresses found it prudent to have some nodding acquaintance with the subject, and Queen Caroline subscribed to a copy of Tull's book. Her grandson, George III, delighted in the title of Farmer George, considered himself more indebted to Arthur Young than to any man in his dominions, kept a model farm at Windsor, formed a flock of merino sheep and experimented in stock-breeding. Royal example reinforced the country tastes of the peers themselves, and helped to create the climate where, in the last quarter of the century, great landowners and statesmen like the first Earl of Leicester, the Duke of Bedford and Lord Althorp, were happy to be painted in farmyard scenes.

This was a much healthier state of affairs than that of the sophisticated Versailles nobility, fluttering in their gilded cage; and the tradition of the eighteenth century was a lasting one. In the early years of the next century John Grey of Dalston visited Lord Althorp, then Chancellor of the Exchequer, at Downing Street, at a moment of serious crisis in the nation's affairs. Althorp's first question was: 'Have you been at Wiseton on your way up? Have you seen the cows?'[8]

Even in the twentieth century it was natural for Evelyn Waugh, excessive admirer of the aristocratic virtues, to characterise the English peeress, in the person of the Countess of Circumference (*Decline and Fall*) as a plain-speaking, down-to-earth countrywoman, whose advice to 'dig it and dung it' reverberated round the school sports field.

In the eighteenth century the peers who gave a personal lead were an important minority but they helped to set the tone in society. Most landowners did not rush to adopt the new techniques and kept only a small home farm for supplying their households, but few of them were actively hostile to experiments on the part of their tenants. The traditional role of the landowner helped to establish conditions where experiment and progressive farming were possible. They protected tenants in bad times by remitting rents when cattle disease, droughts or ruinous harvests occurred, and allowed in practice great security of tenure even when, as was often the case, the tenants only had year-to-year leases. Far from being diehard or reactionary, most peers took a liberal attitude to agricultural change, and the increased productivity which made possible the feeding of a growing town population owed much to the tolerance of the majority and the enthusiasm of a few.

In industry, too, active participation in schemes unconnected with their estates was limited to an energetic few. One or two peers had long had an eye to the main chance unthinkable to their equals in Spain. As early as 1698 the Marquis of Carmarthen, an English Rear-Admiral who did much to whet Peter the Great's interest in ships during his visit to England, seized the opportunity of obtaining a concession to import Virginia tobacco into Russia. He promptly afterwards sold the concession to a group of merchants. Other peers were more versatile; the Duke of Chandos promoted oyster-fishing for pearls off Anglesey, and digging of pipe-clay near Southampton, and he dabbled in a composition supposed to protect ship's bottoms from worms, had shares in Covent Garden Playhouse, and personally experimented in extracting precious metals from various ores in his laboratory at Canons, his country seat.

The peers who participated in business as usual were unusual, but most were eager to exploit the resources of their own land. They were usually quick to appreciate the possibilities of iron or coal deposits, although leasing them out to entrepreneurs rather than developing them direct. The second Duke of Montagu was not slow to realise the potential of his Beaulieu estate, which was heavily timbered with oak, contained an ironworks founded before 1603 by his great-grandfather Henry, 3rd Earl of Southampton at Sowley pond, where the great forge-hammer was worked by a water wheel, and claimed the privileges of a free harbour. As the Duke at that time was granted the sugar-producing islands of St Vincent and St Lucia in the West Indies, he planned to develop a port on the Beaulieu river as a depot for the West India trade. He offered long leases at Buckler's Hard for a yearly rental of 6s. 8d., building sites and trading facilities to merchants and others giving three loads of free timber for every house erected. The Duke was unable to carry out his original West Indian plan, but with great versatility turned Buckler's Hard into a shipyard and for sixty-two years ships of war, including Nelson's *Agamemnon*, were built there.

Several peers were quick to grasp the significance of transport for the development of mineral deposits. The Duke of Bridgewater's canal from Worsley, the centre of the coalmines of his estate, to Manchester, was the first of a network of waterways. Other peers followed suit with important and lesser-known enterprises. In 1773, the Earl of Thanet built the Skipton Castle canal to carry lime and limestone from his estates to the Leeds and Liverpool canal. The Marquess of Stafford cut a canal to serve his ironworks in Shropshire. The majority of peers were at least open to change, and their guests were expected to take an interest in engineering. Aristocratic house-parties would sometimes go to watch a loch being constructed or a fen being drained. Far from representing a backward-looking group, obstructive to industry, peers were prepared to promote, invest and support, even if not participating directly themselves. A substantial minority showed real enthusiasm, drive and entrepreneurial skill, and their attitudes, perpetuated by their descendants, were to be a boon to the country. The crude petroleum lying neglected on the Youssoupoff family estates by the Caspian Sea would have been inconceivable to their opposite numbers in England.

An aristocracy so flexible in its attitude to industry and agriculture could well afford to leave the leadership in fashion, manners and conversation to the French. 'It must be owned,' Lord Chesterfield wrote to his son in 1747, 'that the Graces do not seem to be natives of Great Britain; and I doubt, the best of us here have more of the rough than the polished diamond. Since barbarism drove them out of Greece and Rome, they seem to have taken refuge in France, where their temples are numerous, and their worship the established one.'

The Grand Tour of the continent, which followed university and became almost *de rigueur*, at least for the eldest sons of great families, did something, from the mid-century onwards, to polish manners of the leaders of society. Some of the cruder social solecisms – the scratching, spitting and picking of the nose which disgusted Lord Chesterfield – were eradicated in the fastidious female company of the Paris and Geneva salons. But as late as 1784, Francois de La Rochefoucauld, on a visit to the Duke of Grafton, wrote that, 'Very often I have heard things mentioned in good society which would be in the grossest taste in France. The sideboard too is furnished with a number of chamber-pots and it is a common practice to relieve oneself whilst the rest are drinking; one has no kind of concealment and the practice strikes me as most indecent.'[9]

But if the English peers tended to neglect what Chesterfield called 'those lesser talents, of an engaging, insinuating manner, an easy good breeding, and genteel behaviour and address', they were far from being philistines. The fashion set during the Renaissance in Italy that a gentleman must have at least the elements of culture and a respect for the Arts had been widely adopted in England. The first cultivated court, in the new style, had been that of Queen Elizabeth, who presided over an artistic circle with a passion for literature, music and the theatre. The patronage of the peers was most valuable in the theatre, which reached such a glorious peak at that moment. The organisation of travelling troupes into companies under some lord's name greatly improved standards: the first important company was the Earl of Leicester's, while Lord Strange, heir to the Earl of Derby, boasted for a time Burbage in his company. Shakespeare wrote his earlier plays for the Earl of Pembroke's company, but it was Henry Wriothesley, Earl of Southampton, and grandson of the first lay owner of Beaulieu, who earned himself the greatest lasting fame as the patron of Shakespeare, his 'Lord of my love', and the inspiration of the sonnets.

The Elizabethan and Jacobean courts were unusually cultivated and throughout the seventeenth century, whenever possible, peers had provided patronage for writers, artists and dramatists. In two centuries the English peerage had transformed itself from the quarrelsome territorial warlords of the fifteenth century into a generally cultivated set of men, taking trouble at least to write elegant and amusing letters, and able to dispute classical translations with their sons' tutors. The third Earl of Shaftesbury helped to make the process more self-conscious – his *Characteristics of Men, Manners, Opinions, Times,* published in 1711, set out to make refinement in art and morals a fashionable

151

concern, and had a big impact on the age. The eighteenth-century peerage contained of course its share of sots, rakes and club-boors, but taken in all they provided the most cultivated leadership this country has ever had, and their patronage of the finest works of literature, music, art and architecture made a priceless contribution to posterity.

A new note of admiration and respect appeared in peers' attitude to the great creative writers. The first Duke of Montagu was proud to be numbered amongst the friends and benefactors of La Fontaine. Several distinguished writers were usually to be found enjoying the magnificent hospitality which he dispensed at Montagu House in Bloomsbury, on the site of the present British Museum. One of his favourite guests was Pope, who began to find that the five guineas which the Duke's servants expected in tips was too much for his purse. He accordingly wrote the duke a letter stating that he would be forced to decline all future invitations to Montagu House unless accompanied by five guineas to permit him to fulfil the expectations of the duke's servants. The reply was a note containing five guineas and an invitation to dinner the following night, and this form was followed thereafter.

Some of the most original thinkers of the century found that, as tutors to noble families, they had some time at least to write undisturbed. The economist Adam Smith was tutor to the sons of the third Duke of Buccleuch, who gave him an opportunity to travel abroad and a life pension.

The system of patronage did not always work well. It could produce humiliation for the artist and toadying to the patron, 'fed with soft dedication all day long' as Pope said of another Montagu, Charles Montagu, first Earl of Halifax, and treated to lines like, 'Thus gracious Chandos if beloved at sight'. Dr Johnson, notoriously independent of patronage, composed the bitter lines:

> There mark what ills the scholar's life assail,
> Toil, envy, want, the patron and the jail.[10]

But most often, the mingling of the worlds of fashionable society and of letters was of benefit to both parties and to taste. The peers were patrons of music second only to the Austrian nobility and one of the great figures here, as in literature, was the first Duke of Chandos, whose magnificent country seat of Canons near Edgeware, built with the public money diverted to his pockets when Paymaster-General of the forces, was a forcing-house of talent. Handel lived at Canons from 1717 until 1720, and wrote for the Duke's choir the twelve Chandos anthems, the source from which he later drew material for his oratorios. Life at Canons brought Handel into close contact with leaders of English literary and artistic circles. The poets Gay, Arbuthnot and Pope often joined the vast resident household who sat down to dinner each evening to the musical accompaniment of the choir. They prompted Handel to turn his attention to music drama: Gay wrote the libretto for Handel's *Acis and Galatea* in 1719; and it was from another masque, *Haman and Mordecai,* with libretto by Pope and produced at Canons with full-scale costumes and scenery, that Handel later reconstructed his first English oratorio, *Esther.* Canons was obviously a stimulating environment for Handel's talents, although His Grace's guests were not always entirely to his taste. Handel, we are told, 'used to say that, to an English audience, music joined to poetry was not an entertainment for an evening and that something that had the appearance of a plot or fable was necessary to keep their attention awake'.[11]

It was the visual arts that benefited most from aristocratic patronage. The Dilettanti Society, founded in 1734 by some fifty peers or peers' sons who had been on the Grand Tour, had as its objects the cultivation of artistic tastes in congenial surroundings, and the encouragement of promising artists, who were financed to travel abroad. By 1764 it had accumulated sufficient funds to make possible an expedition to Asia Minor to collect details of its monuments of antiquity. Volumes on Ionian antiquities were published in 1769 and 1797 and, under its aegis, Egyptian, Etruscan, Greek and Roman sculptures were bought. Charles Sackville, Earl of Dorset, himself a poet, some of whose work has been published in the *Oxford Book of English Verse,* was a friend of poets and writers and there is a room at Knole where their portraits still hang. Nor must be forgotten the famous Kit Kat Club of which John, Duke of Montagu was an enthusiastic member and the likenesses of whose members now hang in the National Portrait Gallery.

Architecture was an interest natural to peers who were, next to the Crown, the largest owners of real estate in the country. Pope's friend, Lord Burlington, stayed as a young man for a considerable period in Italy, became a devotee of Palladian architecture, and when he returned to England formed a school of young architects to design buildings in the new style. Burlington suggested the general ideas and left detailed work to be done by such protégés as Kent, Colin Campbell, Isaac Ware and Flitcroft. Perhaps no peer initiated as important a scheme as the Prince Regent's plans for London, which transformed the West End at the beginning of the next century, but for numerous country houses from Blenheim Palace to Chatsworth, for what remains of Chippendale furniture, Adam interiors and Capability Brown gardens, we have much to thank the eighteenth-century peerage. In the return they obtained for money spent, they could well bear comparison with the Arts Council.

In their patronage of the arts the eighteenth-century peers were conforming to an international code of behaviour binding on their class from Russia to Spain. The characteristic which completely set apart the English peerage was their political power. The English peers, alone in Europe, had been on the winning side in the international contest between monarchy and nobles. While the Austrians, French and Spanish had been out-manoeuvred and reduced to impotence by their sovereigns – and the Russians had hardly even got started – the boot had been firmly on the other foot in England. The peers and the gentry had exploited the folly of seventeenth-century kings, their reliance on parliamentary votes of taxes, and had imposed conditions, explicitly or implicitly, with every change of dynasty. The peers were the senior partners and they had triumphed, not as irresponsible territorial magnates, but as parliamentarians, depending on the alliance of the gentry and bound by constitutional rules. Their victory, and the use they made of it, paid dividends far into the future. The political expertise of the English peerage had always been its most priceless possession.

In the eighteenth century the peers and their sons, with the gentry, dominated political life in London and local government in the shires. The peers' commanding position was based on membership of the upper house, the lion's share of cabinet posts, and partial control over membership of the House of Commons. In 1726 a quarter of the peerage held government or court office, and most other places were held by their relatives or dependants. At the accession of George III in 1760, one hundred and eleven patrons, most of them peers, influenced or determined two hundred and five elections for borough seats in their neighbourhoods. The first Duke of Newcastle, the virtuoso performer at the art of patronage, deployed his main talents in marshalling government influence, but he also enjoyed in his own right the nomination of twelve members of parliament, four from Yorkshire, four from Nottinghamshire, and four from Sussex.

Apart from this powerful lever, the peers dominated the countryside through the office of Lord Lieutenant, who recommended names to the bench of magistrates. The peerage as we have seen had few legal privileges, but no continental nobility had anything like its political power.

There were, of course, abuses of authority. The peers, like most of the politicians of the day, were inclined to treat the offices of the crown as a generous form of outdoor relief for dependants and relatives. Horace Walpole, fourth son of Robert Walpole, 1st Earl of Orford, drew a quarter of a million pounds from his government sinecures in the course of a long life. It was considered only proper that public money should be diverted to the pockets of peers too impoverished to live up to their station in life. Lord Hardwicke declared that:

'I look upon such pensions as a kind of obligation upon the Crown for the support of ancient noble families, whose peerages happen to continue after their estates are worn out.'[12] The peers manipulated affairs to their advantage. The ferocious game laws and the corn laws protected the special interests of the landowning class. There were numerous private members' bills to serve private ends, whether industrial, enclosing or matrimonial. Attempts to allow other classes to participate in political power were firmly blocked well into the nineteenth century. The peers and gentry sustained the sublime conviction that only they had the right and the capacity to govern the country. But in spite of all that, compared with other privileged minorities they set a fine example of public service.

155

The House of Lords, no less than the Commons, was prepared to consider the national interest. Peers made no attempt to use their power to evade taxes for themselves or their order. While most of their equals abroad enjoyed wide exemptions from the most burdensome demands of their governments, the peers voted for taxes, when need arose, which pressed heavily on themselves. The land tax, the standard resource during war time, pressed more heavily on landowners than on tenant farmers. Most people's patriotism stops short of volunteering taxes to the government, and the peers' readiness to pay up says much for their essential public spirit as a class. Furthermore, it was not only hope of financial gains which committed the peers to public life. Although they may have hoped for lucrative office as recognition of their efforts, many peers attended the Upper House, took an intelligent part in debates, studied reports and promoted the government interest at election time without any real chance of reward. Public work was an accepted obligation binding on the privileged, and the attendance at House of Lords debates was far higher than in the twentieth century.

At local level, there were fewer returns for the time most peers devoted to unpaid, often arduous and sometimes tedious public work. Here again, there were numerous examples of bullying, injustice and blatant self-interest. Many peers were callous of poverty, disease and injustice, watched unmoved the sort of horrors depicted by Hogarth or the deprived life of the agricultural labourers revealed so horrifyingly by the Hammonds. As La Rochefoucauld said, 'We can always find strength to bear the misfortunes of others.' But most peers were conscious of the obligations which their good fortune imposed. They lived in a world of deep curtsies, tugged forelocks and obsequious addresses, without descending to power without responsibility, 'the prerogative of the harlot throughout the ages', in Baldwin's phrase. They set the tradition of public duty which the diarist Charles Greville was to describe so finely, in his assessment of the Duke of Rutland in 1838 :

'The Duke of Rutland is as selfish a man as any of his class – that is, he never does what he does not like, and spends his whole life in a round of such pleasures as suit his taste, but he is neither a foolish nor a bad man, and partly from a sense of

156

duty, partly from inclination, he devotes time and labour to the interest and welfare of the people who live on his estate. He is a guardian of a very large union, and he not only attends regularly the meetings of Poor Law Guardians every week or fortnight, and takes an active part in their proceedings, but he visits those paupers who receive out-of-doors relief, sits and converses with them, invites them to complain to him if they have anything to complain of, and tells them that he is not only their friend but their representative at the Assembly of Guardians, and that it is his duty to see that they are nourished and protected.'[13]

The public spirit of the English peerage left the continental nobilities standing. It helped to ensure their survival as a class far into the future.

Chapter Seven

English Peerage (II)

The English peerage saw out the nineteenth century in splendid style. In 1800 the peers held nine of the twelve seats in the cabinet. One hundred years later, nine of the nineteen cabinet ministers still sat in the Lords. A country which had in the course of the century become the foremost industrial power in the world, which had more than two million trade unionists, a mass of humanitarian legislation on the statute book, and had extended the vote to two thirds of the adult male population, was still led in 1900 by Robert Arthur Talbot Gascoyne-Cecil, ninth Earl and third Marquess of Salisbury, whose illustrious ancestor had served Queen Elizabeth. His colleagues included the Marquess of Lansdowne, Secretary for War, whose subsidiary title of baron went back to 1181 and whose great-grandfather had been Prime Minister under George III; and the Duke of Devonshire, Lord President of the Council, who owned one hundred and eighty-six thousand acres in eleven counties, and whose ancestors had served in parliament since the fourteenth century. At a time when the French nobility lingered on as a quaint anachronism in a republic they hated, when the Italian nobility were politically irrelevant, and the Russians obedient minions of a monarch soon to be swept away, the English peerage was still parading its staggering instinct for survival.

The record of the House of Lords during the nineteenth century was not always an enlightened one. The Upper House neither initiated nor welcomed most of the important measures of social reform passed as the country adapted to a new industrial economy. With a few obvious exceptions, the peers accepted with equanimity the fate of climbing boys, women miners and factory children. There must have been many peers, surrounded

158

like Lord Marney in Disraeli's novel *Sybil* with villages full of wretched tenements, open drains and typhus, who declared over dinner that 'the people are very contented here'. The prejudices of the Upper House were more glaring than those of the Lower, it was more hostile to Catholics and to Jews. As for democracy, the House of Lords was on every occasion reluctant to extend the vote. At this level, the peerage was dragged into the twentieth century, tetchy and complaining.

But this reactionary record is more than redeemed by two great qualities: the reluctance of the Lords to push their opposition to extremes, and the existence of individual peers prepared to give a lead to current demands. The Whig peers generally took the line that graceful and judicious concessions would strengthen, not weaken, their order. The Tories were often prepared, when it came to the crunch, to face up to the demands of a changing world. From these sophisticated and realistic views there followed the survival of the peerage as a force to be reckoned with well into the twentieth century, and the absence of violent revolution in English history.

It was the Duke of Wellington, leading a solidly Tory cabinet from the benches of the House of Lords, who first demonstrated a curious and very English phenomenon. The Duke, a third son of the Earl of Mornington, was a Tory of the deepest dye, a champion of aristocracy, who had favoured 'sprigs of nobility' in the army, held that family and fortune should influence promotion, and despised 'low, vulgar popularity'. But when, in 1828, the Duke, as Prime Minister, was faced with the breakdown of government in Ireland, he persuaded his party, much against their will, to abandon one of the dearest principles of Toryism and remove the old penalties against Roman Catholics. The Duke's standing and prestige were able to sway both the king and a majority of his peers as a lesser figure might not have done – though feelings ran so high that Lord Winchilsea challenged him to a duel, at which both noble lords judiciously missed. The precedent was an important one: the most stalwart defender of the old order had been prepared to sacrifice his opinions and split his party so that the business of government might be carried on. There may be something in the belief that those to 'whose career office is incidental but not essential, who

159

nor hope to rise nor fear to fall, can take an unimpassioned view of practical questions.'[1] After Wellington, flexibility, realism and a readiness to compromise were to be longstanding characteristics of the English peerage.

Four years later an even more vital change, the 1832 Reform Bill, was carried by one of the most aristocratic cabinets of the century. The Bill cut back the influence of numerous peers and strengthened the Commons at the expense of the Lords. But its sponsor, Lord Grey, the Prime Minister, was a grand seigneur who set out to show that 'in these days of democracy and Jacobinism it is possible to find real capacity in the high aristocracy'.[2] His cabinet of thirteen contained only three commoners, and it passed an Act in flat contradiction to the apparent interests of their order and one vital to the peaceful and democratic evolution of Britain. The majority of the peers, of course, bitterly resented this 'betrayal'. A few were prepared to use force to defend their position. But the Duke of Buckingham, who brought his cannon ashore from his yacht to fight reform, found himself in a tiny belligerent minority. In general, moderation and good sense prevailed. Only a few peers would have succumbed to the hysterical fears of Disraeli's Countess of Marney (*Sybil*) who predicted that 'a revolution was inevitable, that all property would be instantly confiscated, the poor deluded king led to the block or sent over to Hanover at best, and the whole of the nobility and principal gentry guillotined without remorse'. The fate which befell the French nobility was never really likely in England because the English peers did not panic. Lord Fitzwilliam wrote that, 'if landlords think to get the better of right reason by means of great power, they cannot expect to be shown consideration'.[3] This enlightened self-interest was in the country's interest as well, and helped to preserve the peerage to retreat another day.

Fourteen years later the Duke of Wellington piloted the next aristocratic sacrifice through the House of Lords. Faced with another national crisis – this time famine in Ireland – the Duke persuaded a reluctant majority of his peers to repeal the corn laws, a repeal which clearly gave urban interests priority over agricultural ones, and which was, by a delayed reaction, to bring financial hardship to the great landlords at the end of

160

the century. The Duke's motives were again disinterested: he supported the unpalatable measure because it was no longer a question of the corn laws but of government; and my great-grandfather, the 5th Duke of Buccleuch said that in such circumstances he too would not desert the queen's service. They were able to carry with them a majority in their House because, as the Prime Minister wrote to Lord John Russell, 'there are many peers who, whatever their opinions might be about the Corn Laws, would be anxious that any measure which passed the House of Commons should pass the House of Lords, and would do all they could to assist it.'[4] The sacrifice of dearly held opinion in the face of a national crisis was becoming characteristic of the peerage. It is a responsible use of power hard to parallel amongst other privileged minorities.

In 1867 the Conservatives, under the leadership of the Earl of Derby, the richest peer in England next to the dukes and a man secure enough to speak with a broad Lancashire accent, passed a massive reform of Parliament. The reform nearly doubled the electorate, gave votes to working class men in the towns, and, in the eyes of Lord Cranborne, 'doomed the aristocratic principle'. But most of the peers of both parties were sensible enough to avoid collision with the new forces which a rapidly changing society was producing. The same Lord Cranborne, who in 1867 had been a stalwart opponent of the Reform Act, was to prove adaptable in his turn when, as Marquess of Salisbury, he became Prime Minister.

Until Lord Salisbury became premier in 1885, it was generally accepted that a landed estate was the essential accompaniment of a peerage, and the great majority of new peers had made their way in the 'gentleman's professions', the armed services, the law or politics. Most of them came from the landed gentry or had close connections with the aristocracy. When my grandfather, a second son of the 5th Duke of Buccleuch and holder of the Beaulieu estates, became first Baron Montagu of Beaulieu in 1885, his elevation was of the traditional kind which was just being challenged. The close and powerful connections of my grandfather were underlined by the letter, written by Queen Victoria in her own hand to my great-grandmother, widow of the 5th Duke of Buccleuch:

F   161

Windsor Castle.

Dear Duchess,

I am anxious to announce to you myself that with Lord Salisbury's entire concurrence I shall confer the Barony of Montagu on your son Henry. It gives me great pleasure to do this, and I am sure you will be glad that the name so long born by your dear Husband's uncle should be revived again.

I hope to soon see you, and pray believe me always,

Yours affectionately,

V.R. & I.

This was an elevation of the traditional type for political and public services, but during Lord Salisbury's first ministry one third of the new peers had made money in business, a tacit recognition by this most patrician of patricians that it was necessary to move with the times. Lord Salisbury, a peer deeply convinced of the virtues of rank, helped to broaden the base and widen the sympathies of his class. Under his leadership, old prejudices mellowed. In July 1885, Nathan Mayor de Rothschild took his seat in the Upper House swearing the holy Jewish oath on a Hebrew bible, his head covered with the ceremonial Jewish headgear. The House of Lords, which twenty-seven years before had opposed Jewish members of Parliament, was still prepared to compromise. I doubt, however, if his family received a warm personal letter from Queen Victoria.

By the end of the century, although individual peers were still prominent at cabinet level, the House of Lords had already peacefully surrendered the real basis of its power. Lord Salisbury was to be the last premier to sit on its benches. The working classes outnumbered all other voters. The growth of party organisation and of public meetings had virtually eliminated lordly influence. Merit had supplanted aristocratic connections as a means of entry to the civil service. County Councils elected by direct vote had replaced the magistrates sitting in quarter sessions – men appointed on the recommendation of the Lord Lieutenant – as governors of the counties. All that was left for the peerage as a whole by the end of the century was the House of Lords' veto and, after the substance of power had been peaceably and generously surrendered, the peers were tempted to make a show of fight for the shadow. Even here, there was much more fighting talk than fighting deeds. The habits of centuries were not lightly abandoned.

True, the Conservative majority in the Lords broke the spirit, if not the letter of the constitution. It used its vote to throw out Liberal measures ranging from land reform to education, while leaving untouched the programme of the Conservatives. It forgot the wise counsel of Lord Beaconsfield that partisan use of the veto would ultimately rebound on the position of the Lords themselves. It behaved in a way which offended the instincts for fair play of most ordinary Englishmen. By throwing out the 1909 budget which increased income taxes, death duties and introduced new land taxes, the Conservative peers not only abandoned the constitutional practice of 250 years, but presented themselves as rich men trying to avoid their due contribution to the exchequer. Lord Willoughby de Broke, the leader of the diehards, whose fighting spirit had perhaps been whetted as one of the finest masters of foxhounds of the century, made in 1911 a fire-raising speech more in keeping with the rigid inflexibility of the Austrian nobility than the moderation of English peers.

Fortunately, this was not the whole story. As always, a substantial number of peers were to be found on the side of change and reform. As early as 1907, before there was any real threat of imposed reform, my father proposed a balanced and detailed scheme which was much in advance of his time. He suggested that the Upper House should draw from three sources: the first such peers as had been cabinet miinsters, privy councillors, colonial administrators or members of the Commons for more than ten years; second, government nominations including *ex officio* a number of distinguished men such as the Governor of the Bank of England; and third, two hundred peers elected to serve for a session. My father recognised so early that all hereditary peers could not expect a permanent seat, regardless of the part they played in public life, and after more than sixty years, his ideas on the subject still have something to offer.

In 1911, one hundred and eighty-one Liberal peers voted for the Parliament Bill which ended the absolute veto of their order, and the cabinet which drafted the Bill contained its share of aristocratic talent – one baron, one viscount, three earls and a marquis. Winston Churchill, the Home Secretary and the grandson of a duke, was more anxious than almost any of his colleagues to take tough measures against the peers. Even Balfour and Lansdowne, amongst the Conservatives, were not merely selfish oligarchs, anxious to preserve the privileges of their class for their own sake : it was their fervent belief that England owed the greatness of her history to patrician rule, and that the quality of leadership and judgement showed by the upper classes could not lightly be sacrificed. The quality of leadership since 1911 had not yet proved them wrong.

In any case, as a major confrontation between mass forces and a privileged minority, this was a good-humoured affair by international standards, an anticipation of that very British phlegm displayed during the general strike, when trade unionists and police played football, to the despair of the Communists. True, the Prime Minister was in 1911 shouted down with cries of 'traitor' – in the House of Commons, not the Lords – but he did not hesitate to attend Lord Winterton's ball at Claridge's that same month. And when the pressure was put on, and the Unionist majority threatened with swamping, the majority of the peers gave way, with nothing more than pugnacious gestures. Lord Curzon of Kedleston persuaded thirty-seven of his Conservative peers, not just to abstain on the vote, but actually to support the Parliament Bill. The British peerage, bred for gallantry and the heroic virtues, has in fact shown an almost civilian reluctance to fight at the last ditch. But then, perhaps like the best generals, it has known just when to retreat.

The English have been blessed with an exceptionally peaceful history, without violent revolution or recent civil wars which have troubled so many of her continental neighbours : and the credit for this lies not with her radicals – not essentially more moderate in their demands than radicals elsewhere – but with her aristocracy, who for nearly a hundred years made concession after concession to the forces of change and democracy. There is nothing more difficult or more unusual than the voluntary surrender of power. The peers themselves benefited from their calculated sacrifices : while their equals abroad had to console themselves with the purely social prestige of euphonious titles, individual British peers have been prominent political leaders

164

far into the democratic age. As my survey in Appendix One shows, they still as a group retain the respect of large numbers of Englishmen. But the main beneficiary has been the nation.

The peerage, which accepted such far-reaching changes in the course of the nineteenth century, remained a very traditional body of men in most other respects until the 1880s. Until as late as 1885 the view prevailed that a man, however eminent, was only fitted to become a peer if he possessed a landed estate. Between 1833 and 1885 only one fifth of the new peers possessed less than three thousand acres. As distinguished a statesman as Benjamin Disraeli had been careful to buy three thousand acres in Buckinghamshire, on a loan from the house of Rothschild, to give him the right landowning ambience before becoming Earl of Beaconsfield in 1876.

For two thirds of the century the great landowners were in a secure financial position : the proportion of land held in the great estates was growing every year until 1873. Security perpetuated the old ways. Tenants were supported in bad times and entertained in good. While labourers existed on minute wages, efforts to combine into unions were firmly resisted and the game laws upheld, a tradition of almsgiving spasmodically relieved the worst distress and brought warmth and colour into drab lives. A classic description of the best kind of aristocratic benevolence in action was given by the diarist Charles Greville, who stayed at Petworth in May 1834, and attended Lord Egremont's open air feast for the poor of the neighbourhood :

'A fine sight it was, fifty-four tables, each fifty feet long, were placed in a vast semi-circle on the lawn before the house. The tables were all spread with cloths and plates and dishes : two great tents were erected in the middle to receive the provisions which were conveyed in carts, like ammunition. Plum puddings and boiled and roast beef were spread out, while hot joints were prepared in the kitchen, and sent forth as soon as the firing of guns announced the hour of the feast. Tickets were given to the inhabitants of a certain district, and the number was about four thousand; but, as many more came, the old Peer could not endure that there should be anybody hungering outside his gates, and he went out himself and ordered the barriers to be taken down and admittance given to all. They think six thousand were fed.'[5]

A band paraded through the grounds while the people, dressed in their best clothes, tucked in ravenously. In the evening ten thousand people were treated to a firework display, and the enjoyment of the crowds was eclipsed by the satisfaction of the earl :

'There was something affecting in the contemplation of that old man – on the verge of the grave – rejoicing in the diffusion of happiness and finding keen gratification in relieving the distresses and contributing to the pleasures of the poor.'

A jamboree on this scale was sufficiently unusual to warrant long description in Greville's diary, but almsgiving of some kind was universal. In the mid-nineteenth century it was normal, it has been estimated, for between four and seven per cent of the gross income of an estate to be paid out in charities. The more modest schemes of Lord Montagu of Boughton, who built at Beaulieu in the 1830s a school for one hundred boys and a school for one hundred girls, or of my grandfather, who provided a house in the village and a salary for a district nurse, were no doubt more typical than Lord Egremont's feast, but all were continuing a traditional pattern of behaviour which stretched far back into the past.

Charity encouraged an atmosphere of forelock-tugging and gaping servility. Occasionally, independent men preferred to starve rather than truckle to the landlord. Lord Rosslyn was not alone in believing that, while his Christian duty was clearly to succour his dependents, 'those who served had no right to an opinion'. Almsgiving was an unpredictable and erratic way of relieving distress. But it was clearly preferable to be a labourer in the orbit of a large estate than the servant of a small proprietor. Even the manufacturer Richard Cobden, a fierce critic of the peerage, admitted that its strength depended on 'strong prejudices' in its favour among 'all ranks and classes in the country'.[6] And even today proud men have been known to refuse the payments of the Ministry of Social Security.

Charity payments declined only at the end of the century. In other fields too, the first three quarters of the century were traditional ones. Peers continued to patronise the arts. They commissioned portraits of themselves and their families, patron-ised architects, and supported the theatre and the opera. The Earl of Egremont launched Turner on his career by providing him with a studio at Petworth, and was a generous friend to Constable, Flaxman, Nollekens and others of their circle. Joseph Paxton, en route from the gardens of Chatsworth to the Crystal Palace, built Mentmore Towers for Baron Meyer de Rothschild. But real interest and discrimination were harder to find after the older figures like Egremont, bred in the eighteenth century, died out. The new century did not produce quite the enthusiasm and discernment which had led their great-grandfathers to found the Dilettanti Society a hundred years before.

A peer was still expected to appreciate the Arts. The literary giants – Trollope, Thackeray and Browning – were welcomed at aristocratic dining tables, but the eighteenth-century patron had become a mere nineteenth-century host. Gems of dining table wit, not fulsome dedications, were now their repayment. Really cultured tastes were harder to find. Mathew Arnold, writing in 1868, called the aristocracy barbarians. They might still possess sweetness, he admitted, but they had far too little light.[7]

In the more practical fields of agriculture and industry, the eighteenth-century interest prevailed, although here again there was less distinction. Peers were still very much countrymen, ready to talk of crop-rotation and silage, presiding over agricul-tural shows, reading the farming magazines, and planting trees. But the big names in agricultural history, the Townshends and the Leicesters, were not found again.

Peers did not usually take long to appreciate the potential of railways. Well prepared, by the experience of canals, for the beneficial results of extended markets and lowered costs, few peers completely blocked the building of lines across parkland and farms, and several had a sharp eye for a bargain which promised well for their survival in a competitive future. The conversation which Disraeli sets down in *Sybil* must have been paralleled at other stately dinner tables :

'There is nobody so violent against railroads as George,' said Lady Marney. 'I cannot tell you what he does not do ! He organised the whole of our division against the Marham line.'

'I rather counted on him,' said Lord de Mowbray, 'to assist

me in resisting the joint branch here; but I was surprised to learn he had consented.'

'Not until the compensation was settled,' innocently remarked Lady Marney. 'George never opposes them after that. He gave up all opposition to the Marham line when they agreed to his terms.'

Peers rarely invested in main line railways and there was no nineteenth-century equivalent of the Duke of Bridgewater's pioneer work in canals, but several peers supported branch lines. Once again, the peerage did not set its face against the new industrial society which was developing around it. Neither did it, until the end of the century, go over to it in large numbers. Peers on boards of companies were still a rarity.

It was the last twenty years of the century which really brought an alteration in the position and way of life of the peerage. Until then, although fewer outstanding peers had been bred, the traditions and standards of the eighteenth century had been handed on. My great-great-great-grandfather, the third Duke of Buccleuch, who came into possession in 1751, would not have been too disconcerted if placed in the shoes of his great-grandson, the sixth Duke, who inherited the title in 1884. But the next twenty years brought changes in almost every aspect of life. The dominant role of the landed aristocracy in politics and society began to crumble. Peers had to adapt more fundamentally than before or go under. The process began which is still transforming the peerage today.

The depression in agriculture, which began in the 1870s with falling prices, bad harvests and ruinously cheap wheat imports, was to hit most of the peerage hard. There was a powerful and substantial minority with large city estates: the five great London landlords, the Duke of Portland, the Duke of West-minster, Duke of Bedford, Duke of Norfolk and Lord Cadogan, could afford to look with relative indifference on agricultural fortunes, but to most peers the price of wheat was crucial. As it fell from 56s. 9d. a quarter in 1877 to 46s. 5d. in 1878 and then to 31s. in 1886, the prospects of many a titled house slumped too. The aristocratic tradition that the landlord pro-tected his tenants in bad times put the burden squarely on to them. In Essex, one of the worst hit counties, an average of

168

twenty per cent of rents were remitted, and even then it was difficult to find tenants to occupy empty farms. On the Countess of Warwick's Easton Lodge estate seventy thousand pounds had to be provided out of capital to make the farms more attractive to tenants, and thirty thousand pounds was spent on farming tenantless farms direct, to prevent them from going out of cultivation.

In some areas where stock raising or mineral deposits cushioned the impact, peers survived in almost the old style. But the imposition of death duties in 1889, coming at a time when the landowning aristocracy was already in trouble, was resented more than its low scale might suggest. In an article written in 1907 my father demonstrated that in the previous forty seven years the rent on his ten thousand acre estate at Beaulieu had halved, while the burden of rates and taxes had doubled. Peers had never looked on their estates purely as investments, and were used to benefiting in prestige, position or sport rather than in big cash returns, but the depression of the eighties, coinciding with a more critical attitude to the landlord class, made the first tiny dents in that unquestioned assumption. A few peers were prepared to agree with Lady Bracknell, in Wilde's *The Importance of Being Earnest* (1895) that :

'What between the duties expected of one during one's lifetime and the duties enacted from one after one's death, land has ceased to be either a profit or a pleasure. It gives one position, and prevents one from keeping it up. That's all that is to be said about land.'

Faced with this challenge, which continued with little sign of abatement for more than two decades, a small number of peers abandoned their traditional way of life. Land sales were an early sign. From 1873 the proportion of land held in the great estates began to decline; and the 1880s and 1890s saw steadily increased land sales, often of outlying properties rather than whole estates, although this was not unusual where bad times coincided with a feckless holder of the title. In all, there was a larger transfer of land from old to new hands than had occurred for more than two hundred years; and in the 1890s Ernest Terah Hooley, one of the more unsavoury operators in this fluid market, made a million by the age of thirty-five out of his land

169

deals. Most peers remained in possession of intact estates, but some cut down expenditure in ways that radically altered the usual aristocratic tradition. A few gave up the London season, participation in which had always distinguished the aristocracy from the gentry. In the eighties the story was widely repeated of one peer, who had sold off his town house, closed up his uneconomic family mansion, and was showing surpluses instead of deficits for the first time in decades. Others cut down on charity payments, another traditional obligation which their ancestors had kept up even in bad times : the average percentage of income devoted to charity from the landed estates went down in the last quarter of the century.

These were all essentially negative reactions to the problems of the time. It was not paring down and economising that was to save the peerage as a vital group but new thinking and new initiative, and this was not wanting at the time when it was needed most. Peers had never entirely divorced themselves from business : now, the more enterprising of them began to seize its possibilities on a scale which had never been attempted before.

The spectacular opportunities for making fortunes on the newly developing frontiers of the Empire gripped the imagination of many peers. The fluid society in which they moved was an advantage quickly seized, and peers used their contacts with successful businessmen for information, favours and advice. Cecil Rhodes became a favourite guest at house parties. Kenyan timber, South African diamonds, Mexican gold and Rhodesian copper became as common topics of conversation as hounds, cattle-breeding or the Turf. At home, the world of stocks, shares and company promotion was embraced with more enthusiasm than ever before. From the 1880s there was a general movement by landowners to spread their assets by investing on the stock exchange. Until the 1880s it was not at all usual for peers to become company directors. By 1896 more than one quarter of the peerage held directorships, most of them in more than one company. The peerage, never hostile to industrial interests, was now adopting them on a scale never seen before, and was even borrowing business techniques to improve the efficiency of their own estates. The Earl of Warwick formed a limited liability company in 1899 to run his family estates, with a board of directors which included his brother-in-law, the Duke of Sutherland. The scheme, which aimed at running the estates on more businesslike lines and at cutting taxation, was widely emulated. Taken all in all, the British peerage was quickly learning to compete in a competitive world.

The cost, of course, was the abandonment of some of the dignity and civilised habits of the past. The circle of the Prince of Wales, whose own investments were handled by the millionaire Ernest Cassel, had a philistine flavour which contrasted poorly with their eighteenth-century predecessors. Practical jokes, dropping ice down the royal neck or pouring treacle over the head of a docile courtier, were preferred to poetry reading or musical recitals. The Souls, an intellectual group which earnestly discussed science and philosophy and revolved around Lord Salisbury's nephew, Arthur Balfour, were objects of a wondering curiosity inconceivable in the days of the Dilettanti Society. An air of almost indecent opulence and vulgar display began to permeate society.

Some of the old aristocracy, more conservative than the rest, blamed the lower tone on the new men, the swollen class of plutocrats favoured by the Prince of Wales and more conspicuous than ever before at aristocratic gatherings. The Prince openly enjoyed the company of rich men. Baron Maurice de Hirsch, a rich Bavarian Jew who was constantly snubbed by the Austrian nobility, excluded from the Austrian jockey club and never received at court, became in England a prominent member of the Prince of Wales' set. A conspicuous class of plutocrats, the Rothschilds, the Sassoon brothers, Sir Thomas Lipton and Arthur Wilson of Tranby Croft, were prominent in society and overshadowed many peers, even the more businesslike ones, in wealth. There was some resulting bitterness. Some of the bad feeling aroused by the Tranby Croft affair, when a host exposed one of his guests cheating at cards, was aroused because the host, the shipowner Arthur Wilson, was a new man, allegedly ignorant of the aristocratic code of hospitality. But philistinism, vulgarity and the occasional smell of jealousy were less damaging phenomena than rigidity. In any case, the Marlborough House Set was only ever a small section of the brighter blades of the aristocracy. The ambitions of many others,

171

from Lord Rosebery – twin desires, to win the Derby and become Prime Minister – to the young Lord Randolph Churchill, drew them to public life, and success in this field carried a prestige which quite outshone the purely social glamour of the Prince of Wales' circle. Even the most frivolous retained their local ties and some sense of responsibility to tenants and labourers; 'duty' was not ignored even by the Prince's favourite beauties, and the Countess of Warwick at the peak of her royal favour spent time feeding jellies and beef tea to sick employees. The court never became of the Versailles type.

The peerage entered the twentieth century in a basically healthy condition, enjoying, in addition to its other advantages, one further valuable asset – it was indubitably English. At a time when the French élite, Anglophile almost to a man, watched *le Derby* at Chantilly, *le steeplechase* at Auteuil, or might even be unfortunate enough to be *black-boulé* at *le Jockey Club;* when the German nobility assiduously copied English manners, sport and dress; and the fashionable Russians affected only to speak French and English, the peers had an inestimable advantage in being, in nearly every case, the epitome of an Englishman. Their Englishness was a large part of their popularity. Lord Riblesdale, himself the very model of the handsome English patrician, might well write in 1898 that to be a lord 'is still a popular thing'.

The hereditary peerage grew more rapidly than ever before from 1885 onwards – although the number of titles was still small by continental standards – and although the new creations were bringing in brewers, bankers and businessmen, the great majority of the House was still from traditional stock. In 1911 only one in eleven of the hereditary peers originated from the business world.

That year, which saw its capitulation to the Liberals, brought another spate of land sales, prompted by the continuing low returns and an anxiety about the future. Most peers still held on to their estates as best they could. The attachment to acres won, planted and built up by one's ancestors, and handed down through succeeding generations, was a force difficult to break and perhaps hard for an urban society to imagine. In spite of

172

this, several peers felt that realism demanded a new look at the assumptions of land ownership. Agricultural fortunes had improved only slowly, and the prestige of land ownership was not what it had been. Education at a major public school and at Oxford or Cambridge was becoming to be regarded as a test of status as valid as that of a landed estate or good pedigree. In the past, even a radical statesman like Gladstone had recognised that land carried special burdens and special responsibilities. Twentieth-century taxation increasingly treated landowners as an idle and privileged class to be mulcted at every opportunity. As a result, more peers than ever before were forced to look on their estates as investments like any others which, if they did not pay adequate returns, should be liquidated. In 1912, nineteen peers had large estates on the market, not all of them driven to these lengths by desperate straits. A few peers decided to sell out to business altogether.

What the agricultural depression had begun, and egalitarian ideas of taxation continued, the First World War accelerated. Although less military minded than most of the continental nobility, the English aristocracy had traditionally closer ties with the armed services than any other English class. Peers usually served at least as honorary colonels of their local regiments, and the yeomanry week was a recognised part of the aristocratic year. When war came, the old tradition that those who had the largest stake in the country were first to fight for her persisted, even when, by 1914, peers were not necessarily the richest men in the country. Physical courage, inculcated in comfortless and sometimes brutal public schools and fostered in the hunting field, was still an inescapable requirement of good breeding. An aristocrat was above all expected to know how to die, and the few peers who were young enough were amongst the first to enlist when war broke out. Twenty of them died in the fighting services. The state sometimes demanded a double sacrifice, of money as well as life. The second Earl of Feversham, who was killed in action in 1916, had only inherited his title the year before, and the repetition of death duties was crippling. But the greatest sacrifice of all came from their sons, who were much more often of fighting age. Forty-nine direct heirs to peerages died in the course of the war, not to mention a host of younger sons. Viscount St Davids and my uncle Lord Forster both lost their first and second sons in the space of two years. One strange and unfair anomaly was that until World War II only officer's estates paid death duties, other ranks were exempt.

No peer escaped a heavy financial contribution. The revival of agriculture which accompanied the war rarely benefited the great landlords. The tradition was still strong in most areas that, while rents were remitted in hard times, they were not raised in good. Tenants, not landlords gained from the rising prices; but the peers, with their large establishments to maintain, were hit hard by rising prices, rising wages and escalating taxation. Whole wings of the great mansions which had some of them seen a glittering last season the year before the war, were shut up, dustsheeted and empty. It was clear that armistice must bring another fundamental appraisal of the finances and way of life of the great landlords.

The end of the war brought the biggest land sales of all. In the four immediate post-war years one quarter of the land of England changed hands, the biggest transfer of land since the Norman Conquest. Most of the peers who now abandoned their estates had only been driven to this repugnant course by many years of setbacks, not forgetting the loss of their sons and heirs in the war. Most of them had sufficient background in business to make their way in a landless world. In the short run, the sales were advantageous : many peers congratulated themselves on their timely action when prices tumbled later in the twenties. The new owners, most of them former tenants, were left to face the new depression without the umbrella of their landlords' protection. The landless peer, hitherto a freak phenomenon, was still not common, but estates were usually much shrunken from their former size. 'The old order is doomed,' proclaimed the Duke of Marlborough.[8]

In London, there was an accompanying but less spectacular series of town house sales, as the Mayfair streets were, one by one, made over to offices, night clubs and property companies. The old London season continued in a modified form, but to those who could remember pre-war days, society was unrecognisable. Trade union leaders, newspaper proprietors and radical critics of the class system joined the peerage on a scale which was completely new. In 1919 the first coloured peer, the Calcutta lawyer, Satyendra Sinha, received a seat in the Upper House. The peers had a long history of adaptability to help them adjust to the new realities but even so a whole generation of older men sat down to write their memories of a more congenial past.

The upheaval naturally seemed great to peers brought up in Victorian days, but compared with what the Austrians and Russians were undergoing, these were merely 'little local difficulties'.

Individuals, prompted by the changing times, began to make their way in fields unknown to their predecessors. Peers, often under plebeian pseudonyms, were to be found on the stage, in the cinema world, in journalism, motoring and exploration, as well as the by now familiar business world and the still more traditional armed services. Several peers had acted as pioneers in the new technological world of the twentieth century, and were well equipped to deal with their new role. My father had worked on the South Western Railway when he left Oxford in 1885, that being the fastest kind of transport then available. He was one of the first to recognise the enormous potential of motor and air transport : in 1902 he started as a sixpenny weekly the magazine *Car Illustrated*, 'a journal of travel by land, sea and air,' and this was before the Wright brothers flew. In later years, he campaigned for bigger air preparations before the First World War, and publicised the need for motorways and fly-overs. The peerage to which he belonged was never stick-in-the-mud or effete, and was well equipped after 1918 to adapt to the new circumstances of life.

There was, before the second war, little sign of a reinvigoration of the surviving estates, although a few peers were making a new beginning, on a small scale, in opening their homes to the public. It seemed in this field as though the cumulative blows of a generation had temporarily deprived the peerage of its old vigour and initiative. It took another war, and another social revolution, for the peerage to bounce back with energy and enterprise, starting booming stately homes businesses, transforming run-down estates into flourishing concerns as rising land values doubled and trebled the value of their land, and exploiting the glamour of their ancient titles in a new mass society, more curious about them than any of its predecessors.

The British peerage has survived into the space age culture of the twentieth century more completely than any of its continental counterparts. Compared with them, it has shown a disproportionate ability to compete, prosper and prevail.

Chapter Eight

Peerage Today

Sadly we refer to most European aristocracies in the past tense. We have seen how popular discontent and aristocratic silliness combined to bring about the decline and in some cases the absolute fall of every aristocratic class except the British.

Earlier chapters have, I think, highlighted the ways in which the nobles of Europe connived at their own demise. Sometimes they were over-snobbish, sometimes they lacked a proper acquisitiveness. Most often of all they mistook the trappings of power for the reality.

Here the aristocracy is not so muddled. The appearance and the actuality are combined in one institution : the House of Lords. Britain alone has a legislative chamber in which the sole qualification of most of its members is that they have succeeded as the eldest sons of English Lords.

In an increasingly egalitarian age the institution has been much criticised. Mr Wilson's Labour Government even went so far as to instigate joint party talks on its future. The talks were shelved in a fit of pique and so was the Bill for Lords Reform which the government subsequently introduced. (This was largely to make time for anti-Trades Union legislation which suffered a similar fate !)

The basis of most criticism – including the Wilson Government's – was not that the House didn't work (it did and does) but that it was illogical. This feeling is not restricted to commoners. Some peers are consumed with similar feelings of injustice.

Indeed, in the course of the long debate on the future of the House of Lords, in November 1968, there was a widespread feeling that the issue of the hereditary peers was dead; that no one could possibly pretend that such a system could be continued.

This was interpreted by those outside the House as a total surrender. So widespread was this feeling that in the following spring Garter King of Arms, Sir Anthony Wagner, took us to task in *The Times* for not standing up for ourselves.

His arguments were that democracy and the electoral process did not always produce fine legislation and management; and that where comparisons could be made the peerage were often better. 'The belief that peers of old lineage often have some special quality of behaviour is not just snobbery. It is attested by reliable, disinterested observers,' he wrote.

Perhaps no hereditary peer in the last three days of debate in the House ventured such an immodest claim, but the hereditary system does have its defenders.

It needs to.

The most virulent attacks came late on the evening of the 19th November. Young Lord Gifford, a hereditary peer, referred to us as an 'abomination'.

'I supported these reforms,' he said, 'because they will send the hereditary peers into the backwoods where they belong but I should very much like to send their titles with them.' The inference is that he should join them and one wonders how he could have tolerated his anachronistic position for so long. It is possible to renounce both title and position, and feeling as he does, Lord Gifford could surely have followed the example of men like John Grigg, the erstwhile Lord Altrincham, who did renounce his title on the death of his father.

The Communist, Lord Milford, was still more radical. No half measures for him.

'Even to many noble Lords opposite,' he thundered, 'the hereditary basis of this Chamber has become increasingly difficult to defend. Its abolition was due hundreds of years ago.'

He continued 'The reform of your Lordships' House is a "red herring" and is of no value to the British people. Bring in a White Paper for the abolition of the House of Lords, to get rid of the rank of peers and all titles and privileges, make the first priority the tackling of the real problem facing us today.'

The best defence of heredity and at the same time its most devastating opposition came from Lord Carrington. A hereditary peer himself and as the very respected Leader of the Conserva-

178

tive Party in the Lords, he was largely responsible not only for the White Paper on which Lords Reform is based, but also in persuading Conservative peers to endorse the reform proposals which he negotiated with the Labour Government.

'I think,' he said, 'that the mixture of life peers and hereditary peers which form your Lordships' House makes an admirable assembly; and it works well. There are positive advantages in the hereditary system. Those of us who sit here because our fathers and grandfathers did before us are beholden to nobody for our seat; we are answerable to nobody for what we do or what we say; and if we displease our political superiors they have no remedy save to remove the Party Whip from us – a punishment which might perhaps sadden us but would not, I think, totally crush us. Nobody has chosen us for our merit, because nobody has chosen us. We are here with no axe to grind; and I hope it would not be too presumptious of me to say that there are a very large number of hereditary peers who come to this house out of a sense of inherited duty and obligation, and not for what they expect to get out of it. I do not think that any reformed House, whether it be elected or nominated will be any better in composition than is the present one.'

That was the defence, compelling and convincing. The attack was swifter and devastating. 'I should be happy,' he said, 'to see the continuation of the hereditary system were it not for one thing – and it is of course the most important thing. It is that heredity as a basis for sitting in one of the two legislative Houses in this country is no longer acceptable to the broad mass of the people.'

In a democracy this is surely an unanswerable argument.

The debate and the White Paper which prompted it were both of course complicated, repetitive and often dull. In essence the Proposals were that in future ALL members of the House of Lords should be appointed as life peers are now, that existing peers should retain their right to attend; but that their sons should lose it.

In future only peers of first creation should be allowed to vote. Hereditary peers whose fathers, grandfathers and remote ancestors gained the family title will be able to vote by being

179

appointed life peers. Such is the British aptitude for compromise.

Argument meandered about the House almost endlessly. It lasted until after 1 a.m. on the first day and until midnight on the second. Eventually the White Paper was approved by two hundred and fifty-one to fifty-six against.

Because most peers accepted that a compromise had been hatched between the two parties, opposition was mostly muted and the atmosphere in the House was, as always, good humoured.

Lord Denham said that the House would lose its quota of 'ordinary blokes'; the Marquess of Salisbury said it would lose its quota of young men – a point never yet answered satisfactorily. Quite the most amusing speech was the late Baroness Asquith's. She reserved her greatest scorn for the 'two tier' system of voting and non-voting peers. 'I do not think,' she said, 'that any legislative body anywhere should contain first class and second class citizens. I think that we should all serve on equal terms and have equal rights.

'Have the Government, I wonder, been inspired to suggest this scheme by their experiment in first and second class mail in the Post Office? I devoutly hope that this House is not going to be run like the Post Office.'

She also weighed into the notion that peers should no longer be allowed to vote after the age of seventy-two – except in the case of cabinet ministers (strange exemption). 'I intend,' she concluded with a game flourish,' to cast my last vote in the last ditch against becoming a fourpenny stamp.'

In the event she seems to have abstained.

In all, one hundred and eighteen peers spoke on the Paper. In February 1969 the Commons started on the Committee stage of what was now called the Parliament (No. 2) Bill. Such was the standard of debate that the Liberal M.P. for Orpington, Mr Lubbock, felt moved to describe it in a memorable outburst as 'all piss and wind'. At one time four consecutive hours were spent on points of order alone. Certainly the Lords debates at no time reached such a low standard and if it had no peer would have expressed himself in such terms.

In itself that might be a recommendation for retaining it in its present form, but it is no argument for exhaustive quotation. For those with stamina it is all contained in Hansard.

However not everything is in Hansard; not all peers go to the House of Lords and the scope of my enquiries extends beyond Parliament.

Many of the more interesting peers did not take part in those debates and in the following weeks I dug a few of them out and explored their views not just on the restricted area of Lords Reform but also on related questions like the morality of hereditary privilege.

'The peer who renounced his title' is almost like the title of an H.M.Bateman cartoon. One can imagine the coronets tumbling, owners aghast as one of their number leaves the chamber in a bowler hat. My friend, John Grigg, was the second man to take such a drastic decision.

He did it just fifteen minutes after Anthony Wedgwood Benn (previously Lord Stansgate) who had been largely responsible for making it possible. Until that moment John had been Lord Altrincham. 'The whole question,' he says, 'resolves itself into two aspects which are nearly always confused. On the one hand the political aspect; on the other the titular aspect. Certainly ninety per cent of my reason for doing it is political, rather than titular. The political aspect seems to be this.

'Is it right that in a supposedly democratic state, in the latter part of the twentieth century, there should be hereditary membership of Parliament – a certain group of people, who have a hereditary right to sit in Parliament? That is one aspect of the question. And the other is: Is it right that there should be hereditary titles? Those two questions are distinct. There are a lot of people with hereditary titles who have no right to sit in Parliament, even as things now are; baronets, and Irish peers, and so on. Well, ninety per cent of my reason for renouncing is under the first head. I think it's absolutely wrong there should be hereditary membership of Parliament. When my father died I never took my seat in the House of Lords, although I am a political animal and would have liked to be in Parliament.

'Holding the view I did it would have been a monstrous hypocrisy to make an exception in my own favour. When the legislation permitted it I lost no time in regularising the position.'

181

The remaining aspect – the title itself – worries him much less. I think John was perhaps unduly conscientious.

Few people would argue the case that the hereditary aristocracy are in any way 'better' than any other social group. Aristocrats are no longer better educated or more wealthy. Not necessarily because of any decline in their own virtues, but because of the increase in those of others.

On the other hand when people bet on horses or dogs, raise pedigree cattle, or choose gun dogs they pay a great deal of attention to breeding and training. It is strange that it is now fashionable to dismiss, as irrelevant, breeding and background in human beings. But when you compare the difference in price of a pedigree bull or stallion and that of an equally fine but non-pedigree animal as seen in a nearby field, it can run into thousands of pounds.

Lord Mancroft made the same point well when I spoke to him. He said:

'I think there is a great deal to be said for the hereditary principle. The trouble is that people won't listen to it, it is not an argument in these democratic days that carries any weight. When Herbert Morrison on one occasion was caught out by Lord Salisbury on some political point, I remember one peer saying to another, "You know, Bobbity Salisbury has got all the political onus and cunning of Morrison, but he's been at the game four hundred and fifty years longer!" There's a lot in that, you know. But it's not an easy argument to put forward at a street corner.'

Other peers echo these sentiments. Lord Wakefield, Tory and ex-captain of the England Rugger XV, remarked on seeing in our history: 'Time and time again great contributions are being made to the well-being of the State by great families.'

Opposition to the principle comes generally from the Left Wing Life Peers. Baroness Wootton, for instance, says: 'It's an absolute toss up whether you get wisdom out of certain people's sons. Even the sons of nice and intelligent fathers are sometimes very foolish. . . . Two hundred years ago people believed that the peerage was a sort of natural aristocracy. Well, today we are quite certain that it isn't.'

The young also tend to have suspicions. Lord Lichfield is,

fashionably, a highly successful photographer and a cousin of the Queen. He sides with Barbara Wootton:

'I don't see any reason why I should be allowed to go and speak in public on important issues because my great-great-grandfather was bright, or clever, or a pirate (which he was) and buccaneered round the world, and made or stole a fortune. The King made him a sort of mini-God, and because I could be his moronic great-great-grandson, I don't see any need to allow me the right to speak in public on national affairs.'

Expressed like that heredity certainly sounds indefensible but I don't believe it is. I certainly feel a sense of blood, history, call it what you like. I am proud of being a direct descendant in the male line of Charles II and Mary, Queen of Scots.

In one of his recent interviews, Prince Charles referred to 'the family firm' and there is no doubt that the monarchy is the world's finest example of inherited privilege and responsibility. It may appear morally indefensible, but look at the Royal Family. Clearly they all have a very strong and inherited sense of duty. The same applies to the peerage.

I, for example, have an inherited sense of responsibility to tenants. A *nouveau riche* man who buys an estate has no such sense and misunderstandings often arise as a result.

The forthright Lord Arran put it succinctly:

'If a peer or a policeman gets into trouble – even if it's only a driving offence—then he gets into the *News of the World*. And serve him right!'

Apart from our titles the only absolutely tangible thing we have in common is our membership of Parliament. Lord Arran is one of many who emphasise the fact that we really have very little else in common. 'We're certainly not a clique. Far from it,' he says. 'I have eight cousins in the House of Lords and we don't see eye to eye on anything. We're barely on speaking terms.'

So, leaving aside our entrance qualifications, does the House of Lords work? Is it a good thing?

Our powers, already eroded by the act of 1911 and by legislation under the '45 Labour Government, have been diminishing. It was, however, a Tory Prime Minister, Harold Macmillan, who dealt the real blow to the hereditary peerage by introducing life peers in 1958, and this principle was extensively taken up by Harold Wilson whose life peerage creations drastically reformed the content of the House virtually without the country realising it. Perhaps, inadvertently, he strengthened it.

I personally shall view any further change in the House of Lords with some regret. For years I have accepted the inevitability of some change, and indeed its desirability; but I shall certainly look back at the unreformed House with nostalgia. After all I succeeded to my father's title when I was two-and-a-half, and I took my seat almost immediately after my twenty-first birthday towards the end of 1946.

When I took the opportunity of making my maiden speech on Palestine, where I had just recently spent one year in the army, as usual with maiden speeches I was kindly received; but the message I appreciated most was from Lord Salisbury himself, the leader of the Tory opposition peers. So for twenty-one years I have attended its debates, and even as an undergraduate at Oxford I used it as a more agreeable and prestigious debating society than the Union. I would not be human if I did not view it with affection.

Many peers express similar feelings – and not just hereditary peers. Lord Snow, for instance : 'I always think there is a degree of happiness there which is much greater collectively than any human institution I have ever sat in, or been in before. Now, is this because people are happy because they are there, or because having been happy they find their way there? It is rather remarked, this general air of mild and faintly dotty euphoria. Much more than the House of Commons. The House of Commons on the whole, although in some ways it has great Trade Union spirit, is not a particularly happy place.'

But listen to Barbara Wootton. 'I find it an unnatural sort of audience. I've been speaking all my life, but I have either spoken to a captive audience of students or to a meeting which had come together because, rightly or wrongly, they thought they wanted to hear what I had to say. I've not previously had experience speaking to people, about ten per cent of whom are normally asleep, who have no particular reason to want to hear what I have got to say, and in an Assembly in which the people who might be sympathetic sit with their backs to you, so that you talk to the backs of their heads! I find this grotesque. In other words, I am not a good Parliamentarian, and I find something quite distasteful in the way in which the speeches in the Lords (or the Commons for that matter) are built up into a sort of performance in themselves. If you speak, everybody comes and congratulates you on making such a good speech, or they refrain from congratulating you because it was a bad one. This I think is embarrassing for grown-up educated people. It is all right for the Oxford or Cambridge Unions. There, a speech is a performance, and the speakers are learning the trade, but I would have thought that people in mature years only spoke because they wanted to produce some result, not because they wanted to make a good performance. I find this practice equally distasteful whether people congratulate me, or whether I feel it my duty to congratulate them. It seems to me so childish.'

But despite her strictures there seems to be a general agreement that the Upper House is a very much more impressive forum than the Commons. Here I would be the first to admit that the introduction of life peers – and still more life peeresses – has had a considerable effect.

'I won't say we're much more intelligent than the Commons,' says Lord Arran modestly, 'but we're certainly much less stupid.'

Lord Boothby has been in the House of Commons for thirty-four years, so he is in a good position to make comparisons. 'The standards of debate in the House of Lords where you have got practically negligible Party Whips, and everybody says exactly what he really thinks are,' he says, 'immeasurably superior to those in the House of Commons. I have heard debates on currency lately, on university education, on defence, which I thought were far better than anything that the House of Commons has done, because they always have to have an eye on the votes, and the constituencies and the local papers, and that kind of thing. Whereas the House of Lords says what it thinks.'

Often through some hereditary quirk experts on the most unlikely subject appear as if from nowhere. Lord Mancroft reminded me of one example.

'I remember,' he says, 'one peer getting up during the second reading of the White Fish Bill, and beginning, "My Lords, the

185

last occasion on which I had the honour to address your Lordships was some thirty-seven years ago, this was the last time we
had discussed white fish". That's all he was an expert about. He
was very good on it, made a powerful speech, and was never
seen again.'

That I think is a pertinent anecdote because it demonstrates
one of the great strengths of the House: it's total unpredicta-
bility. What other legislative chamber could give us an ex-
corporation gardener, like the Earl of Buckinghamshire, alongside, say, the top National Trust man, Lord Antrim. Or provide
a retired bus driver, Lord Teviot, to sit in the same chamber
as Lord Stokes, whose company make the world's best buses?
Where else can you find a Chamber which includes numbers of
young men of under thirty?

John Grigg is critical of this sort of defence: 'Some people say
it's a perfect cross-section. That is a lot of nonsense. Because
they are certainly not that. And they are even more weighted
in favour of the higher income groups than jurymen under the
present system. The jury is criticised as being too middle-class,
and the peerage must be criticised for being too upper-class!'

But Lord Boothby insists that with the introduction of life
peers (like himself) the House is virtually perfect. 'I do think that
the advent of life peers has made a great difference to the
House of Lords. It's gingering the whole thing up, and keeping it
up to date, and making it better. I mean you have all sorts of
people, Sainsbury, Crowther, God knows who, who are really
the leaders of industry. You already had the Law Lords, all
the best legal talent, you have all the retired Chiefs of Staff who
know a hell of a lot about it all (and in the Defence Debate can
speak with much more authority than any member of the
House of Commons could hope to). That sort of House I think
you ought to have. A House that can say, "Well, it's all very
well, this has been passed by the Commons, it's quite all right,
but according to our experience, this and that won't do . . . it
won't work". And time and again the Commons will acept that
and have accepted it.'

Lord Lichfield not unnaturally emphasised the importance
of youth. 'The advantage I think of the House of Lords now is
that the young group of peers like Hugh Reay and Gifford

186

and so on, speak very well, are very much closer to the thoughts of the man in the street than my grandfather, who hadn't the least idea what John Smith, who went on a bus every day to work, actually thought about or did. He did, however, know terribly well what one of his game keepers who was illiterate might think or do or actually feel, but he didn't know what the great middle class felt. Whereas we are very much part of that. Very nearly all my friends and a lot of people I meet and talk to are journalists, photographers, clothes designers, the fashion world of models. Which is very much closer to the English way of life than my grandfather's (I talk about my grandfather all the time because I really inherited from him). Therefore, if we are going to make a contribution, we can make a more worthwhile one because one hears much more directly the complaints and feelings of ordinary people, and if I did feel about something very strongly, I could stand up and say it, and I should get nearer the mark than they ever did.'

Lord Mancroft makes a still more valid point about youthful peers: 'It's largely the young men', he says, 'who do the donkey work. You won't get Field Marshals to sit up half the night on Clause 14 of the Rats and Mice Bill.'

In all the palaver about reform of the House of Lords neither point has been effectively answered. No rational system could give us young men, nor could it provide the ordinary person.

The main argument for abolishing the right of the hereditary peer is that by doing so the status of the House will be greatly increased. At the moment anything we do tends to be despised because the opposition say, 'Oh that's just a lot of silly old backwoodsmen who have inherited their position'. Opponents seldom pause to consider whether what we say or do is good. They prefer the red herring.

This is the view of, among others, the Liberal peer, Lord Beaumont, who predictably wants his reformed second chamber to be elected on a system of proportional representation.

At the moment though, it looks as if the House will continue unreformed. I think that is a good thing – if only people would forget their prejudices and take us more seriously. But before I leave the subject – a final word to Baroness Wootton who, as far as I know, is the only one of us to take such an extreme view as this :

'Hardly anybody would consider doing what I think would be reasonable, and that is to do away with the second chamber altogether. I think it is a current cliché that everybody says, "Oh, but you must have a second chamber". Why? And what in this context is a second chamber? I mean, would it do if you took, let us say, a quarter of the members of the House of Commons and put them in a separate room? This, in fact, is what they do in Norway, where they have two chambers. They elect the lot together and then segregate one section. I can see no real reason why you should have a second chamber, and the whole situation was well summed up, I think it was by the late Dr Lees Smith, when he said, "A second chamber is either obstructive or superfluous". However, abolition does not seem to be practical politics at present.'

Well, we have already seen the erosion of freedom which occurs when power is too closely concentrated in the hands of the Prime Minister or a small cabal surrounding him. I would regard any check on the abuse of power by the executive as by definition a good thing.

But though the House of Lords is the great bastion of the peerage, and the one thing above all which gives us real credibility, there are still other aspects. What after all is it like to be a peer? To be called 'My Lord'. Lord Arran for one thinks it's 'jolly'. He would punish peers who don't go to Parliament by removing their titles and going back to being called 'plain Mister'. That would teach them, he thinks.

I succeeded to my title when I was a very young boy and at first the fact of having it was an absolute misery to me. One was being teased constantly. All through school life there seemed to be a continual chorus of, 'Yah Boo, little Lord Fauntleroy'.

During the war, when I went to America and Canada for two years, it was a blessed relief. I could be Edward Montagu again. Authentic titles are neither used nor understood there, and even now when I travel in the States I sometimes find myself referred to as 'Mr Lord Montagu'. They think I'm the same as Duke Ellington or Count Basie – which is, I suppose, not bad company.

188

I have always maintained that the only people who have real respect for a title are those in the service industries. That is largely because they suffer under the illusion that a title means money. Therefore the only value of a title is in booking a table in a restaurant, and even that is based on a misconception. The press naturally like names so that if you court publicity a title makes life easier. Certainly if, like me, you are forced to open your house to a paying public, a title greatly enhances its attraction. The public appear to be less interested in houses owned by plain Misters. There are still those who chase titles to put on their letter heading. Charities and some businesses like 'a Lord on the board'. Even this apparent perk is inhibiting. It is like marriage for the wealthy. Everyone enjoys being sought after, but they want to be loved for themselves, not for money or title.

It is, however, a fact of life in this country. We are a nation of snobs and nothing will change us. What plain Mr Smith does is seldom interesting, however significant. What Lord Smith does, however trivial, is always of interest.

Unfortunately there are still some people who feel a crippling sense of inferiority when confronted with an aristocrat. I feel no corresponding sense of superiority when faced with a commoner. Most of my best friends are commoners! I find that most peers react to their position with mild amusement tempered with pride. Almost all agree with me about servants.

Lord Arran, who succeeded rather late in life, comments: 'If I make a fuss on the phone now and say "Lord Arran" there's usually a discreet pause and I'm through to the supervisor. Before I succeeded they would just say "Mr Gore, well who the hell are you?"'

Lord Thomson of Fleet says rather quaintly that he is able to visit Communist countries with a much enhanced standing now that he is a Baron. 'They don't approve of there being titles', he observes, 'but they pay respect.'

The Scots, of course, are exceptions to most rules and the Duke of Atholl implies that it means more to be Chief of the Clan Murray, than to be a mere duke. 'There are a lot of people who were historically much more powerful than the peerage, and probably weren't peers because of a choice on their part. In Scotland, you see, it's the clan chiefs, who are important. It

189

really means something when you are head of a very large family – and many clan chiefs aren't part of the aristocracy in the sense that they don't have titles. The Macnab of Macnab for instance; Cameron of Lochiel; or Clanranald; and The Chisholm.'

Many peers nowadays feel self-conscious about using their title at all, even though it is their real name. The Marquess of Queensberry for instance is a Professor of Ceramics at the Royal College of Art. He is known as Professor Queensberry, though you may occasionally find a piece of pottery inscribed with the legend 'Designed by the Marquess of Queensberry'. 'I very often am in a room,' he says, 'and I find people are introduced to me as "This is David Smith, or Jack Jones . . . do you know Lord Queensberry?" It is quite unnecessary if everybody else is being introduced by their Christian names to introduce one with a title, using the title. That's snobbery.'

One professional peer who has even more trouble with his title is Lord Lichfield. 'As far as advertising agencies or magazines go,' he says, 'or newspaper editors, picture editors, they may be interested to see you because you are something of a curiosity. But they are going to regard even your greatest photograph as a kind of amateur effort. And, therefore, I work under four different pseudonyms; which is not because I don't want to call myself Lord Lichfield – I do call myself Patrick Lichfield for most purposes – but I do work for various other magazines and newspapers under different pseudonyms which in a sense bolsters up my confidence because they are using me for the quality of my work. In advertising agencies I walk in under a completely different name. I was even once asked to go and photograph myself by a newspaper!'

A similar point is made by my friend, the Marquess of Hertford, who, like me, is in the stately home business but also runs a successful public relations firm. 'It was a slight disadvantage when I began working in Fleet Street, because people tended to think one was an amateur. But I have been here for seven years now, and I am a full member of the Institute of Public Relations, and I think it has dawned on people that I am a fairly well-qualified P.R. man. But then we all start with such advantages that we ought to be able to earn our own livings.

I mean we are mostly brought up in ideal surroundings and given excellent educations. If we can't cope who can? I really have very little sympathy for peers who plead poverty. It's much easier for us than it is for most people to go out and earn their own living. The more acid comments come, predictably, from those who tend to wear their titles like a crown of thorns: John Grigg makes, I think, a pertinent point: 'One of the reasons that being a peer is embarrassing is that you tend to be taken not seriously enough by sensible people and too seriously by silly people. Having a title of any kind means you are walking round every day of your life in a sort of fancy dress. And some people take fancy dress more seriously than others.'

That staunch egalitarian Baroness Wootton is the only person I know who really does seem to object even to the peerage's most trivial perks.

'I occasionally find it irritating', she says, 'if I go, say, to a local butcher myself; then he has got fillet steak. But if somebody else goes for me, he hasn't. I can't stand that sort of thing, and I won't continue going to a shop where it happens.'

That may well sound a small thing, but I think it well illustrates what is borne out in my opinion poll at the end of the book: that the ordinary British public still has a great deal of respect for the British peerage. And I think further that we have earned it, and are earning it.

I have not dealt at any great length with the ties between the peerage and the land. The tax man has succeeded in recent years in decimating many great estates which through the rigid application of the principle of primogeniture had remained intact for centuries. But the ownership of a large estate is not, nor ever has been, the exclusive privilege of the peerage. You will find great landowners in the pages of *Burke's Landed Gentry* as well as the *Peerage* of the same name. At the same time the fact that most peers have had estates has meant a first-hand knowledge of ordinary people and a strong sense of duty to those people. It has also for the most part meant work. Land has usually, I believe, been the symbol rather than the cause of wealth. And if you compare our record with that of any other aristocracy you will, I believe, discover one predominant fact. We have tended to work harder.

191

Lord Snow adds a word on this. Of the future he says, 'You will lose the aristocracy completely if it doesn't work, that is very simple. We know that from other countries, the French and Italian aristocracy have absolutely no function except a rather bizarre snobbery.'

The attempts to drive the hereditary peerage out of Parliament will necessarily result in their having less to do. And certainly the survival of the House of Lords has contributed more to the survival of a credible peerage than anything else. Without our Parliamentary seats some people give us another two generations or less. I have already indicated that we have a staying power and adaptability which ensures our survival far beyond the twentieth century. Some of us may be re-created as life peers; others may be able to sit in the House of Commons AND retain their titles. One absurd compromise on another, and characteristically British.

But as the traditional institutions of the country become increasingly egalitarian, so the traditional class, the aristocracy, are able to branch out into new fields. Taxation, death duties and inverted snobbery may conspire against us but ultimately the effect will be to release a new talent. In politics the convention which has kept peers out of the Commons has been greatly to the detriment of the Commons. And there are many other areas, previously thought unfashionable, which will become increasingly popular among the peerage. Already journalism has been widely infiltrated. Something which would have been unthinkable sixty years ago. Argument may continue about us as a class or a group but as individuals we will increasingly prove the futility of generalisation.

I believe that in a hundred years' time there will be aristocrats prominent in every walk of national life – to an extent previously unknown, even though many titles may have fallen into disuse. At the same time I hope that at least some of the great traditions will have been maintained. That there will still be an hereditary Earl Marshal organising the great State ceremonies; that there will still be Cecils at Hatfield, Churchills at Blenheim, and of course I hope Montagus at Beaulieu. I have no doubt that this will be so. And rightly.

192

Appendix One

Public Opinion Survey on
The Peerage

The British people's attitude to the aristocracy has always seemed ambiguous. A respectful admiration of individuals has often been coupled with an egalitarian dislike of the hereditary system in general.

To find out what people think about the aristocracy I commissioned a small survey. This survey was similar to those organised by market research firms and was carried out independently by a fourth year student of sociology at London University assisted by other students. People were stopped in the street or interviewed in their own homes, and asked straightforward questions about their views. The subjects were not selected by the 'random sampling' methods of the political opinion type of survey as this would have been too costly. But the interviewers were asked to use their judgement to see that a fair cross-section of the population was interviewed. To make it still more representative the interviews were spread regionally across the country. Within these regions, areas were selected on the basis of the type of neighbourhood, i.e. working-class or middle-class. In the last resort the results are only of the one hundred and twenty people interviewed, but it is hoped that they can be made more generally applicable to a wider population than this, despite the lack of the more 'scientific' methods used by more elaborate social surveys.

The interviewer began by making it clear that the survey was concerned with the hereditary aristocracy and not the life peerage. The people interviewed were then asked a series of questions designed to discover their ideas about the aristocracy as a cohesive and self-contained social group.

Ninety-five per cent of those interviewed thought that the aristocracy was an important part of the upper class in British society. This is hardly a surprising result, but the replies to the question, 'Would you say that we still have a society in which the aristocracy is the upper class?' were rather astonishing. Fifty-six per cent of all the respondents said 'Yes'.

Historians and sociologists have long agreed that the social and political élite of British society is a class with extremely heterogeneous origins, and certain fluidity of membership, in which money and the occupation of important administrative and political positions are as important as noble birth. Indeed, if birth still counts, then it is being born into the upper middle class that matters. So it comes as a considerable shock to realise that so many people retain a perception of a British society in which the upper echelons are dominated by hereditary aristocrats. This appears to be contrary to the facts. Combined with this view of the aristocracy as the upper class is the notion that the aristocracy forms a closed group with few outside contacts, or at least that it attempts to maintain its exclusiveness against outsiders.

Eighty-two per cent of those interviewed replied in the affirmative to the question, 'Do you think that members of the aristocracy try to hang together as a group; for example in their social and business life?' The majority (sixty-three per cent) of the sample went even further and said that they thought that the peers tried to ensure that their children married those of other nobles. They saw the aristocracy not merely as a group which has notions of its own exclusiveness, but as something akin to a self-perpetuating caste. Here, too, the facts seem to contradict the prevalent view of the aristocracy; what is known of marriage patterns in the nineteenth and twentieth centuries suggests that intermarriage is not a common phenomenon. As earlier chapters of this book show, the aristocracy has usually tried to marry into commercial wealth, in order to boost declining family fortunes. This idea of the distinct social position of the aristocracy, however, is not held only by those who in some sense look up to old noble families. Later sections of the results reveal that it is to a large extent held by those who are neutral, or even critical in their attitudes.

Nor are there any significant regional differences. The towns are as likely to follow the pattern as the country, the north as likely as the south. There are hints, however, that the Scottish and Welsh respondents have a less positive perception than the English, but the numbers are too small to prove this.

The next section of the survey was designed to find out whether or not people thought that the aristocracy had something to contribute to present day life, or were just historically interested. The results were disappointingly inconclusive. To the question, 'Would you say that the aristocracy had much to contribute to present day life?', the replies were split roughly into equal numbers of yes and no. It was possible that the question itself was at fault, because of its broadness, so a more specific question was then asked: 'Do you think that they do a lot of work for local government and charity?'. Here again the replies were evenly divided, with a large number (fourteen per cent) of don't knows. The impression of the interviewing staff was that more would have preferred to answer don't know and that the yes and no replies should not be taken too seriously. These two questions told us little, except that some people have the notion that the aristocracy contributes something but it also revealed that they don't know what. It may seem surprising that so many said yes, when so few knew what peers did.

The question of the reform of the House of Lords was the next to be raised. This was a topical issue at the time of interviewing, though the Government proposals had not then been announced. Fifty per cent thought that hereditary peers should have seats in the Lords; forty-four per cent thought not, and six per cent did not know. A fairly even division. But the results for the next question were surprising: thirty-nine per cent think that hereditary peers play a useful part in politics, whereas fifty-eight think that they do not (two per cent don't know). So many of those who think that hereditary peers should have seats also think that they are politically useless.

To try and find out what these confusing replies in fact mean, the respondents were then asked whether they thought that the House of Lords should be abolished: sixty-one per cent said no, and thirty-six said yes. This pattern of replies could mean several things. Either people do not associate the House of Lords with hereditary peers, in which case the answers to the two previous

195

questions could not be expected to bear any relation to the replies here, or people's feelings about the House and about peers differ, so that those who wish to throw out the aristocracy, also wish to keep the upper chamber. Or again, perhaps people think that peers are not only of no political consequence, but that the House itself is harmless, in which case there is no need to change anything. Unfortunately the possible interpretations of the replies to this part of the questionnaire only became apparent during analysis of the results; too late for people to be asked questions which might have made their attitude clearer.

The sample was then asked a series of questions to find out whether they looked up to the aristocracy or were in any way deferential. This was a difficult thing to find out, because it was difficult to ask people straight out whether they felt deferential towards aristocrats and expect absolutely valid replies. So the questions were more obliquely phrased. A series of questions such as 'Are you interested in the aristocracy?', 'Do you like reading about peers in the daily papers?', and 'Do you ever visit stately homes in order to see how the aristocracy lives?' produced results of around twenty-five per cent to thirty per cent saying yes, and seventy per cent to seventy-five per cent saying no. Respondents were then asked 'Do you think that most people secretly look up to the aristocracy?', the replies being fifty-six per cent yes, and forty-four per cent no. But when asked 'Do you?' the yesses dropped to twenty-six per cent, a figure which seems surprisingly high for a direct question on deference. However, the next question, 'Would you feel proud if you suddenly discovered that you were related to an old noble family?' produced forty-two per cent yes replies, and this seems to show a deferential attitude towards the aristocracy which the previous question was unable to trap.

The same people said 'yes' to the previous two sets of questions; so those who professed interest in the aristocracy were also those who admitted looking up to it; they represent about twenty-six per cent of the sample. The jump of sixteen per cent on the last question in this section suggests that many more people have a secret regard for the peerage than would openly admit to it, not altogether surprising, but it is interesting to see it demonstrated in this way.

Traditionally, the monarchy and aristocracy have gone hand in hand in this country, so it seemed worth finding out what the people in our survey thought both of the monarchy as an institution, and of its relationship with the aristocracy. The respondents were asked 'Should we still have a monarch?', a question to which eighty per cent said 'yes'. Those who said 'no' were then asked if they would prefer some other type of Head of State. Only fourteen per cent of the total sample said 'yes'. These results are much what one would have expected. The next question was 'Do you think that the Queen and the nobility are close? That is, that the Queen has most of her private friends among the peers?'. This was phrased in such a way because of the widespread view that the monarchy in this country is in some sense a middle class institution. For instance, Roy Perrott in his book *The Aristocrats* suggests that the present monarch has deliberately played down her connections with the aristocracy and has tried to present a public image of a relatively classless rather than aristocratic way of life, in order to bring the monarchy into line with post-war Britain. The press has also put forward the picture of the homely middle class lady primarily concerned with her family. It is a picture of a way of life which is in some respects different to that of everyone else, but with which the man in the street can identify, as it is within his own experience. The Queen is presented as the first monarch of the democratic age, a woman of exaggerated ordinariness. If people really believed this projected image, then one would expect them to disassociate the Queen from the aristocracy, as Perrott asserts that they do, but our figures indicate the reverse.

To the question whether the monarchy and aristocracy are close, the replies were sixty-nine per cent saying yes, eight per cent don't know, and only twenty-three per cent no. One question alone might be thought insufficient to test this view, so the subject was tackled from another angle: 'Would it make sense to have a monarchy in this country without the aristocracy which has always gone with it?'. The response to this was not quite so clear cut as to the previous question, fifty-six saying it would not make sense to separate the two institutions, five per cent not knowing, and thirty-nine per cent thinking it would make sense. But then the question was more strongly worded.

197

The first merely asks people whether they think the two institutions are related; the second asks for views on the implied possibility that they might be divorced. So a third question was presented: 'Should we do away with the ceremonial occasions in which the aristocracy plays an important part?'. Fifty-four per cent said no, a reply similar to that of the previous question; this changed to sixty-five per cent when the second part of the question was present. 'For instance, the Coronation', a number almost the same as that in the first of the three questions in this section. From this consistent pattern of replies it appears that many people still see the monarchy and aristocracy going hand in hand, despite the conscious efforts of the monarchy to present a different picture.

Finally an attempt was made to isolate those who felt in some way hostile towards the aristocracy. A two part question was asked: 'Do you think that the aristocracy stands for our English tradition?', and 'Do you think that it is a good thing that it should be associated with this tradition?' The replies to the first part were seventy-two per cent saying yes, to the second part the replies were only fifty-six per cent saying yes, and forty-four per cent saying no. These were compared with the replies to the next, and final question, which was deliberately chosen for its emotive ring: 'Would the country be better off if we abolished all titles and treated the nobility as ordinary citizens?' Fifty-six per cent thought that the country would not be better off, and forty-four per cent thought it would be.

In both cases the forty-four per cent were the same people. A further check of their views showed that they were also the same people who had said earlier that the hereditary peers should not have seats in the House of Lords. This does show a consistent pattern which helps to isolate at least part of the population hostile to the aristocracy. This percentage is a largish one, but perhaps not as great as one might have expected. Indeed, it came as quite a surprise to find fifty-six per cent of the sample supporting the nobility as the bastion of tradition and opposing the suggestion that the peers should be treated like anyone else. But these replies may be the best indicators of feelings about the aristocracy. Forty-four per cent have been identified as consistently critical of the nobility. The earlier section of the survey showed another forty-four per cent who were basically deferential. Twelve per cent do not really fit either category but support the status quo and the sense of heritage symbolised by the aristocracy. These are the only consistent groupings of replies to be found. On other questions individuals react to the specific subject matter without any general pattern emerging. The sample was also broken down into a number of subsections; region and area, social class, political convictions, and sex. Regional variations were very slight : the only significant findings were that respondents from Scotland and Wales were more likely to be critical of the aristocracy and that urban and rural voters in all regions were identical. This is surprising if one assumes that the countryside is more traditional than the towns.

Occupational groupings, or social classes, were divided into three : professional and managerial (groups A & B), junior non-manual (group C) and manual (group D). These are the breakdowns normally used by market research surveys but correspond roughly to the more usual notions of upper middle, lower middle and working classes. The figures for groups A and B produced one major surprise. This was the large number who saw the aristocracy as a united upper class : sixty per cent saw the aristocracy as the upper class; eighty-nine per cent thought that aristocrats tended to hang together as a group, and sixty-nine per cent reckoned that aristocrats tried to make sure that their offspring intermarry. Otherwise the replies from this class were predictable. On the House of Lords section, only thirty-one per cent thought that peers should have seats, twenty-two per cent thought that the aristocracy play a useful part in English politics, and fifty-four per cent were in favour of abolishing the Lords altogether. Twenty-five per cent admitted to looking up to the aristocracy and thirty-seven thought that they would feel proud to discover that they were related to an old noble family. All these replies show considerably less enthusiasm for the aristocracy than was found among the other social classes. This theme was confirmed by the fact that only thirty-one per cent thought it a good thing that the aristocracy was identified with English tradition; and that forty-three per cent thought the country would be better off if we abolished titles altogether.

The results of the section on the monarchy, however, seem rather inconsistent with the rest of the questionnaire : Eighty per cent wanted to retain the monarchy, the largest percentage of all three classes; eighty-three per cent thought that the Queen and the nobility are close (again the highest percentage); and only forty-three per cent thought that it would make sense to have the monarchy without the aristocracy. These results display what can only be seen as an ambivalent attitude towards the nobility. In themselves apparently peers are not worth supporting, but in terms of the monarchy (which this class values very highly) then one must tolerate them. Only those forty-three per cent who thought that it would make sense to separate the two institutions also came out on the side of abolishing titles for the good of the country.

The lower middle class group replies proved more difficult to analyse, because of their inconsistency. Like both the A/B group and the D group a considerable majority (sixty-two per cent) saw the aristocracy as the upper class, and eighty-one per cent thought that peers tried to stick together as a group. But unlike the A/B group, this one claimed to be less interested in the aristocracy, to be less likely to view the monarchy and aristocracy as close (only fifty per cent saying yes, with twenty-five per cent don't knows) and to be more likely (sixty-three per cent) to say that it would make sense to have the monarchy without the aristocracy. These figures differed significantly from those of group D, which on the questions were more similar to those of A/B. On the other hand, group C had the highest scores of all on the number of people who said they would feel proud to discover that they were related to an old noble family (fifty-six per cent). Fifty-six per cent also believed that the peers should have seats in the House of Lords. On the question, 'Is it a good thing for the aristocracy to be associated with tradition?' fifty per cent said yes. These lower middle class respondents were also the least likely to agree that the country would be better off if we abolished all titles and treated the nobility as ordinary citizens. Twenty-five per cent said yes, as against forty-three per cent in group A/B and fifty-three per cent in group D. They were also the least likely to want to do away with the ceremonial occasions in which the aristocracy plays an important

200

part. What can be made of this pattern of replies is difficult to judge. One interpretation is that the lower middle class attempts to disguise what are basically very strong pro-aristocratic sentiments by giving low scores on direct questions. But this may be an oversophisticated view of their replies. Alternatively, it may be that the people interviewed here are genuinely inconsistent in their attitudes, and that this reflects the lack of any clearly formulated views on the whole subject. However, the small number of respondents in this class, compared with the other two, makes a choice between these interpretations difficult. It only needs a few people with divergent views to upset what would otherwise be a consistent pattern.

The working class replies gave few problems. They were generally more interested than the upper middle class but less deferential than the lower middle class. Forty-two per cent said that they would be proud to be related to the aristocracy and twenty-two per cent admitted openly to looking up to peers. The first figure is considerably less than for group C, while the second is about the same. Interestingly, the figures on the ideas of the aristocracy as the upper class are the same as those of the other social class groups. But only seventy-three per cent as against over eighty per cent for A/B and C, saw the aristocracy trying to maintain itself as a solid social group mixing only with its equals. This is a low figure in terms of the general results of this survey. It is difficult to find an explanation for this. When asked if the country would be better off if we abolished all titles and treated the nobility as ordinary citizens, fifty-three per cent said yes. This is the highest number for all three groups, and seems to indicate a fairly strong critical attitude amongst this social class. This impression is strengthened by the fact that only forty per cent thought it a good thing that the nobility have been associated with our English tradition. (Against fifty per cent of the lower middle class.) The working class, however, seems to be more traditional in its attitudes than the middle classes. Forty per cent thought that the hereditary peers should sit in the Lords, as against thirty-one per cent in class A/B and fifty-six per cent in class C; but only thirty-five per cent thought that the House of Lords as such should be abolished, compared with fifty-four per cent for class A/B and forty-three per cent

for class C. Equally, as regards the relation between the aristocracy and monarchy : thirty-five per cent only thought that it
would make sense to have the one without the other, compared
with forty-three per cent for A/B and sixty-three per cent for C,
even though slightly fewer people thought we should retain the
monarchy than in A/B. One can therefore characterise the
working class as a group with no strong affection for the hereditary aristocracy. But it does have an attachment to at least two
institutions traditionally associated with the nobility : i.e. the
monarchy and the House of Lords.

Conservative and Labour voters were then compared. The
assumption was that the Conservatives were more likely to
favour the aristocracy than the other voters. The Conservative
party has traditionally been identified with the elite groups in
our society, particularly the aristocracy and monarchy. The
socialist basis of the Labour Party has tended to be hostile to
both. The figures from this survey demonstrate the difference
quite clearly. The Conservatives see the aristocracy both as
the upper class and as an extremely exclusive and solid social
group : ninety-one per cent think that they try to hang together
as much as possible. Peers are, in turn, heavily identified with
the monarch : seventy-seven per cent see the Queen and the
peers as close, and only twenty-seven think it would make sense
to have the one without the other; or to do away with the
ceremonial occasions in which the aristocracy plays an important
part. Labour supporters have a similar idea of the aristocracy
as a class, but emphasise the peers' 'groupness' far less strongly,
and are less likely to see aristocracy and monarchy as close
(sixty-six per cent). They are also more likely to think that the
monarchy could continue without the aristocracy (forty-eight
per cent) and to oppose the ceremonial aspect (seventy-four
per cent). The Conservatives emerge from the rest of the
questionnaire as being extremely deferential; sixty-two per cent
openly admit to looking up to peers, and seventy-two per cent
say that they would be proud to be related to nobility. Labour
voters score only eight per cent and twenty-six per cent respectively on these questions. Although fairly evenly divided on
whether peers perform a useful function in the Lords (fifty-five
per cent say yes), sixty-seven per cent of the Conservatives wish

to retain seats for the hereditary aristocracy and seventy-six per cent wish to retain the Lords as an institution. The corresponding Labour figures are twenty per cent, twenty per cent and fifty-six per cent. This consistent pattern, in which Conservatives support privilege, and defer to the nobility, can be seen at its sharpest in the replies to the question 'Do you think the country would be better off if we abolished all titles and treated the nobility as ordinary citizens?'. Conservatives had a total of fourteen per cent saying yes, as against Labour's fifty-six per cent. Conservatives were pro-peerage; Labour supporters were anti.

After this division into political parties, we decided to see how far political preferences affected the results when social class was added. For this purpose, class A/B was compared with D. As regards people's ideas of the aristocracy as a group, party preference is more important than social class. Labour voters in both working and upper middle classes are less likely to see the aristocracy as a solid clique than Conservatives in these classes. But this does not hold good for the section dealing with the House of Lords. When asked whether peers should sit in the Lords, both Conservative groups had a majority saying yes (sixty-five per cent to seventy per cent), the upper middle class Labour group were one hundred per cent against, but the working class Labour group had thirty per cent saying yes. Similarly, on the usefulness of the peers in British politics, upper middle class Conservatives were overwhelmingly in favour, Labour voters in the same class were entirely against, but working class Labour and Conservative respondents were now split in the same proportion (forty per cent saying yes). On the subject of abolition of the Lords altogether, the major difference is still more a class one – not a political one. Conservative and Labour in the upper middle class are both strongly in favour of abolition. In the working class they are strongly against.

When asked about looking up to the aristocracy, class played a less important part. Both Conservative groups did not look up (sixty per cent approximately), upper middle class Labour supporters did not do so at all, and only thirteen per cent working class Labour voters said that they did. This seems to be part of a consistent pattern : on all the questions implying deference

203

to peers, the Conservatives had a majority in both classes looking up to the nobility, but all Labour voters were opposed. When the subject was a traditional institution, such as the House of Lords or the monarchy, then Labour working class replies were complicated by typical class attitudes towards traditional institutions. Labour voters in A/B remain very consistent in their replies, so do both Conservative groups. But Labour voters in D vary enormously. For example, Labour working class answers agreed with the Conservatives in this class about the connection between monarchy and aristocracy, but not with A/B Conservatives, nor with A/B Labour supporters. Though for different reasons. Similarly, both working class groups are less likely to think that it would make sense to have the monarchy without the aristocracy than either of the upper middle class groups. So class attitudes in the working class can be seen influencing their answers on many questions. Within the working class there are only slight differences between Labour and Conservative voters which can be explained by political convictions.

Finally, we made a brief comparison between men and women. This showed an agreement about aristocracy as a group, and of the relation between the aristocracy and monarchy. But there are major differences in attitudes towards the House of Lords and the subject of looking up to peers. Women are more likely than men to want to keep the peers in the Lords, to say that they are useful, and to favour retaining the Lords as an upper chamber. (Even so less than fifty per cent of women favoured the upper house and the peers' role in this). Women were also more likely openly to look up to peers than men and more likely to admit that they would feel proud to discover that they were related to an old noble family.

The tabulated results of the survey can be found in the Appendix.

Appendix Two

Questionnaire and Results

1.   Do you know what a hereditary peer is?   ....

2. (a) Would you say that we still have a society in which the aristocracy is the upper class?   ....

   (b) Or in which the aristocracy is an important part of the upper class?   ....

3. (a) Do you think that members of the aristocracy try to hang together as a group?   ....
e.g. in their social and business life?   ....

   (b) Do peers try to make sure that their children marry those of other nobles?   ....

4.   Would you say that the aristocracy had much to contribute to present day life?   ....
If so, what sort of things?

5.   Do you think that they do a lot of unpaid work for local government and charity?   ....

6. (a) What is the peerage's main source of income?   ....

   (b) Are most lords well off?   ....

7.   Should hereditary peers have seats in the House of Lords?   ....

8.   Would you say that hereditary peers play a useful part in English politics?   ....

9.   Should the House of Lords be abolished?   ....

10.   Are you interested in the aristocracy?

   (a) For instance, do you like reading about peers in the daily papers?   ....

   (b) Do you ever visit Stately Homes to see how the aristocracy lives?   ....

11. (a) Do you think that most people secretly look up to the nobility?   ....

   (b) Do you?

   (c) If not, do you despise them?   ....

205

12. Would you feel proud if you suddenly discovered that you were related to an old noble family? ....

13. not used.

14. (a) Should we still have a monarchy? ....
    (b) Or would you prefer to have some other type of Head of State? ....

15. Do you think that the Queen and the nobility are close? That is, that the Queen has most of her private friends amongst the peers? ....

16. Would it make sense to have a monarchy in this country without the aristocracy which has always gone with it? ....

17. Would you like to see more old English homes taken over by the nation for the benefit of the people? ....

18. (a) Should we do away with the ceremonial occasions in which the aristocracy plays an important part? ....
    (b) For example, the Coronation. ....

19. (a) Do you think that the aristocracy stands for our English tradition? ....
    (b) Do you think that it is a good thing that they should be associated with tradition? ....

20. Do you think that the country would be better off if we abolished all titles and treated the nobility as ordinary citizens? ....

21. Age ....

22. Sex ....

23. Political party: if there was an election tomorrow, how would you vote? ....

24. Occupation: ....

25. Education: at what age did you leave school? ....

QUESTIONNAIRE AND RESULTS

Table 1

Total results for whole sample, in percentages (corrected to
nearest whole number). (Absolute number in sample = 120.)

Question Number			Yes	No	Don't Know
1.			80.0	20.0	
2.	(a)		56.0	44.0	
	(b)		95.0	5.0	
3.	(a)		82.0	13.0	5.0
	(b)		63.0	22.0	15.0
4.			39.0	59.0	2.0
5.			42.0	44.0	14.0
6.	(a)	Land = 40%			
		Inheritance = 33%			
		Business = 16%			
	(b)		72.0	20.0	8.0
7.			50.0	44.0	6.0
8.			39.0	58.0	2.0
9.			36.0	61.0	3.0
10.	(a)		28.0	72.0	
	(b)		26.0	74.0	
11.	(a)		56.0	44.0	
	(b)		26.0	74.0	
	(c)		3.0	97.0	
12.			42.0	58.0	
13.	This question was deleted during interviewing.				
14.	(a)		80.0	20.0	
	(b)		14.0	86.0	
15.			69.0	23.0	8.0
16.			39.0	56.0	5.0
17.			69.0	31.0	
18.	(a)		46.0	54.0	
	(b)		35.0	65.0	
19.	(a)		72.0	28.0	
	(b)		56.0	44.0	
20.			56.0	44.0	

207

Table 2
Selected results for social class groupings in sample, in percentages (corrected to nearest whole number).

Question No.	Group A/B Yes	No	D.K.	Group C Yes	No	D.K.	Group D Yes	No	D.K.
2. (a)	60.0	40.0		62.0	38.0		60.0	40.0	
(b)	93.0	7.0		87.0	13.0		93.0	7.0	
3. (a)	89.0	11.0		81.0	19.0		73.0	18.0	9.0
(b)	69.0	14.0	14.0	56.0	44.0		65.0	22.0	13.0
6. (b)	57.0	37.0	6.0	63.0	37.0		71.0	24.0	5.0
7.	31.0	69.0		56.0	44.0		40.0	60.0	
8.	22.0	78.0		31.0	69.0		31.0	69.0	
9.	54.0	46.0		43.0	51.0		35.0	65.0	
10. (a)	29.0	71.0		19.0	43.0	38.0	18.0	82.0	
11. (a)	66.0	34.0		50.0	50.0		60.0	40.0	
(b)	25.0	75.0		13.0	87.0		22.0	78.0	
12.	37.0	63.0		56.0	44.0		42.0	58.0	
14. (a)	80.0	20.0		75.0	25.0		73.0	27.0	
15.	83.0	9.0	8.0	50.0	25.0	25.0	71.0	29.0	
16.	43.0	57.0		63.0	37.0		35.0	65.0	
17.	63.0	37.0		44.0	56.0		73.0	27.0	
18. (a)	54.0	46.0		38.0	62.0		58.0	42.0	
(b)	43.0	57.0		20.0	80.0		36.0	64.0	
19. (a)	71.0	29.0		63.0	37.0		60.0	40.0	
(b)	31.0	69.0		50.0	50.0		40.0	60.0	
20.	43.0	57.0		25.0	75.0		53.0	47.0	

Table 3

Selected results for voting preferences in sample, in percentages (corrected to the nearest whole number).

Question Number	Conservatives			Labour		
	Yes	No	D.K.	Yes	No	D.K.
3. (a)	91.0	9.0		68.0	32.0	
7.	67.0	33.0		20.0	80.0	
8.	55.0	45.0		20.0	80.0	
9.	24.0	76.0		56.0	44.0	
11. (a)	67.0	33.0		74.0	26.0	
(b)	62.0	38.0		8.0	92.0	
12.	72.0	28.0		26.0	74.0	
14. (a)	95.0	5.0		71.0	29.0	
15.	77.0	23.0		66.0	34.0	
16.	27.0	73.0		48.0	52.0	
17.	62.0	38.0		80.0	20.0	
18. (a)	27.0	73.0		74.0	26.0	
20.	14.0	86.0		56.0	44.0	

Table 4

Selected results comparing voting and class factors in the sample, in percentages (corrected to the nearest whole number).

Occupational Group A/B

Question Number		Conservatives Yes	No	D.K.	Labour Yes	No	D.K.
3.	(a)	100.0	0		64.0	36.0	
7.		65.0	35.0		0	100.0	
8.		73.0	28.0		0	100.0	
9.		82.0	18.0		82.0	18.0	
11.	(a)	73.0	27.0		82.0	18.0	
	(b)	64.0	36.0		0	100.0	
12.		44.0	56.0		0	100.0	
14.	(a)	100.0	0		64.0	36.0	
15.		91.0	9.0		64.0	18.0	18.0
16.		82.0	18.0		73.0	37.0	
17.		55.0	45.0		73.0	37.0	
18.	(a)	82.0	18.0		82.0	18.0	
20.		9.0	91.0		73.0	37.0	

Occupational Group D

Question Number		Conservatives Yes	No	D.K.	Labour Yes	No	D.K.
3.	(a)	80.0	20.0		70.0	30.0	
7.		70.0	30.0		30.0	70.0	
8.		40.0	60.0		40.0	60.0	
9.		30.0	70.0		44.0	56.0	
11.	(a)	60.0	40.0		70.0	30.0	
	(b)	60.0	40.0		13.0	87.0	
12.		50.0	50.0		39.0	61.0	
14.	(a)	90.0	10.0		74.0	26.0	
15.		60.0	40.0		70.0	30.0	
16.		40.0	60.0		35.0	65.0	
17.		70.0	30.0		83.0	17.0	
18.	(a)	40.0	60.0		70.0	30.0	
20.		20.0	80.0		48.0	52.0	

Table 5
Selected results for sample divided by sex, in percentages (to nearest whole number).

Question Number		Men Yes	No	D.K.	Women Yes	No	D.K.
2.	(a)	54.0	46.0		55.0	45.0	
	(b)	95.0	5.0		95.0	5.0	
3.	(a)	84.0	12.0	4.0	79.0	20.0	1.0
	(b)	65.0	20.0	15.0	60.0	26.0	14.0
6.	(b)	72.0	17.0	11.0	74.0	26.0	
7.		41.0	50.0	9.0	67.0	32.0	1.0
8.		37.0	61.0	2.0	45.0	52.0	3.0
9.		38.0	58.0	4.0	32.0	66.0	2.0
10.	(a)	23.0	77.0		40.0	60.0	
11.	(a)	61.0	39.0		48.0	52.0	
	(b)	23.0	77.0		31.0	69.0	
12.		29.0	71.0		64.0	36.0	
14.	(a)	80.0	20.0		79.0	21.0	
15.		66.0	27.0	7.0	73.0	18.0	9.0
16.		38.0	55.0	7.0	40.0	60.0	
17.		72.0	28.0		65.0	35.0	
18.	(a)	46.0	54.0		47.0	53.0	
	(b)	34.0	66.0		35.0	65.0	
19.	(a)	72.0	28.0		74.0	26.0	
	(b)	56.0	44.0		60.0	40.0	
20.		41.0	60.0		48.0	53.0	

Notes

Foreword

1. Rather an adolescent pun.

2 The King and Lloyd George were really very distant kinsmen: both descending in the female line (like Lord Snowdon) from the old Welsh kings.

3. To give another example; there is some reason to suppose that the alleged *jus primae noctis* or *droit de seigneur* (which was never a law as such) was an occasional customary survival where the lord was heir of a formerly pagan sacral royal or priestly house who had had the duty of ritual defloration. Such a duty has been carried out ceremonially by Brahmins on the Malabar coast until modern times, especially among the polyandrous Nayar, and also survived in Western Europe with the devils of witch-cults until at least the seventeenth century (who were often driven to using an artificial phallus with the more unattractive of their duty-virgins). I'm sad to say the *droit,* if we ever had it, is no longer exercised in the territorial barony of Easter Moncreiffe, though that boastful old goat Glengarry is *said* to have revived it at Invergarry as late as the Regency.

4. The Rurikid equivalent of the Norse hird was the *druzhina* (corresponding also to the Welsh kings' *teulu,* who never left the battlefield without their sovereign lord) as witness the heathen Wodenborn Grand Prince of Kiev – from whom both Lord Montagu and I descend through several girls, doubtless exquisite creatures all – who said he could not become a Christian 'because my *druzhina* would laugh at me'.

5. According to my calendar of Celtic Saints, my own birthday (9th April) is appropriately enough St Dotto's Day. So far, however, I haven't yet been able to establish any blood relationship with him. But although he is said to have been an abbot in the Orkneys who died in 502, the book adds the rather depressing comment: 'the Bollandists doubt his existence'.

6. A good example is Ludovic Kennedy, who combines both roles, T.V. and aristo. For he springs from the ancient princes of Galloway through the Kennedy earls of Cassillis, of whom the old saying was that they were 'kings of Carrick' and so fierce that:

> 'From Wigtoun to the Toun of Ayr,
> Portpatrick to the Cruive of Cree,
> There's no man dare to bide him there
> That will not ride with Kennedy.'

7. Who seriously supposes that the Moor Murderers or even Colin Jordan are the 'equals' (whatever that means) of Lord Crawford or Thomas Pakenham, let alone of Bertrand Russell? And how can I claim to be the equal of any good honest London cabby, when I can't even drive a motor car? Nor could he claim to be my equal, for I bet he doesn't know who won the decisive battle of Sekigahara, when nor where nor why. The real point is: we're all different. And nobody in his senses would have it otherwise.

8. In Sweden, for example, they are actually numbered off, so that Civil Engineer C. H. M. Silfwerbrand is head of noble family No. 508 (ennobled 1650). There is a further point: another qualified engineer, H. C. G. Montgomery, is head of noble family No. 1960 (only enrolled among the Swedish nobility in 1756), but his forefathers were noble in Scotland from the twelfth century, and were already so before they came here as Norman immigrants. These Montgomerys are thus both immemorial nobles (probably Norse) and yet also paper-dated nobles in Sweden.

Chapter One – French Nobility
1. M. A. Chaletier. Académie de Sciences, 1875.
2. Quoted V. H. H. Green, *Renaissance and Reformation,* 1952, p. 269.
3. Quoted Harold Nicolson, *The Age of Reason,* Readers Union, 1962, p. 7.
4. Quoted Franklin L. Ford, *Robe and Sword,* 1965, p. vii.
5. Memoires of the Comte de Ségur, translated by Gerard Shelley, 1928, p. 62–63.
6. *Selected Letters of Lord Chesterfield,* O.U.P., 1929.
7. Quoted C. B. A. Behrens, *Ancien Régime,* 1967, p. 64.
8. Quoted ibid. p. 73.
9. Quoted A. Goodwin (Ed.), *European Nobility in the Eighteenth Century,* 1953, p. 38–39.
10. Edith Sichel, *The Household of the Lafayettes,* 1910, p. 10.
11. Quoted ibid, p. 67.
12. Ségur, op. cit.
13. Ibid.
14. *The Memoirs of Chancellor Pasquier,* translated by Douglas Garman, 1967, p. 31.
15. Quoted Edith Sichel, op. cit.
16. Quoted Margery Weiner, *The French Exiles,* 1960, p. 106.
17. Pasquier, op. cit., p. 48.
18. Ibid, p. 72–73.
19. Quoted Jean Robriquet, *Daily Life under Napoleon,* translated by Violet M. Macdonald, 1963, p. 56.
20. Pasquier, op. cit. p. 218.
21. Alfred Cobban, *A History of Modern France,* 1862, Volume II, p. 86.

22. D. W. Brogan, *The French Nation,* 1957, p. 55.
23. Editor's note to Victor Hugo, *Things Seen,* edited by David Kimber, 1964, p. 156.
24. Ibid, p. 126.
25. Ibid, p. 256.
26. Quoted Barbara Tuchman, *The Proud Tower,* 1966, p. 193.
27. George Wyndham, *Life and Letters,* edited by J. W. Macneil and Guy Wyndham, n.d., Volume I, p. 480.
28. *The Genealogists' Magazine,* June 1936.

Chapter Two – Spanish Nobility
 1. Quoted William C. Atkinson, *History of Spain and Portugal,* 1960, p. 80.
 2. Quoted Gerald Brenan, *The Spanish Labyrinth,* Cambridge, 1964, p. 14.
 3. Quoted Sir Charles Petrie, *Philip II,* Readers Union, 1964, p. 41.
 4. Ibid, p. 42.
 5. Cervantes, *Don Quixote,* translated by J. M. Cohen, Penguin, 1950, p. 707.
 6. Quoted Brenan, op. cit., p. 35.
 7. Ibid, p. 35.
 8. Ibid, p. 35.
 9. Quoted R. Carr, *Spain,* 1966, p. 42.
10. Quoted Goodwin, *European Nobility in the Eighteenth Century,* 1953, p. 55.
11. Ibid, p. 59.
12. Joseph Townshend, *Journey through Spain,* 1791, Volume II, p. 158.
13. Antonio Marichalar, *The Perils and Fortune of the Duke of Osuna,* translated by Harriet de Onis, 1932, p. 244.
14. Escandon y Barron, Marqués de Villavieja, *Life has been Good,* 1938, p. 82–83.
15. Brenan, op. cit., p. 86.
16. Quoted Carr, op. cit., p. 602.

Chapter Three – Austrian Nobility
 1. E. Vehse, *Memoirs of the Court of Austria,* translated by Franz Demmler, 1856, Volume I, p. 467.
 2. *The Complete Letters of Lady Mary Wortley Montagu,* edited by Robert Halsband, 1965, p. 273.
 3. Quoted Ilsa Barea, *Vienna,* 1966, p. 95.
 4. Alec Harman and Wilfred Mellers, *Man and his Music,* Readers Union, 1964, p. 633.
 5. Vehse, op. cit. Volume II, p. 305.
 6. Ibid, p. 304.
 7. Mrs Frances Trollope, *Vienna and the Austrians,* 1837, Volume I, p. 218.
 8. Quoted Ilsa Barea, op. cit., p. 357.

9. Edward Crankshaw, *The Fall of the House of Habsburg*, 1963, p. 60.
10. Ilsa Barea, op. cit., p. 283.
11. Norah, Countess Wydenbruck, *My Two Worlds*, 1956, p. 65.
12. Consuelo Vanderbilt Balsan, *The Glitter and the Gold*, New York, 1952, p. 82.
13. Quoted Barbara Tuchman, *The Proud Tower*, 1966, p. 327.
14. Countess Wydenbruck, op. cit, p. 161.

Chapter Four – Italian Nobility
1. Quoted Burckhardt, *The Civilisation of the Renaissance in Italy*, Phaidon Press, 1944, p. 218–219.
2. Quoted John Gage, *Life in Italy at the time of the Medici*, 1968, p. 21.
3. Quoted Ibid., p. 21–22
4. Quoted Philippe Erlanger, *The Age of Courts and Kings*, 1967, p. 64.
5. Quoted A. Goodwin (Ed.) *European Nobility in the Eighteenth Century*, 1953, p. 68.
6. Ibid, p. 72.
7. Maurice Vaussard, *Daily Life in Eighteenth Century Italy*, 1962, p. 70.
8. Ibid, p. 62.
9. Ibid, p. 70.
10. Ibid, p. 69.
11. Ibid, p. 66.
12. Quoted Harold Acton, *The Bourbons of Naples*, 1956.
13. Ibid.
14 Dennis Mack Smith, *Italy*, 1959, p. 38.
15. Margaret Blunden, *The Countess of Warwick*, 1967, p. 165.

Chapter Five – Russian Nobility
1. *John Evelyn's Diary*, edited by Philip Francis, 1963.
2. Quoted A. Goodwin (Ed.), *European Nobility in the Eighteenth Century*, 1953, p. 177.
3. *The Russian Journals of Martha and Catharine Wilmot 1803–1808*, 1934, p. 224.
4. Quoted Lionel Kochan, *The Making of Modern Russia*, 1962.
5. Prince Felix Youssoupoff, *Lost Splendour*, translated by Ann Green and Nicolas Katkoff, 1953, p. 22–23.
6. Kochan, op. cit. p. 116.
7. Quoted *A Western View of Russia*.
8. *Memoirs of Princess Daschkaw*, 1840, Volume I, p. 44.
9. Youssoupoff, op. cit., p. 66.
10. Goodwin, op. cit., p. 81.
11. Leo Tolstoy, *Anna Karenina*, translated by Louise and Aylmer Maude, O.U.P., p. 25.
12. H. Seton Watson, *The Russian Empire*, 1967, p. 466.

215

13. Quoted Kochan, op. cit., p. 143.
14. Princess Catherine Radziwill, *Those I Remember,* 1924, p. 149–150.
15. Quoted in *Witnesses to the Russian Revolution,* edited by Roger Pethybridge, 1964, p. 149.

Chapter Six – English Peerage (I)
1. Quoted Godfrey Davies, *The Early Stuarts,* 1960, p. 267.
2. Quoted J. Steven Watson, *The Reign of George III,* 1960, p. 36.
3. Quoted G. E. Mingay, *English Landed Society in the Eighteenth Century,* 1963, p. 285.
4. Ibid.
5. *Selected Letters of Lord Chesterfield,* O.U.P., 1929, p. 381.
6. Quoted Lord Ernle, *English Farming Past and Present,* Heinemann, 1961.
7. Oscar Wilde, *The Importance of Being Earnest.*
8. Quoted Ernle, op. cit., p. 208.
9. Quoted Mingay, op. cit., p. 147.
10. Quoted Boris Ford (Ed.), *From Dryden to Johnson,* 1957, p. 276.
11. Quoted Alec Harman and Wilfred Mellers, *Man and his Music,* 1964, p. 515.
12. Quoted Basil Williams, *The Whig Supremacy,* 1939, p. 140.
13. *The Greville Memoirs,* edited by Henry Reeve, 1888, volume IV, pp. 45–46.

Chapter Seven – English Peerage (II)
1. Quoted Bernard Holland, *The Duke of Devonshire,* 1911, Volume I, p. 156.
2. Quoted Asa Briggs, *The Age of Improvement,* 1959, p. 236.
3. Quoted F. M. L. Thompson, *English Landed Society in the Nine-*
4. *The Greville Memoirs,* edited by Henry Reeve, 1888, Volume V, *teenth and Twentieth Centuries,* 1963, p. 281.
   p. 348.
5. Ibid, volume III, p. 86–87.
6. Quoted Asa Briggs, op. cit., p. 408.
7. Mathew Arnold, *Culture and Anarchy,* C.U.P., 1957, p. 102.
8. Quoted Thompson, op. cit., p. 330.

Index

217

INDEX

Doria family, 117
Dorset, Duke of, 146
Dorset, Charles Sackville, Earl of, 153
Dostoevsky, Fyodor, 58
Dreyfus affair, 59, 60
Duclos, Charles Pineau, 38
Duma, the, 127

Edward VII, 75, 77
Egremont, Lord, 165–6, 167
Elizabeth I, 139, 150, 158
Elizabeth II, 197, 200, 202
Erasmus, 64
Esseville, Comte d', 39
Esterházy family, 87, 88
Evelyn, John, 121

Ferdinand the Catholic (of Austria), 83–5
Fernan-Nuñez, Duke of, 74
Flaxman, John, 167
Foscarini family, 114
Francis I (of France), 30, 31
Franco, General, 79, 80
Frangipani family, 108
Franz Joseph (of Austria), 95, 96, 99
French cuisine, foundation of, 31
French nobility, ways of acquiring, 36–7
French revolution, 29, 30, 31, 35, 37, 44, 45, 50, 51, 52, 94, 96, 112, 132; of 1830, 52; of 1848, 54–5
Friess, John, 92
Fuchs, Joseph John Nepomuch, 92

Gedimin, 121
Genovesi, Antonio, 116
George II, 148
George III, 129, 148, 155, 158
Gifford, Edward, Earl of, 178
Gladstone, W. E., 173
Gobelin tapestries, 36
Golden Book (Venice), 106, 116

Goya, Francisco de, 71
Grafton, Duke of, 140, 151
Gramont, Duc de, 57
Grand Tour, the, 121, 150, 153
Greville, Charles, 156, 165, 166
Grigg, John, 178, 181, 182, 186, 191
Guéry, Comtesse de, 44
Guelphs and Ghibellines, 108
Guise, Duc de, 32
Guildford, Lord, 145
Gutther-Schoder, Marie, 98

Habsburg, House of, 65, 82, 83, 84, 90, 92, 100, 101, 110, 111
Halifax, Charles Montagu, Earl of, 152
Hambledon Club, 146
Hamilton, Duke of, 144
Handel, George Frederick, 152
Hardwicke, Lord, 155
Haydn, Joseph, 88, 97
Heira, Gutierre de (Marqués de Réal Transporte), 66
Henri IV (Bourbon), 32, 33
Henry VII, 138
Henry VIII, 139
Hertford, Hugh, Marquess of, 104, 190
Hervey, Lord, 122
Hidalgos, categories of, 67
Hirsch, Baron Maurice de, 97, 171
Hitler, Adolf, 99, 101
Hofkirchen, Lord of, 83
Hogarth, William, 156
Hoyos family, 82, 88; Alice, Countess, 99
Hooley, Ernest Terah, 131, 169
Howe, Lord, 147
Hugo, Victor, 52, 53, 54, 55

Isabella (of Spain), 62
Iruja y Artazcoz, Don Luis Martinez de, 81
Italy, unification of, 103
Italy's Hopes (Balbo), 118

219